WELCOME to
The Taste of Scotland Guide 1991

J M B MacMillan MBE MC *Chief Executive*

One of the more interesting features of international culinary competitions recently has been the great success of Scottish chefs.

Competing with the best in the world at London, Frankfurt and Singapore, the Scots have emerged with medals and distinctions galore, in individual as well as team events.

Food critics have singled out and acclaimed specific Scottish hotels and restaurants as the best of their kind in the United Kingdom.

Such distinctions reflect the great changes in the standards of food selection, preparation and presentation that have taken place in Scotland over the last decade or so. Alongside this there has evolved a similar improvement in front-of-the-house behaviour.

Warm, friendly well-mannered service seems to go naturally with pride in servi⋯⋯l that guests are going to enjoy.

Taste of S⋯⋯ ⋯siderable rol⋯ ⋯he best ⋯em.
⋯⋯els and
r⋯ ⋯em as
th⋯ ⋯pected and
se⋯

Whi⋯ ⋯ ⋯ength of Scotland is its incor⋯ ⋯able country house hotels – the jewels in the crown – the aim of Taste of Scotland is to present a cross-section of the best so that there is something for everyone at whatever price they wish to pay.

Thus you may find five star hotels and farmhouses on the same page. One is not being compared with the other. Each has been chosen because it is, in our view, the best in its category and someone wants that specific category at that price.

The diversity of scenery and of cultural heritage and leisure facilities in Scotland ensures that there is something for everyone.

The magnificent scenery of the west coast particularly and of the islands of the Outer and Inner Hebrides has not changed much in the last few thousand years.

It is still primitive, unspoiled, undeveloped – and hauntingly beautiful. So, in different ways, is much of the rest of the country.

What has changed very much for the better, is the standard of comfort and the excellence of cuisine the visitor can expect.

Enjoy the scenery, be comforted by good accommodation at the end of the day – and take pleasure in the food.

Jack Macmillan

CONTENTS

TASTE OF SCOTLAND current members are identified by the 1991 Certificate of membership which should be on display.

The Taste of Scotland Scheme Ltd

is sponsored by:

The Scottish Tourist Board

The Highlands & Islands Development Board

The Scottish Milk Marketing Board

The Scotch Quality Beef & Lamb Association Ltd

The Scottish Salmon Board

HOW TO USE THIS GUIDE

Sample entry

location number →

— GRANTOWN ON SPEY —
107   D6

← grid reference

The Ardlarig
Woodlands Terrace
Grantown-on-Spey
Moray
PH26 3JU
Tel: 0479 3245

address & tel no etc →

On A95 as it enters Grantown-on-Spey. ← how to find it

description →

Unique among the hotels and guest houses of the Spey Valley is the Ardlarig – a tastefully decorated Victorian house set amidst its own gardens. Guests return time after time to enjoy the welcoming and relaxing atmosphere, the high standards of service and, above all, the quality cuisine based mostly on traditional Scottish recipes, freshly prepared on the premises, nothing from the freezer here! The herb garden is a chef's delight and an extensive range of wines and spirits will complement your meal in the elegant candlelit dining room. Leisure events include short cookery courses, painting weekends, champagne breaks in the four poster bedroom to say nothing of impromptu musical evenings! French, German and Italian spoken. Well behaved children and pets are welcome.

any seasonal limitations →

Open all year

Rooms: 7 ← accommodation

Picnic Lunches by arrangement
Dinner 7 - 8 pm (b) - later by arrangement ← meal times & prices
Non-residents welcome – reservation essential

No smoking throughout

specimen inclusive terms quoted on per person per night basis →

Bed & breakfast from £18
Dinner B & B from £30

Own pastries, breads and preserves. Prime Highland beef with fresh oranges and Courvoisier; local venison steaks with wild cherry sauce, fresh Speyside salmon poached in cream and Drambuie. Quality vegetarian dishes. ← specimen food specialities

STB ratings →

STB 2 Crown Commended

No credit cards ← credit cards accepted

Proprietors: Kevin W Gee &
Andrew Hunter

Entries

- Establishments selected by Taste of Scotland are listed in this Guide in alphabetical order under the nearest town or village.
- Island entries are shown alphabetically by island or island group, e.g. Skye or Orkney.
- A full list of hotels etc is given in alphabetical order in the index at the end of the Guide.

3

Special diets or requirements

- Vegetarian meals are more readily available nowadays, but we would advise that you mention this requirement when making your booking.
- Other special needs, such as diet or facilities for disabled guests, should also be arranged in advance.

Wines and spirits

- Except where otherwise stated, all hotels and restaurants are licensed for the sale of wines, spirits, beers etc.
- Most unlicensed establishments – which tend to be small guest houses or farmhouses – will welcome your taking your own wine, but again please enquire in advance.
- Where an establishment is shown to have a restricted licence it generally means that residents and diners may be served alcoholic beverages, but it is not open to members of the public to call in for a drink.

Lunches

- Nowadays lunchtime eating has become much less formal except in city centre hotels and restaurants. Bar snacks are more usual in some smaller establishments and rural hotels.
- From this edition of the Guide, we are trying to simplify the choice available by specifying Dining Room/Restaurant Lunch or Bar Lunch.

Restrictions on smoking

- Within the information on each establishment, we have noted where there is no smoking permitted in the dining room or restaurant.
- Where an area is set aside for non-smokers the entry will show "No smoking area in dining room or restaurant".
- Entries which do not give any such information are taken to have no restriction on smoking.

Pets

- Pets are accepted in some establishments with forewarning. It is wise to check this also as there may be a small charge and sometimes there is a restriction on the areas within the establishment where they are permitted.

- Restaurants generally do not accept dogs.

Foreign languages

- This year we have asked establishments to provide us with details of foreign languages spoken and this has been noted within the description of the establishment where appropriate.

PRICES

- The price category ranges have been updated for 1991. As always, Guide readers should check prevailing prices.
- The information on estimated prices as at November 1990 is provided by the establishments for a guest choosing a three course meal, excluding drinks.

(a)	under £10.00
(b)	£10.00 - £15.00
(c)	£15.00 - £20.00
(d)	£20.00 - £25.00
(e)	£25.00 - £30.00
(f)	over £30.00

- **Please note:** these prices are **for guidance only** and should be checked on booking or arrival.
- Inclusive terms are listed **as a guideline**. Where a price range is given, the lower price normally indicates the rate per person sharing a double room and the higher price the rate for a single room or a higher quality room.
- Times of food service are listed to show first and last orders, unless otherwise indicated.

HOW TO AVOID DISAPPOINTMENT

- Make an advance reservation whenever possible.
- Mention you are using the Taste of Scotland Guide.
- Remember that many dishes are seasonal and that the specialities listed are selected as examples of what may be available – but such items will only be offered to guests if the top quality produce can be obtained.
- Check if any changes to prices have occurred since the publication of this Guide.
- Confirm that credit cards are accepted.

Comments

Taste of Scotland welcomes comments – both good and bad.

However if you have an unsatisfactory meal, we would always advise you to speak to the restaurant or hotel manager or proprietor at the time.

It gives an immediate opportunity for the situation to be explained.

Write to the Taste of Scotland Scheme if this fails to solve the problem.

But do let us hear of your good experiences too!

We like to give our members feedback on comments from the public, and to simplify this we provide a comment slip at the end of this Guide for your use.

STB Grading and Classification scheme

The Scottish Tourist Board's quality assurance schemes help you to choose a place to stay that's right for you.

The schemes let you know in advance about the quality and range of facilities and services that are guaranteed in hotels, guest houses, B and Bs, self catering places and holiday parks.

So you are assured a quality experience on your holiday or business trip in Scotland.

All over Scotland you'll find the distinctive quality symbols that signify a quality Scottish welcome in places to stay.

And the schemes cater for disabled visitors, with STB accommodation guides carrying symbols showing a range of accessibility for disabled people.

Grading

Quality is indicated by:

APPROVED	An ACCEPTABLE quality standard.
COMMENDED	A GOOD quality standard.
HIGHLY COMMENDED	A HIGH quality standard.

All graded establishments are independently checked for quality each year by the Scottish Tourist Board's trained visiting officers. They look for the things that add up to a traditionally excellent Scottish holiday experience – warmth of welcome, atmosphere and personal comfort, efficiency and friendliness of staff, condition of decorations and furnishings, appearance of buildings, and tidiness of grounds and gardens. The quality of food and its presentation are also very important in hotels, guest houses and B and Bs.

These quality grades can apply to all types and sizes of accommodation from a small bed and breakfast or self catering place to a large hotel. The grade reflects the establishment's quality, irrespective of its range of facilities and services, its classification or number of crowns.

A Highly Commended Two Crown establishment offers a higher quality than a Commended Four Crown establishment although not offering as many facilities and services.

Classification

The range of facilities and services offered is indicated by crowns, with awards ranging from one to five crowns. Hotels, guest houses and B and Bs with the minimum required facilities are indicated as "listed."

As the requirements for each crown level are continuously monitored and subject to improvements and modifications an establishment indicating a lower number of crowns from previous years does not imply a reduction in quality. Quality is not measured in crowns.

The Scottish Highlands and Islands – *where all the signs point to peace and contentment*

Starting with Argyll and the Isles . . .

From the Mull of Kintyre to Oban and beyond, Argyll stretches serenely across mountains, forests, glens and lochs. Like a necklace around it lie the Isles: Mull, Coll, Tiree, Iona, Colonsay, Jura, Islay, Gigha, Arran, Cumbrae and Bute.

Here you can visit some of Britain's most beautiful gardens: all kinds of flowers flourish in the gentle Gulf Stream climate. You can play golf amid some of the finest scenery in Europe; visit prehistoric standing stones; go cruising in waters Saints and Vikings have sailed; walk wooded mountain trails; and enjoy unrivalled hospitality.

The Heart of the Highlands . . .

embraces Mallaig, Fort William, Inverness, Nairn and the Spey Valley. It's a region of superlatives: Britain's highest mountain, Ben Nevis; Britain's deepest loch, Loch Morar; Britain's oldest monster, Nessie (she may also be the shyest but could well pop out to see you); and Britain's biggest inland waterway, the Caledonian Canal. Here, naturally, you'll have a superlative holiday, whether you're visiting castles, beaches, wildlife centres or the sites of ancient battlefields.

The Northern Highlands and Islands . . .

Within the broad scope of the Northern Highlands and Islands you'll find far-flung islands: Skye and the Inner and Outer Hebrides. On the mainland you'll discover the dramatically varied scenery of Ross and Cromarty, Caithness and Sutherland.

This is a land of remarkable contrasts. In the course of a day you can come across towering mountains, gentle moors, quiet beaches, stone-age remains and magnificent castles. You can enjoy boat trips, visit bird sanctuaries, go hill-walking or fish for record-breaking skate and halibut. And at the end of the day, you can frequently enjoy a *Ceilidh*, where the music and dancing continue into the wee small hours.

Orkney and Shetland . . .

Just about where ancient mariners thought the world ended, the Orkneys start. And beyond the Orkneys, only 200 miles from the coast of Norway, lie the Shetland Isles. The nearness of Scandinavia has influenced life in these islands down the centuries. Listen carefully to the locals: you'll find their accents owe more to the Viking than the Pict.

Explore the countryside, the ragged cliffs and sandy beaches: you'll see the work of the wild Atlantic and the North Sea everywhere. (You'll also find the work of early man in the ancient forts and burial mounds that dot the landscape.)

Above all, be ready to make new friends. If you were expecting to find these islands peopled by inward-looking folk, wrapped in splendid isolation, you'd be wrong. Orcadians and Shetlanders have been welcoming visitors from over the seas since time immemorial. Make this year the year they welcome you.

How do you get there?

Easily – by road, rail or air. Excellent roads bring you into the Highlands, some leading you to drive-on, drive-off ferries which connect you to the main islands. For train-lovers, the Inter-City service goes to Inverness, and the tracks in the Highlands lead you along some of the most beautiful rail journeys in the world.

Information and Bookings

For further information and bookings for holidays in the Scottish Highlands and Islands contact Hi-line on (0349) 63434.

A Warm Welcome From The Scots . . .

Perhaps the first picture of Scotland is of its scenic attractions – the grandeur of its hills and lochs or the drama and the spectacle of Edinburgh, its capital city. Scotland certainly has beautiful landscapes and it offers an even more valuable attraction: friendly people.

Lively Cities and Dramatic Scenery

The two great cities of the central belt of Scotland, Edinburgh and Glasgow, head the list of urban options. Beyond the cities, the countryside includes not only the grandeur of the Highlands and the special magic of the islands, but the rugged, wooded landscapes of the Borders and Galloway, and the unspoilt seascapes of the east coast. Best of all, in the countryside of Scotland, you can still enjoy clean clear air and the sparkle of pure water.

Wherever you choose, you can be sure of a friendly welcome. The Scottish people are fiercely proud of their nation and its strong identity – and always happy to help visitors make the most of their stay. Start your Scottish holiday adventure with this guide. We look forward to meeting you in Scotland.

Scotch Whisky –
Spirit of Scotland

Scotch whisky is the national drink of Scotland. It is also the natural drink of Scotland, made only from the purest natural ingredients – golden barley, clear water and cool Scottish air.

Scotch whisky can only be called Scotch if it is distilled and matured in Scotland – by law it must be left to mature for a minimum of three years, but in practice most Scotch whisky is left to mature for much longer.

Few would venture to assert the precise moment at which Scotch whisky was first distilled. What is certain is that the ancient Celts practised the art, and had an expressive name for the fiery liquid they produced – 'uisge beatha' – the water of life.

For generations the Scots kept their whisky to themselves, distilling it in homes and farmhouses throughout the Highlands, Islands and glens alike. Then came the Government determined to tax it.

For more than 150 years, the wily Scots continued to distil their whisky, smuggling it down to the towns and cities, and outwitting the hated excise officers and revenue men, who are today the stuff of legend.

However, by the mid-19th century, most distilleries had legalised their businesses, and the foundations of today's Scotch whisky industry were laid.

There are four main stages in the pot still process – malting, mashing, fermentation and distilling. First the barley is steeped in water and then allowed to germinate, before being dried in a peat-fired kiln, the smoke of which contributes to the flavour and aroma of the final product. Next, hot water is added to the ground malted barley in a mash tun to convert the starch into sugar. Then the mixture is transferred to a fermenting vat where yeast is added and fermentation converts the sugar into alcohol.

Finally, in the distinctively shaped swan-necked copper pot stills, distillation of the new spirit takes place. Most malt whisky is distilled twice, and only when the spirit reaches a high enough standard is it filled into oak casks and stored in cool dark warehouses where the long process of maturation takes place.

Unlike grain whiskies, malt whiskies vary enormously from one distillery to the next and one geographical region to another. The flavour of a malt depends on the water used, the distillation technique unique to that distillery, the size and type of cask, and the atmospheric temperature and humidity during maturation. There are over 100 different distilleries in Scotland, each producing its own distinctive malt whisky. The distilleries are divided geographically into Highland, Lowland, Islay and Campbeltown malts.

Highland malts are often subdivided into five further categories: the most famous whisky producing area is Speyside where some of the best known Highland malts are produced – Glenfiddich, Macallan, Cardhu, Glen Grant, Tamdhu and The Glenlivet to name but a few. The four other types of Highland malt are Eastern, Northern (of which Glenmorangie is probably the best known), Perthshire, e.g. Glenturret, and the Islands, which include Highland Park on Orkney and Talisker on Skye.

Islay malts range from the lighter peated Bunnahabhain and Bruichladdich through to the more heavily peated Laphroaig and Bowmore. Although close to Islay, on mainland Kintyre, the two remaining Campbeltown malts, Springbank and Glenscotia, have a distinctive style of their own, while Lowland Scotland is more associated with grain whisky production. However, there are ten malt whisky distilleries in that region, which extends as far south as Bladnoch in Wigtown.

"Westering Home"...

SINGLE ISLAY
MALT SCOTCH WHISKY

Bunnahabhain
UNSPEAKABLY GOOD MALT

See Glassmaking at Caithness Glass

Perth

Visit the Caithness Glass Visitor Centre and Factory.
Factory Shop and Restaurant. Monday to Saturday 9.00am to 5.00pm.
Sunday 11.00am to 5.00pm. (open 'till 6.00pm during July and August –
7 days a week). October to Mid April Sundays open at 1.00pm.
Glassmaking – Monday to Friday 9.00am to 4.30pm.
Car and Coach Parking.

Caithness Glass PLC, Inveralmond, Perth PH1 3TZ. Tel: 0738 37373.
On the north side of Perth on the A9, Perth Western Bypass.
Also at Wick, Oban and King's Lynn.

CAITHNESS GLASS
PRESTIGE AWARDS

In 1988, Caithness Glass PLC, one of Scotland's foremost glass manufacturers and designers, launched the Caithness Glass Prestige Award Scheme.

The object is to give recognition to existing high standards in the hotel and catering trade in Scotland and, by so doing, encourage others to emulate the winners.

The awards are restricted to establishments which are members of the Taste of Scotland Scheme and thus already identified as leaders in their particular category.

The public is invited to help the judging panel by nominating hotels and restaurants in which they have experienced particularly good standards of food and service.

Taste of Scotland is pleased to record and congratulate the 1990 award winners in each category. These were:

Best Hotel	Turnberry Hotel Turnberry
Best Country House Hotel	Knockie Lodge, Whitebridge nr Inverness
Best Restaurant	The Triangle Glasgow
Best Hospitality & Welcome	Ardanaiseig Hotel Kilchrenan
Special Distinction & Merit	The Gleneagles Hotel Auchterarder
Outstanding Newcomer to Taste of Scotland	Shieldhill Country House Hotel, Quothquan nr Biggar

We invite you to help us to select the 1991 winners by submitting nominations.

In 1991 the categories under competition are:

> *Best Hotel*
> *Best Restaurant*
> *Best Country House Hotel*
> *Best Hospitality & Welcome*
> *Best Newcomer to Taste of Scotland*

The sixth trophy will be awarded at the discretion of the Judging Panel to an establishment identified as worthy of special merit.

You will find details and nomination coupons on page 160 and 162 of this Guide, but letters and/or postcards are equally acceptable.

Closing date for entries: 15 September 1991.

The trophy symbol is shown against the 1990 winners' entries in the Guide.

ROLL OF HONOUR

1989

Cromlix House, Dunblane

North West Castle Hotel, Stranraer

The Cross, Kingussie

Ostlers Close, Cupar

Smugglers Restaurant, Crieff

Auchterarder House, Auchterarder

1988

Caledonian Hotel, Edinburgh

Murrayshall Country House Hotel, Perth

Tiroran House, Isle of Mull

Taste of Speyside, Dufftown

Martins Restaurant, Edinburgh

Broughton's Restaurant, Blair Drummond

A Wine Appreciation
by Robin D Kinahan M W

Director of Wine,
Waverley Vintners Ltd

Scotland and its visitors are lucky with our restaurants and wine merchants. There is a tradition of croft cooked food and good wine that goes back much further than in most parts of England. Indeed, Leith was the major port for Bordeaux wines in the British Isles until the turn of the century.

This gives a clue to some of the tradition of good wine in Scotland – our long association with France. A solid foundation was laid by this and has led the Scots to become a receptive market for the excellent wines of the New World of California, Australia and New Zealand. The Scots are often more adventurous drinkers than our visiting tourists.

So – what wine goes well with what food? There are two answers really. First, whatever you like. Ignore the experts and drink whatever you like. Second, if you don't know what you like, consider these ideas.

Traditionally, white wine drinks well with white meats such as chicken and fish and red wine drinks well with red meats such as beef and venison. The idea is that wine and food should balance each other – one should not dominate the other.

Fish, for example, usually has a fairly oily texture and often has a creamy sauce with it. Therefore, you need a dry white wine with a nice acidity to cut through and balance the texture of the fish and the sauce. You might drink a Chablis with plaice, whilst stronger tasting fish, such as salmon or fish in a more piquant sauce could be balanced by a Sancerre, which has a strong gooseberry flavour, or a more lemony flavoured Alsace Riesling.

Less acidic and broader tasting white wines are better with chicken or veal dishes. Meursaults, Puligny and Chassagne Montrachets and Pouilly Fuisses are delicious with these foods. Sadly, they are expensive now. Good quality Californian or Australian Chardonnays are often better value.

Red wines lack the delicacy to partner fish and white meats – similarly, white wines would be swamped by the richer flavours of red meats. Scotland's ancient connections with Bordeaux mean that the claret section on many wine lists is well chosen and priced. Claret is a delicious partner with beef and venison as long as the sauces are not too rich. Meat with richer sauces are best partnered by a richer wine from the Rhone Valley, such as a Cote Rotie or a Chateauneuf du Pape.

Red Burgundy is the difficult one, because the wines have two completely different styles. Beaujolais wines are deep red, easy quaffing wines – try them chilled at lunchtime. The more northern Burgundies from the Cote d'Or, such as Nuits St Georges and Beaune are much softer and lighter wines. People often think that these Cote d'Or wines are rich and fat. They are not. They are light and delicate and are splendid partners with all meats, but not rich sauces.

I have been discussing almost exclusively French wines so far, which is not surprising, given our history and traditions. There is, of course, excellent value elsewhere.

A wine revolution has recently swept through Italy. The white wines have improved enormously. No longer are they the dull, over-alcoholic wines of the 1970s. Be careful of the cheaper wines, but the better quality Soaves or wines from Tuscany and Umbria are delicious with fish and veal. The recent improvement in Chianti, which was ordered by government decree, has created delicately fruity red wines. As good as many Bordeaux, but with more of a taste of cherries than the blackcurranty flavours of Bordeaux.

In fact, our world of wine is changing everywhere. Germany is producing super dry white wine now in an attempt to get away from the dreary image of Liebfraumilch that they have had up to now The Germans are also trying to regain their reputation for fine sweeter wines. Germany produces far better wines than Liebfraumilch and Piesporter.

Much of the revolution started in California and spread from there to Australia, New Zealand and South Africa. California produces very fine rich red Cabernet Sauvignons in the Napa Valley and delicious dry white Chardonnays in the Sonoma Valley. Further north in Oregon, some delightful Pinot Noir red wines are made, which are almost Burgundian in their lightness and complexity. Australia has the sometimes astonishing ability to consistently produce excellent wines at reasonable prices. Of particular note are their red Shiraz wines, which are made from the Syrah grape of the southern Rhone. They are excellent with venison. New Zealand has been "the" discovery of recent years. Their Sauvignon wines are some of the most fragrant dry white wines I have ever tasted.

With the arrival of wines from all over the world, the choice gets wider and wider and more and more fascinating. In Scotland, we are blessed with a great tradition of fine food from excellent raw materials, such as local salmon, beef and venison and we have a tradition of excellence in wine that goes back many generations.

You will enjoy browsing through many wine lists in Scottish hotels and restaurants. I hope you will find this little essay useful in making your choice. If you already know what you like, you can ignore this!

Taste of Scotland

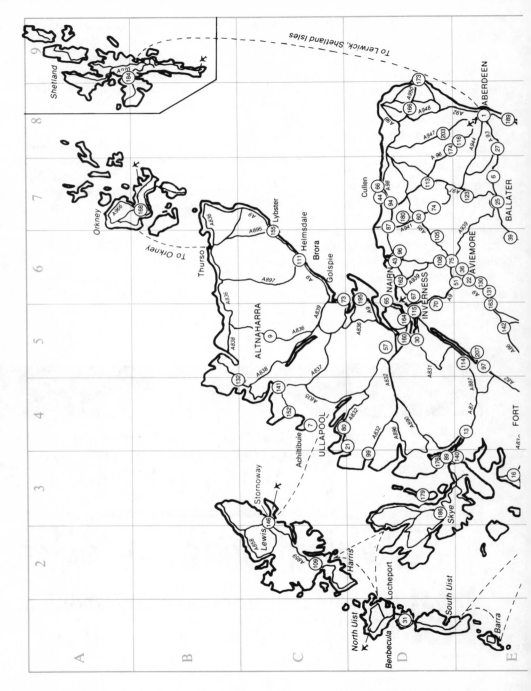

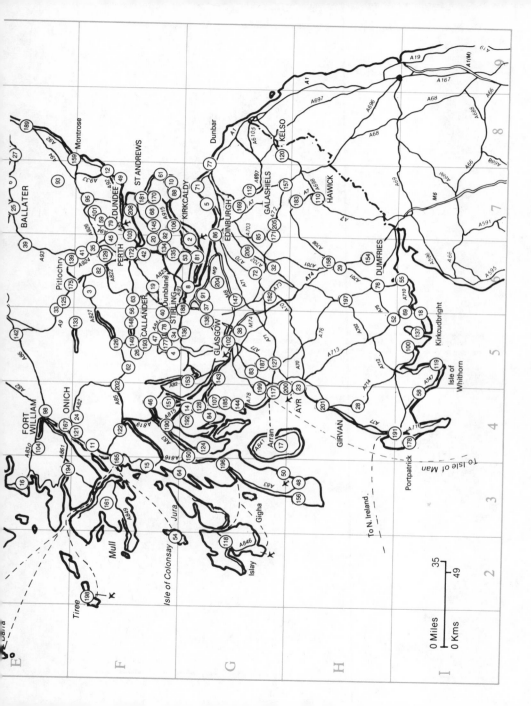

15

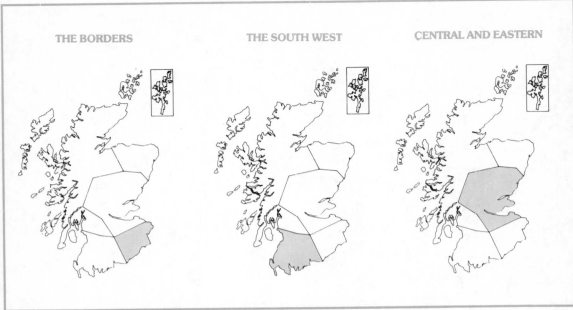

THE BORDERS

THE SOUTH WEST

CENTRAL AND EASTERN

For more details about the locations of hotels and restaurants, car touring routes and general holiday information, contact the Area Tourist Board for the area you are planning to visit. Details on page 22.

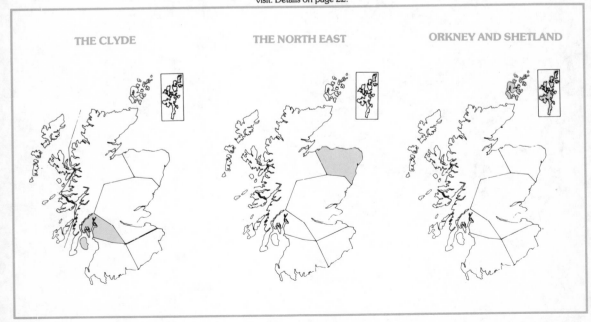

THE CLYDE

THE NORTH EAST

ORKNEY AND SHETLAND

THE BORDERS

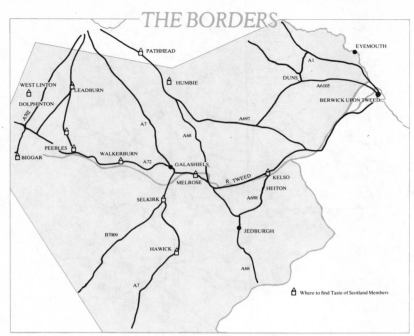

WEST LINTON
DOLPHINTON
LEADBURN
PATHHEAD
HUMBIE
DUNS
EYEMOUTH
A1
A6105
BERWICK UPON TWEED
A702
A697
PEEBLES
A7
A68
BIGGAR
WALKERBURN
A72
GALASHIELS
MELROSE
R. TWEED
KELSO
HEITON
SELKIRK
A698
B7009
JEDBURGH
HAWICK
A68
A7

⌂ Where to find Taste of Scotland Members

THE SOUTH WEST

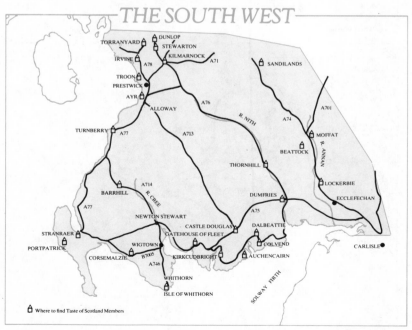

TORRANYARD
DUNLOP
STEWARTON
KILMARNOCK
IRVINE
A78
A71
SANDILANDS
TROON
PRESTWICK
AYR
ALLOWAY
A76
R. NITH
A74
A701
TURNBERRY
A77
A713
MOFFAT
R. ANNAN
BEATTOCK
THORNHILL
A714
BARRHILL
R. CREE
DUMFRIES
LOCKERBIE
ECCLEFECHAN
A77
NEWTON STEWART
A75
STRANRAER
PORTPATRICK
WIGTOWN
B7005
CASTLE DOUGLAS
GATEHOUSE OF FLEET
DALBEATTIE
COLVEND
CARLISLE
CORSEMALZIE
A746
KIRKCUDBRIGHT
AUCHENCAIRN
WHITHORN
ISLE OF WHITHORN
SOLWAY FIRTH

⌂ Where to find Taste of Scotland Members

17

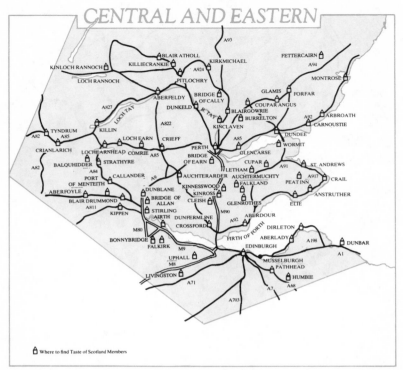

Where to find Taste of Scotland Members

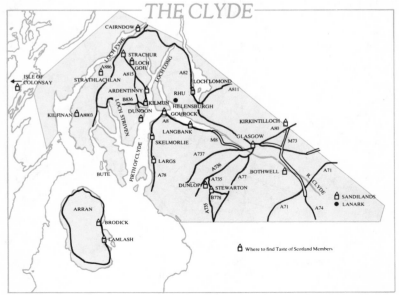

Where to find Taste of Scotland Members

ORKNEY AND SHETLAND

BIRSAY

ORKNEY

STENNESS

KIRKWALL

ST MARGARET'S HOPE

HILLSWICK

BRAE

WALLS

SHETLAND

LERWICK

⌂ Where to find Taste of Scotland Members

THE NORTH EAST

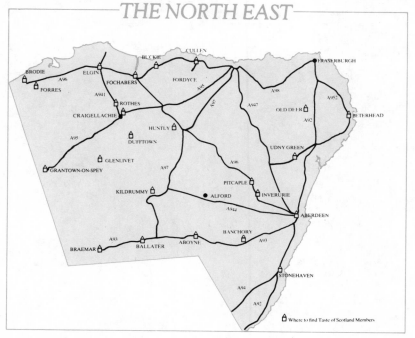

CULLEN

BUCKIE

FRASERBURGH

BRODIE

A96

ELGIN

FORDYCE

FORRES

FOCHABERS

A98

A941

ROTHES

A95

A947

OLD DEER

A952

PETERHEAD

A92

CRAIGELLACHIE

HUNTLY

A95

DUFFTOWN

UDNY GREEN

GLENLIVET

A96

GRANTOWN-ON-SPEY

A97

PITCAPLE

KILDRUMMY

ALFORD

INVERURIE

A944

ABERDEEN

BANCHORY

BRAEMAR

A93

BALLATER

ABOYNE

A93

STONEHAVEN

A94

A92

⌂ Where to find Taste of Scotland Members

19

THE HIGHLANDS

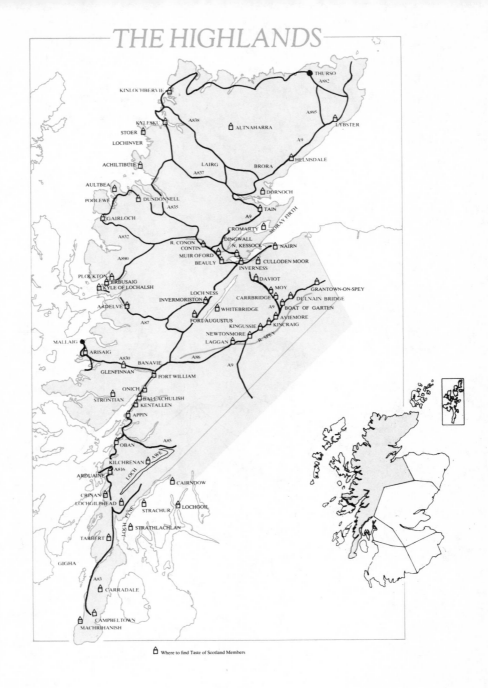

⌂ Where to find Taste of Scotland Members

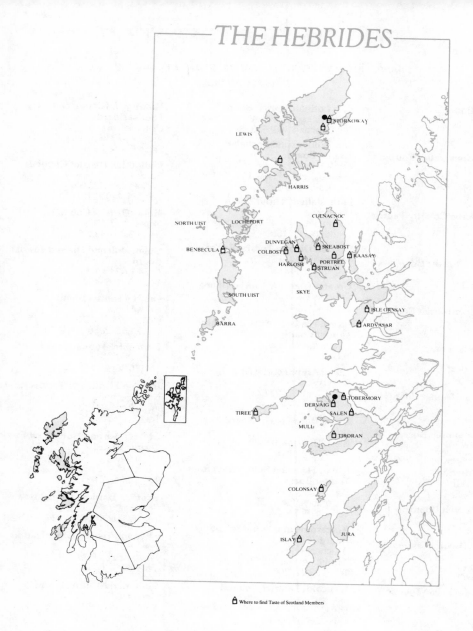

THE HEBRIDES

LEWIS

HARRIS

STORNOWAY

CUI.NACNOC

NORTH UIST

LOCHEPORT

DUNVEGAN

SKEABOST

BENBECULA

COLBOST

RAASAY

HARLOSH

PORTREE
STRUAN

SOUTH UIST

SKYE

BARRA

ISLE ORNSAY

ARDVASAR

TIREE

DERVAIG

TOBERMORY

SALEN

MULL

TIRORAN

COLONSAY

ISLAY

JURA

⌂ Where to find Taste of Scotland Members

LOCAL TOURIST INFORMATION

*For specific information on a particular part of Scotland
contact the following:*

Angus Tourist Board
Arbroath
Angus DD11 1HR
Tel: (0241) 72609/76680

Aviemore and Spey Valley Tourist Board
Aviemore
Inverness-shire PH22 1PP
Tel: (0479) 810363

Ayrshire and Burns Country Tourist Board
Ayr KA7 1BG
Tel: (0292) 284196

Ayrshire Valleys Tourist Board
Kilmarnock
Ayrshire KA1 1ER
Tel: (0563) 39090

Banff and Buchan Tourist Board
Banff AB4 1AU
Tel: (026 12) 2419

Caithness Tourist Board
Wick
Caithness KW1 4EA
Tel: (0955) 2596

City of Aberdeen Tourist Board
Aberdeen AB9 1DE
Tel: (0224) 632727

City of Dundee Tourist Board
Dundee DD1 3BY
Tel: (0382) 27723

Edinburgh Marketing
Edinburgh EH2 2QP
Tel: (031) 557 1700

Clyde Valley Tourist Board
Lanark ML11 7LQ
Tel: (0555) 2544

Cunninghame District Council
Largs
Ayrshire KA30 8BG
Tel: (0475) 673765

Dumfries and Galloway Tourist Board
Dumfries DG1 4TH
Tel: (0387) 50434

Dunoon and Cowal Tourist Board
Dunoon
Argyll PA23 8AB
Tel: (0369) 3755

East Lothian Tourist Board
Musselburgh EH21 6AE
Tel: Dunbar (0368) 63353

Fort William and Lochaber Tourist Board
Fort William
Inverness-shire PH33 6AJ
Tel: (0397) 3781

Forth Valley Tourist Board
Linlithgow
West Lothian EH49 7AH
Tel: (0506) 84 4600

Gordon District Tourist Board
Aberdeen AB9 1DE
Tel: (0224) 642121

Greater Glasgow Tourist Board
Glasgow G1 2ER
Tel: (041) 204 4400

Inverness, Loch Ness and Nairn Tourist Board
Inverness IV1 1EZ
Tel: (0463) 234353

Isle of Arran Tourist Board
Brodick
Isle of Arran KA27 8AU
Tel: (0770) 2140

Isle of Bute Tourist Board
Rothesay
Isle of Bute PA20 9AQ
Tel: (0700) 2151

Isle of Skye and South West Ross Tourist Board
Portree
Isle of Skye IV51 9BZ
Tel: (0478) 2137

Kincardine and Deeside Tourist Board
Banchory
Kincardineshire AB3 3XX
Tel: (033 02) 2066

Kirkcaldy District Council
Leven
Fife KY8 4PF
Tel: (0333) 29464

Loch Lomond, Stirling and Trossachs Tourist Board
Stirling FK8 2LQ
Tel: (0786) 75019

Mid Argyll, Kintyre and Islay Tourist Board
Campbeltown
Argyll PA28 6EF
Tel: (0586) 52056

Midlothian District Council
Roslin
Midlothian EH25 9PF
Tel: 031 440 2210

Moray District Council
Elgin IV30 1EG
Tel: (0343) 543388

Oban, Mull and District Tourist Board
Argyll PA34 4AN
Tel: (0631) 63122

Orkney Tourist Board
Kirkwall
Orkney KW15 1DH
Tel: (0856) 2856

Perthshire Tourist Board
Perth PH1 5LH
Tel: (0738) 27958

Ross and Cromarty Tourist Board
North Kessock
Inverness IV1 1XB
Tel: (0463 73) 505

St Andrews and North East Fife Tourist Board
St Andrews
Fife KY16 9TE
Tel: (0334) 72021

Scottish Borders Tourist Board
Selkirk TD7 4JX
Tel: Jedburgh (0835) 63435/63688

Shetland Tourist Organisation
Lerwick
Shetland ZE1 0LU
Tel: (0595) 3434

Sutherland Tourist Board
Dornoch
Sutherland IV25 3SD
Tel: (0862) 810400

Western Isles Tourist Board
Stornoway
Isle of Lewis PA87 2XY
Tel: (0851) 3088

See entry page . . . 85

Scottish Salmon – *one of nature's finest foods*

Scottish salmon is a magnificent species, well worthy of its title "King of Fish" and is part of the Scottish culinary tradition.

Once, Scottish rivers held such abundant stocks of wild salmon that rich and poor alike could feast on them at will. Poached in vast copper kettles, they graced the laird's table. The sea captain dined on salmon – pickled, smoked and salted – during his long voyages under sail. So common was it, that historical sources note a clause in Perth apprentices' indentures limiting the number of salmon meals to no more than three per week!

Wild Scottish salmon have always been a seasonal delicacy, but several factors have caused the numbers landed to decline over the years. With fewer numbers available, the price of Scottish salmon increased. Some 20 years ago, the concept of salmon farming became a reality, offering the potential for salmon to become once more accessible to all.

Scottish salmon, reared in the security of the clear, unpolluted inshore waters of the Scottish lochs, is now available all year round. It is a luxury food at an affordable price and of consistently high quality.

Cheeses of Scotland

Meals play a very important part in the enjoyment of a holiday. One of the pleasures in life is food and Scotland can provide an excellent variety. The cheeses of Scotland are often full of flavour and texture and the discovery of a new variety can add such pleasure at the end of a meal.

As you travel around take the opportunity to look out for the different cheeses available and try them; you will find cheeses to suit every palate. A cheese, or a piece from a large cheese makes a very acceptable gift to take home to a friend or relative. On the islands of Orkney, Arran and Islay, individual Dunlop cheeses are made and the Orkney cheeses come in three types – white, coloured and smoked. Most of the cheddar cheese is made on the mainland along with a wide range of soft cheeses.

The nutritional value of salmon is undisputed. A 4 oz portion contains under 200 calories (steamed or poached). It contains protein, calcium and iron, vitamins A and D, riboflavin and thiamin. Its natural oil includes two fatty acids similar to polyunsaturated vegetable oils. Current medical opinion suggests that these may help reduce the risk of heart disease by altering the blood clotting mechanism, reducing the likelihood of arterial blockage.

Scottish salmon is a truly fine example of the taste of Scotland. It is available all year round and is one of life's affordable luxuries. Scottish salmon is delivered fresh, with minimal handling, to fishmongers, market stalls, stores and supermarkets, throughout the world.

Today, more international chefs serve Scottish salmon than ever before. You will find it in any five star restaurant in London, Paris or New York. Airlines, hotels and restaurants, keen to provide ever better food and service in a competitive market, choose Scottish salmon to ensure their clients can enjoy the best.

Easy and quick to prepare, Scottish salmon can be served for a family supper or as part of a special celebration meal. It is available fresh or smoked, as whole fish, steaks, fillets or darnes, adding variety, quality and flavour to a healthy diet.

The range of soft Scottish cheese is now extensive and ingredients such as oatmeal, nuts, whisky, pepper and fruits are blended with local cheese to give a unique experience of one of Scotland's oldest industries. See how many Scottish cheeses you can find in shops and cheeseboards as you travel round Scotland and make your holiday a real *"Taste of Scotland"*.

This is the symbol of quality for Scottish Cheddar and Dunlop Cheese.

Here are some names to look our for –
"Crowdie, Caboc, Howgate Brie and Camembert, Arran, Islay, Orkney, Gruth Dhu, Langskaill, Peat Smoked, Ettrick, Galic, Crowdie and Cream.

EAT AT A GREAT LITTLE FISH RESTAURANT TONIGHT.
(YOUR OWN).

Dinner

SAUTE OF SCOTTISH SALMON AU POIVRE VERT

Strips of salmon tossed in butter with shallots and crushed green peppercorns, flamed in brandy and finished with cream.

Served with saffron rice and mangetout peas.

or

SCOTTISH SALMON STEAK BAKED WITH A YOGURT, FRESH HERB AND LIME DRESSING

 A salmon steak coated with a dressing of yogurt, herbs and lime juice and cooked in a hot oven or under a grill for 5 or 6 minutes.

Beautiful with a crisp salad and new potatoes.

or

SCOTTISH SALMON STEAK ROASTED WITH PAPRIKA.

A traditional salmon steak topped with a mixture of paprika and fresh breadcrumbs, then roasted in a hot oven with butter for 5 or 10 minutes, the pan juices swirled with white wine.

Accompanied by buttered broccoli spears and Parisienne potatoes.

Fishing for compliments?
David x x x

*I*t is surprisingly simple to create your own, quite sensational menu from fresh, Scottish Salmon. It doesn't take hours to prepare, all it takes is a little imagination. So go on. Turn a quiet night into a special evening. Tonight.

SCOTTISH SALMON
Simply Delicious

FOR FURTHER SCOTTISH SALMON RECIPES CONTACT THE SCOTTISH SALMON INFORMATION SERVICE, 26 FITZROY SQUARE, LONDON W1P 6BT.

ch Carron, Inverness-shire

Loch Lomond near Inverbeg

△ Montrose

Loch Laggan ▽

Portree Harbour & Raasay

△ North Uist

△ Loch Morlich

Callanish, Isle of Lewis ▽

Ben More

River Tay by Luncarty

△ Harris

△ Eilean Donan Castle

Loch Lochy ▽

△ *Sweetheart Abbey, near Dumfries*

Near Torridon, Wester Ross ▽

View from the shore at Ullapool

Quality Assured
Scotch Beef and Lamb

Look for the thistlehead motif –
it's your guarantee of quality.

In September 1988, the Guild of Scotch Quality Meat Suppliers was formed by a group of thirteen quality conscious wholesalers. Their aim was, and still is, to provide the finest quality beef for the consumer.

What makes 'Quality Assured' Scotch Beef so extra tender and so very tasty, is that it has been 'Specially Selected', and only 'Quality Assured' Scotch Beef carries the distinctive Quality Assured mark in the shape of a thistlehead on all its packaging.

Only prime Beef is chosen and the finest is allowed to carry the Quality Assured mark. The meat is matured in the traditional manner, which is vital to the tenderness, flavour and cooking qualities of the meat, to produce beef that is tender and succulent with a mouthwatering flavour.

The Guild has now grown to include seventeen wholesalers representing all the major meat plants in Scotland and in September 1989 a similar scheme for Scotch Lamb was launched 'Quality Assured' Specially Selected Scotch Lamb.

Only premium lamb which is reared and processed in Scotland and conforms to the strict specifications laid down by the Guild is allowed to be classified as 'Quality Assured'. The lamb is carefully examined and is only available through stockists approved by the Guild of Scotch Quality Meat Suppliers. Specially selected Scotch lamb gives you the opportunity to enjoy the very best in taste, tenderness and quality.

Look out for the mark of eating quality and excellence.

'Quality Assured' specially selected Scotch Beef and Lamb.

Ardoe House Hotel
Blairs
South Deeside Road
Aberdeen
AB1 5YP
Tel: 0224 867355

B9077, 3 miles west of Aberdeen.

A very impressive-looking granite mansion with lofty turrets and inscriptions of heraldry and now a high class country house hotel. It stands in its own grounds and wooded parkland on the south Deeside road, just five minutes out of Aberdeen. There is a splendid terrace with superb views of Deeside. The staircase and the public rooms are especially elegant and the dining room offers high standards of cuisine with plenty of the fresh fish and beef for which Aberdeen is famous.

Open all year

Rooms: 19 with private facilities
Bar Lunch 12 - 2 pm (a)
Dining Room/Restaurant Lunch 12 - 2 pm (a-b)
Dinner 7 - 9.30 pm (b-c)
No dogs
Bed & breakfast £40 - £65
Dinner B & B £55 - £80.50

Local game and seafood.

STB 5 Crown Commended

Credit cards: 1, 2, 3, 5, 6

Caledonian Thistle Hotel
Union Terrace
Aberdeen
AB9 1HE
Tel: 0224 640233
Telex: 73758
Fax: 0224 641627

City centre

This large traditional city centre hotel is right in the heart of Aberdeen, overlooking Union Terrace Gardens and just a hundred yards or so from Union Street, the main shopping street of the Granite City. The restaurant and adjacent cocktail bar are well furnished and dignified and offer good standards of food and service. Less formal is Elrond's Cafe, a spacious bar and restaurant with an interesting range of light meals representing excellent value for money. Vince Toimil, the restaurant manager, speaks various languages including French, Spanish and Italian.

Open all year

Rooms: 80 with private facilities

Bar Lunch 12 - 2.30 pm (a)
Dining Room/Restaurant Lunch 12.30 - 2 pm (b)
Dinner 6.30 - 10 pm (c)
Bed & breakfast £36.30 - £96.50
Dinner B & B £53.75 - £114.00

Fresh local game, poultry and locally caught fish are featured on all menus. The head chef offers a speciality fish of the day fresh from the market.

STB 5 Crown Commended

Credit cards: 1, 2, 3, 5, 6 + Trumpcard

Craighaar Hotel
Waterton Road
Bucksburn
Aberdeen
AB2 9HS
Tel: 0224 712275

Turn off A96 at Greenburn Drive. Follow to end then turn left up Waterton Road. Near airport.

A great deal has been done over the past year to upgrade and improve this fine privately run hotel which has a good reputation with both the business community and local residents. It is not the easiest place to find if you are a visitor to Aberdeen, but persist; it is a good oasis. Food is imaginative with strong emphasis on fresh local produce and is pleasingly presented.

Open all year

Rooms: 41 with private facilities
Bar Lunch 12 - 2 pm (b)
Bar Supper 6.30 - 10 pm (b)
Dinner 7 - 9.30 pm (d)
No dogs
Bed & breakfast from £48
Dinner B & B from £78

Gairloch scallops and crab claws with shallots and cream flavoured with basil then served in a puff-pastry shell. Medallions of Highland venison with shallots and juniper berries flamed with gin.

STB 4 Crown Commended

Credit cards: 1, 2, 3, 5

Craiglynn Hotel
36 Fonthill Road
Aberdeen
AB1 2UJ
Tel: 0224 584050

Midway between Union Street and King George IV Bridge. Car park access from Bon Accord Street.

Craiglynn, an impressive granite building with many unique features is run in a relaxed yet efficient manner. The theme being "Victorian elegance with modern comforts". The bedrooms are tastefully furnished and decorated, all having direct dial telephones and colour TVs. No smoking is requested in the bedrooms. Tea/coffee-making facilities are always available in one of the fine lounges. Dinner menus are decided upon daily and offer an interesting choice of dishes carefully cooked using local produce when available.

Open all year

Rooms: 9, 6 with private facilities
Dinner 7 - 7.30 pm (b)
Reservations required for non-residents
No smoking in dining room
Restricted licence
No dogs
Bed & breakfast £19 - £35.50
Dinner B & B £31 - £47.50

Leek and potato soup, grilled Dee salmon, apple and bramble crumble . . . A sample of the many and varied dishes frequently offered.

STB 3 Crown Commended

Credit cards: 1, 2, 3, 5

Proprietors: Chris & Hazel Mann

New Marcliffe Hotel
51-53 Queens Road
Aberdeen
AB9 2PE
Tel: 0224 321371

Direct access north and south from A92. West end of Aberdeen.

Relaxing and comfortable accommodation with a sophisticated surrounding. Elegant table settings and a quietly efficient service. West end rendezvous for the business community and visitors to the city. Carvery lunches and à la carte dinner. The "in-season" produce of Scotland's fields, moors, rivers and seas is cooked with flair in traditional and innovative ways.

Open all year except 26 Dec, 1 + 2 Jan

Rooms: 27 with private facilities
Bar Lunch 12 - 2.30 pm (b)
Bar Supper 6.30 - 9.30 pm (b)
Dinner 7 - 9.45 pm (d)
No dogs
Bed & Breakfast from £60
Dinner B & B from £75

Medallions of venison with bramble and port sauce, collops of monkfish with spring onion and ginger sauce, roulade of pork fillet with smoked goose, asparagus and pine kernels. Seasonal fruit pavlova.

STB 4 Crown Commended

Credit cards: 1, 2, 3, 5, 6

Proprietors: Stewart & Sheila Spence

Westhill Hotel
Westhill
Aberdeen
AB3 6TT
Tel: 0224 740388
Telex: 739925
Fax: 0224 744354

On A944, 7 miles west of Aberdeen city centre.

Situated in pleasant suburban surroundings this modern hotel is only 15 minutes drive from the centre of Aberdeen. The hotel has 52 bedrooms (all en suite facilities), lounge, cocktail and public bars, restaurant and function suite. Recently refurbished "Castles Restaurant" is highly popular and serves excellent local and international cuisine.

Open all year
Rooms: 52 with private facilities
Bar Lunch 12 - 2 pm (a)
Dining Room/Restaurant Lunch 12 - 2 pm (b)
Bar Supper 5.30 - 9.30 pm (a)
Dinner 7 - 10 pm (c)
Dinner not served on Christmas Day
Facilities for the disabled
Bed & breakfast £30 - £46
Dinner B & B £42 - £58
Weekend breaks 2 nights Dinner B&B £70 per person.
Prime Aberdeen Angus steaks grilled or in special sauces and seasonal fresh fish caught locally, all with fresh local produce.
STB 3 Crown Commended
Credit cards: 1, 2, 3, 5

ABERDOUR
2   **G6**

Hawkcraig House
Hawkcraig Point
Aberdour
Fife
KY3 0TZ
Tel: 0383 860335

Follow Hawkcraig road, through large car park, then down very steep access to Hawkcraig Point.

Elma Barrie has earned a fine reputation for the high standard of food, hospitality and comfort she offers in her old ferryman's house. Situated at the water's edge, next to the harbour, the views across Aberdour bay to the golf course and Inchcolm's 12th century abbey are superb. Seals and seabirds abound, yet the village is only 30 minutes from Edinburgh by road or rail (best by train to avoid the city's traffic and parking problems). The East Neuk of Fife,

Gleneagles and St Andrews are all within a pleasant hour's drive and there is much to see and enjoy on the way. Children over eight years welcome.
Open Feb to Nov
Rooms: 2 with private facilities
Dinner 7 - 9 pm (c)
Open to non-residents – booked meals only
Unlicensed – take your own wine
No smoking throughout
No dogs
Bed & breakfast from £15
Dinner B & B from £28
Home cooking par excellence, using prime Scottish produce.
STB 2 Crown Highly Commended
No credit cards
Proprietor: Elma Barrie

ABERFELDY
3   **F6**

Farleyer House Hotel
Aberfeldy
Perthshire
PH15 2JE
Tel: 0887 20332
Fax: 0887 29430

On B846, 2 miles west of Aberfeldy.

One can use up one's stock of superlatives very quickly here. Farleyer is as near to perfection as any hotel can be. The house itself has its foundations in the 16th century with subsequent extensions. It stands in 70 acres of ground discreetly secluded by mature trees in the geographical centre of Scotland. Frances and Gerald Atkins have furnished it with consummate care so that everything about it looks and feels right. But it is for the food that the ultimate acclamation is reserved. Adventurous, imaginative, exciting, superb – Atkins Restaurant at Farleyer is all these things and more. The rich natural larder on their doorstep gives Frances Atkins and Tony Heath even more opportunity to demonstrate their skills. Quite one of the most outstanding new openings in Scotland in years.

Open all year
Rooms: 11 with private facilities
Dining Room/Restaurant Lunch 12.45 - 1.30 pm except Mon (c)
Dinner 7.30 - 8.30 pm (e)
No smoking in restaurant
Bed & breakfast from £50
Dinner B & B from £80
Terrine of sea trout and langoustine, local woodland chanterelle soup. Salmon with

a sauce of broad beans, samphire and garden herbs. Stuffed breast of Guinea fowl with raspberry and peppercorn sauce.
Credit cards: 1, 2, 3, 6
Proprietors: Gerald & Frances Atkins

Guinach House
by The Birks
Aberfeldy
Perthshire
PH15 2ET
Tel: 0887 20251

On A826, south-west outskirts of Aberfeldy, on road to 'The Birks' Guinach is signposted from Urlar Road.

Luxurious country house hotel in its own secluded garden grounds, with friendly atmosphere and glorious views of the Perthshire Highlands. Superb cuisine and wines are served in the elegant dining room at candlelit tables.

Open all year
Rooms: 7 with private facilities
Dinner 7 - 9.30 pm (e)
No smoking in restaurant
Bed & breakfast from £30
Dinner B & B from £47
Four course dinners, imaginative menus incorporating Scottish specialities – fresh Tay salmon, pan-fried trout, haunch of Atholl venison, medallions of Scotch lamb, prime beef. Full Scottish breakfast.
STB 3 Crown Highly Commended
Credit cards: 1, 3
Proprietor: Albert Mackay

ABERFOYLE
4   **F5**

Forest Hills Hotel
Kinlochard
by Aberfoyle
Stirling
FK8 3TL
Tel: 08777 277

4½ miles from Aberfoyle on B829 to Loch Lomond.

Country house hotel and country club on timeshare estate in the beautiful Trossachs area. Extensive leisure centre. Imaginative food and wines with a wonderful selection of malts. All rooms with private facilities, satellite TV, telephone and tea-making facilities. Emphasis on good presentation of food.
Open all year.
Rooms: 16 with private facilities   ▶

Lunch (Leisure Club) Sun to Sat 12.30 -
2.30 pm (a)
Snack Lunch (Sun Lounge) Mon to Sat
12 - 2 pm
Carvery Lunch 12.30 - 2 pm Sun only (b)
in hotel
Dinner 7.30 - 9 pm (c)
Dogs by arrangement
Bed & breakfast from £35
Dinner B & B from £45
*Salmon, trout, venison, grouse,
pheasant and other game. Delicious
steaks and Scottish lamb. Roasts of pork
and beef.*
STB 4 Crown Commended
Credit cards: 1, 2, 3, 5

ABERLADY
5   G7

Kilspindie House Hotel
Main Street
Aberlady
East Lothian
EH32 0RE
Tel: 087 57 682
On A198 in centre of Aberlady village.
Kilspindie House is a small hotel
personally run by the Binnie family for the
last 24 years. Centrally situated in the
conservation village of Aberlady, the hotel
is only 20 minutes' drive from Edinburgh
and within easy reach of East Lothian's
tourist attractions.
Open all year
Rooms: 26 with private facilities
Bar Lunch 12 - 2.15 pm (a)
Bar Supper 5 - 9 pm
Dinner 7.30 - 8.30 pm (c)
Bed & breakfast from £28
Dinner B & B from £39
*Trout Rob Roy, Steak Balmoral, Scampi
Maison. Accent on local produce.*
STB 4 Crown Commended
Credit cards: 3, 5, 6
Proprietor: Raymond Binnie

ABOYNE
6   E7

Hazlehurst Lodge
Ballater Road
Aboyne
Aberdeenshire
AB34 5HY
Tel: 03398 86921
On A93 in Aboyne.
You can enjoy art, music and award
winning cuisine by the chef/proprietrix in
the intimate atmosphere of this
picturesque former lodge to Aboyne

Castle, once home to Queen Victoria's
photographer at Balmoral. The
accommodation is of a high standard in the
three charming bedrooms overlooking the
large wooded garden and there is a private
lounge. It is an ideal centre for exploring
Royal Deeside, with opportunities for
fishing, shooting, gliding, riding, or just
enjoying the beautiful surroundings.
Open Feb to Dec
Rooms: 3, 2 with private facilities
Dining Room Lunch available for special
bookings
Dinner from 7.30 pm (c)
Bed & Breakfast from £19
*Game from the ancient Caledonian
forests of Deeside, specially selected
fresh seafoods, river salmon, wild
mushrooms and fruit enhanced by an
imaginative, generous use of herbs and
vegetables.*
STB 2 Crown Commended
Credit cards: 1, 3
Proprietor: Anne Strachan

ACHILTIBUIE
7   C4

Summer Isles Hotel
Achiltibuie
Ross-shire
IV26 2YG
Tel: 085 482 282
*Ten miles north of Ullapool turn west off
A835 and continue for 15 miles along
single track road.*
Leaving the main road is like leaving one
world and moving into another, and the
terrain to Achiltibuie is primitive,
enchanting and hauntingly beautiful. The
village itself is a haphazard layout of
cottages, but its piece de resistance is the
Summer Isles Hotel, a haven of civilised
comfort and culinary standards of
astonishingly high level. Mark and
Geraldine Irvine are utterly charming
hosts, bent on ensuring that in this remote
corner of Ross-shire you will want for
nothing – and indeed you won't. There is
everything here, and overlying it is the
sheer tranquillity and beauty of the place.
You will feed on the finest harvest of
seafish, shellfish and the freshest of fresh
locally grown vegetables, fruit and farm
products all prepared with skill and
presented with flair. Like everyone else
who has been there, you will leave
reluctantly, determined to return.
Open Easter to mid Oct
Rooms: 11 with private facilities
Dinner from 8 pm (e)
Lunch is not served in the hotel, but is

available in the adjoining Achiltibuie Cafe
No smoking in restaurant
Bed & breakfast from £37
Dinner B & B from £65
*Local shellfish - lobster, scallops,
langoustine etc*
No credit cards
Proprietors: Mark & Geraldine Irvine

AIRTH
8   G6

Airth Castle Hotel
Airth, by Falkirk
Stirlingshire
FK2 8JF
Tel: 0324 83 411
Telex: 777975
Fax: 0324 83 419
Junction 7 of M9.
Airth Castle stands on a small hill and looks
out over the lush grazing of the Forth
Valley. It has been part of Scotland's
history since the 14th century. The public
rooms are spacious and elegant enjoying
fine views over the surrounding
countryside and designed for guests to
make themselves at home in. There is a
splendid air of permanence about this
building which has several interesting
features both externally and internally and
has earned a good reputation for its food
and service.
Open all year
Rooms: 47 with private facilities
Bar Lunch 12 - 2 pm (a)
Dining Room/Restaurant Lunch 12.30 -
2 pm (b)
Bar Supper 6 - 8 pm (a)
Dinner 7 - 9.45 pm (c)
No dogs
Facilities for the disabled
Bed & Breakfast from £70
Dinner B & B from £85
Credit cards: 1, 2, 3, 5, 6

ALTNAHARRA
BY LAIRG
9   C5

Altnaharra Hotel
Altnaharra
Sutherland IV27 4UE
Tel: 054 981 222
A836, 21 miles north of Lairg
One of Scotland's most famous fishing
hotels situated in the heart of beautiful
Sutherland offering comfort and warmth.
Open to non-residents and non-sporting
guests. Specialising in all requirements ▶

for the angler and outdoor enthusiast with an emphasis on comfort and cuisine.

Open Mar to Nov

Rooms: 20 with private facilities
Bar Lunch 12 - 2.15 pm (b)
Dinner 7.30 - 8.30 pm (c)
No smoking in dining room
Bed & breakfast rates on application
Dinner B & B from £40

Scottish beef, lamb, fresh salmon (subject to availability), home-made soups and desserts.

Credit cards: 1, 3

Proprietor: Paul Panchaud

ANSTRUTHER
10   F7

Craw's Nest Hotel
Anstruther
Fife
KY10 3OS
Tel: 0333 310691
Telex: 727049

Centre of Anstruther on A917 coast road, south of St Andrews.

This is very much a family owned and run hotel in what was originally an old Scottish manse, with recent additions. Well placed for the many interesting towns and harbours of the East Neuk of Fife, and offering straight forward presentation of good local produce, especially fish. Children welcome. French spoken.

Open all year.

Rooms: 50 with private facilities
Bar Lunch 12.15 - 1.50 pm (a)
Dining Room/Restaurant Lunch 12.15 - 1.50 pm (a)
Dinner 7 - 8.45 pm (c)
No dogs
Bed & breakfast from £32
Dinner B & B from £37

Roast Aberdeen Angus, Craw's Nest stuffing; local scampi; Pittenweem haddock, fresh salmon, crab, prawns in season.

STB 4 Crown Commended

Credit cards: 1, 2, 3, 5, 6

Proprietors: Mrs E. Clarke & Family

APPIN
11   F4

Invercreran Country House Hotel
Glen Creran
Appin
Argyll
PA38 4BJ
Tel: 063 173 414/456
Fax: 063 173 532

Just off Oban-Fort William road A828 at head of Loch Creran, 14 miles north of the Connel Bridge.

Superlatives are often overused. But not here. This is a gem of a place, strikingly different. A uniquely styled modern mansion house luxuriously appointed and with truly magnificent views of the hills and glens. Marie and John Kersley with their family have created a haven of total relaxation and enjoyment. Children over five years welcome.

Open Mar to mid Nov

Rooms: 7 with private facilities
Dining Room/Restaurant Lunch 12 - 2 pm (b)
Dinner 7 - 8.15 pm (e)
No dogs
No smoking in the restaurant
Bed & breakfast £35 - £47.50
Dinner B & B £55 - £67.50

Filo pastry of scallops, prawns and mussels in chive and champagne sauce; salmon set on spinach with tarragon butter cream sauce; collops of Highland venison with cranberry, mushroom and port sauce.

STB 4 Crown Commended

Credit card: 1, 3

Proprietor: John Kersley

ARBROATH
12   F7

Byre Restaurant
Redford, Carmyllie
Arbroath, Angus
DD11 2QZ
Tel: 02416 245

B961 Dundee to Brechin route.

Original stone-built byre on a dairy farm. The unpretentious restaurant occupies the full length of the building opening into a peaceful garden where tables are available for service also. Home-made jams, marmalade and honey together with a variety of local soft fruits are for sale. The restaurant is also decorated with a selection of pottery.

Open all year

Dining Room/Restaurant Lunch 12 - 2 pm (a)
Dinner 6.30 - 8 pm (bookings only)

Food service from morning coffee 10 am - 12 noon, afternoon tea, and high tea 4.30 - 6.30 pm

No smoking area in restaurant

Home-made steak pie, chicken with oatmeal stuffing, steak bridie, bannocks and cheese, Arbroath smokie pie with cheese and potato topping. Farmhouse soups. Vegetarian selection. Cloutie dumpling.

No credit cards

Proprietor: Anne Law

ARDELVE
13   E4

Loch Duich Hotel
Ardelve
by Kyle of Lochalsh
IV40 8DY
Tel: 059 985 213

7 miles from Kyle of Lochalsh/Skye ferry on A87 from Fort William and Inverness (via Loch Ness).

A superb location for a country hotel at the junction of three sea lochs and looking out over what is probably Scotland's most photographed ancient monument – Eilean Donan Castle. There are also fine views of the mountains of Kintail and Skye. This is a cosy hotel with comfortable public rooms, well appointed bedrooms and a cheerful dining room in which carefully prepared and presented food is served, utilising to a considerable degree the abundance of fresh fish and shellfish for which the West Coast is famed. French and German spoken.

Open mid Mar to Nov

Rooms: 18
Bar Lunch 12.30 - 1.45 pm (a)
Dinner 7 - 9 pm (c)
No smoking in dining room
No dogs
Bed & breakfast from £22
Dinner B & B from £37

Potato and Stilton soup, smoked haddock loaf, queenie scallop crumble, oysters and mussels, wild salmon, local langoustines, lobster, crab, wild duck, pigeon, venison, heather lamb, walnut tart.

Credit cards: 1, 3

Proprietor: Rod Stenson

ARDENTINNY

14   G4

Ardentinny Hotel
Loch Long
nr Dunoon
Argyll
PA23 8TR
Tel: 036 981 209
Telex: 777205
Fax: 036 981 345

M8 to Gourock, Ferry to Dunoon, A815 then A880 – or drive round Loch Lomond.

Enchanting old coaching inn circa 1720 fully modernised but retaining many old features. Lovely gardens to the sea and lying in the mountainous Argyll Forest Park. The hotel dining room and buttery are very popular with yachtsmen, fishermen and walkers. All bedrooms with private facilities and good views of the loch or mountains.

Open Mar to Nov

Rooms: 11 with private facilities
Sunday Brunch 12 noon - 3 pm
Bar Lunch 12 - 3 pm (a)
Bar Supper 6.30 - 9.30 pm
Dinner 7.30 - 9 pm (d)
No smoking in dining room
Bed & breakfast £25 - £38
Dinner B & B £35 - £57

Stronchullin steaks, lobster salads, prawn soup, Glenfinnart venison casserole, Loch Long langoustine, Argyll lamb with heather honey; sweets prepared daily, speciality coffees with Ardentinny mints.

STB   3 Crown Commended

Credit cards: 1, 2, 3, 5

Proprietors: John & Thyrza Horn,
           Hazel Hall

ARDUAINE

15   F3

Loch Melfort Hotel
Arduaine, by Oban
Argyll
PA34 4XG
Tel: 08522 233
Fax: 08522 214

On A816, 19 miles south of Oban.

This is an interesting old house, former home of the Campbells of Arduaine and extended in such a way as to make the most of its spectacular position looking out to the islands across Asknish Bay. There are glorious uninterrupted outlooks.

The dining and drawing rooms are elegant with good personal touches. The menu, rightly, is not over long and the food is of high standard. As one would expect in this part of the west country there is excellent shellfish. Presentation is good and service is discreet and attentive. Informal bar lunches and suppers are also provided.

Open early Mar to early Jan

Rooms: 26 with private facilities
Bar Lunch 12 - 2 pm (a)
Dining Room/Restaurant Lunch (b-c) - by arrangement
Bar Supper 7 - 9 pm (a-b)
Dinner 7.30 - 9.30 pm (d)
Facilities for the disabled
Bed & breakfast from £42.50
Dinner B & B from £47.50 special low season breaks (min 2 nights stay)

In season: oysters, lobsters, prawns, mussels, scallops, salmon. Home-made soups, jams, marmalade, bread, ice-cream. Fresh local produce, and organic vegetables.

STB   Award Pending

Credit cards: 1, 3

Proprietors: Philip & Rosalind Lewis

ARISAIG

16   E3

The Arisaig Hotel
Arisaig
Inverness-shire
PH39 4NH
Tel: 06875 210

At the edge of Arisaig village on A830 Fort William to Mallaig road, 10 miles before Mallaig on Loch Nan Ceall.

This splendid old coaching inn, now a comfortable country hotel, has its roots in the early 18th century and has been added to through Victorian times and recently. It occupies a splendid site on the sea shore at the edge of the village and there are some splendid views, and some good beaches nearby. It is run by the Stewart family almost as a large family home and it is furnished in keeping with the style of the building. There are open fires in the public rooms and comfortably equipped bedrooms. The food is first class with a heavy reliance on the excellent seafood and shellfish so abundant locally. Janice Stewart and her son, Gordon, who normally preside over the kitchen show much flair and imagination in the presentation of meals.

Open all year

Rooms: 15, 6 with private facilities
Bar Lunch 12.30 – 2 pm (a)
Dinner 7.30 - 8.30 pm (d)
No smoking in main dining room
Bed & breakfast £22 - £40
Dinner B & B £37 - £60

Local seafood, lobster, prawns, clams, halibut, turbot etc. Home-made soups and puddings. Traditional breakfast with Mallaig kippers.

Credit cards: 1, 3,

Proprietors: George, Janice &
           Gordon Stewart

Arisaig House
Beasdale
Arisaig
Inverness-shire
PH39 4NR
Tel: 06875 622
Telex: 777279
Fax: 06875 626

Just off A830 (Fort William-Mallaig road), 3 miles east of Arisaig.

This is a haven of tranquillity and bliss and you will not want to leave. It is one of those rare country house hotels with all the features one hopes to find in such places. A fine old building on a commanding site with lovely gardens and woodland, and magnificent views over Loch nan Uamh to the islands beyond. Ruth and John Smither with their son Andrew have set high standards and this is apparent throughout the establishment. The public rooms have been elegantly furnished as have the comfortable bedrooms with private bathrooms. The staff have been trained to a high degree and polite well mannered service follows automatically. The chefs work wonders with the abundance of delicious local produce from sea and land, and food is prepared with care and presented with panache. An experience to be savoured. Children over 10 years welcome.

Open early Mar to early Nov

Rooms: 15 with private facilities
Dining Room/Restaurant Lunch 12.30 - 2 pm (b)
Dinner 7.30 - 9 pm (f)
Restricted Licence
No dogs
Bed & breakfast rates on application
Dinner B & B from £93.50

STB   4 Crown Highly Commended

Credit cards: 1, 3

Proprietors: Ruth & John Smither

ARRAN ISLE OF

Auchrannie Country House Hotel
Auchrannie Road
Brodick
Isle of Arran
KA27 8BZ
Tel: 0770 2234
Fax: 0770 2812

One mile north of Brodick Ferry Terminal and 400 yards from Brodick Golf Club.

Enjoying a unique situation from which to explore Arran's magnificent scenery, 56 miles of varied coastline and its seven golf courses, the Auchrannie offers a new concept in comfort and cuisine. Nestling among six acres of mature wooded and landscaped gardens, this delightful country house has been tastefully refurbished to high standards. All rooms have private facilities. The renowned Garden Restaurant offers varied menus with particular emphasis on fresh local produce including seafood. Superb leisure facilities, including indoor swimming pool, and 16 additional executive bedrooms form part of a tasteful extension due to be completed in Spring 1992.

Open all year.

Rooms: 12 with private facilities
Dining Room/Restaurant Lunch 12.30 - 2.30 pm (a)
Dinner 6.30 - 10 pm (c)
No dogs
Bed & breakfast £20.50 - £39.50
Dinner B & B £35 - £54

Free range fowl. Fresh local dishes such as wild salmon, trout and marinated scallops.

STB 4 Crown Commended

Credit cards: 1, 3

Proprietor: Iain Johnston

Carraig Mhor
Lamlash
Isle of Arran
KA27 8LS
Tel: 077 06 453

In the village of Lamlash.

A worthy and welcome addition to the catering facilities at Lamlash. Carraig Mhor is a converted cottage on the waterfront but the conversion has been carried out with good taste. Primarily a quality restaurant there are also two bedrooms upstairs. Peter and Penny Albrich are warm and friendly hosts with a wealth of catering experience behind them. Peter presides deftly in the kitchen and shows imagination and skill in the preparation of meals based on local seasonal produce.

Open all year except 2 wks in Nov + 3 wks in Feb

Rooms: 2
Dinner 7 - 10 pm (d)
No dogs
No smoking area in restaurant
Bed & breakfast from £18.50
Dinner B & B rates on application

Local seafood and game. Local king scallops with mangetout and lobster sauce. Medallions of venison, brandy juniper cream sauce, pears and redcurrants.

No credit cards

Proprietors: Peter and Penny Albrich

Glenisle Hotel
Lamlash
Isle of Arran
KA27 8LS
Tel: 077 06 559/258

Via car ferry from Ardrossan, Ayrshire (50 minutes), or Clonaig on Kintyre (30 minutes).

The Glenisle Hotel is centrally situated in the sleepy 'laid back' bayside village of Lamlash. Seafront location with attractive garden. Restaurant with unique cocktail lounge – the Talisman Bar – featuring wooden carvings from that famous Clyde steamer. The hotel is centrally heated and open fires keep it extra cosy.

Open all year.

Rooms: 13 with private facilities
Dining Room/Restaurant Lunch 12 - 2 pm (a)
Dinner 6.30 - 9 pm (c)
Bed & breakfast £21 - £26
Dinner B & B £30 - £35

STB 4 Crown Commended

Credit cards: 1, 3

Proprietor: Alice Toomey

CREDIT/CHARGE CARDS

1 Access/Mastercard/Eurocard
2 American Express
3 Visa
4 Carte Bleu
5 Diners Club
6 Mastercharge

AUCHENCAIRN

Balcary Bay Hotel
Auchencairn
nr Castle Douglas
Kirkcudbrightshire
DG7 1QZ
Tel: 055664 217/311

Off A711 Dalbeattie – Kirkcudbright.

A lovely country house hotel with past smuggling associations, dating back to 1625 and standing in over three acres of garden in a secluded and enchanting situation on the shores of the bay. The hotel retains much of its old character and charm while providing modern amenities and comforts for residents, having full central heating and en suite bedrooms with colour TV, radio, telephone, tea/coffee-making facilities and hairdryer. The cuisine is based on local delicacies such as Galloway beef and lamb, lobster and – of course – Balcary Bay salmon. Together with excellent hospitality, good food and a superb setting, it makes an ideal holiday hotel.

Open Mar to Nov

Rooms: 17 with private facilities
Bar Lunch 12 - 2 pm (a)
Dining Room/Restaurant Lunch 12 - 2 pm (c) - by prior arrangement
Dinner 7 - 9 pm (c)
Bed & breakfast £34 - £42
Dinner B & B £49 - £57
Late/early season breaks and 3 or 7 day reductions

Fresh local seafood including Solway salmon and lobster cooked in a variety of ways. Galloway beef and lamb.

STB 4 Crown Commended

Credit cards: 1, 3

Proprietors: Ronald & Joan Lamb

AUCHTERARDER

Auchterarder House
Auchterarder
Perthshire
PH3 1DZ
Tel: 0764 63646/7
Fax: 0764 62939

B8062 Auchterarder-Crieff road.

Ian and Audrey Brown have created a magnificent country house hotel from this fine old mansion house. It stands in 17½ acres of beautifully manicured lawns ▶

and mature trees. The public rooms are exceptional, of gracious proportion and sumptuously furnished. There is a delightful conservatory. The master bedrooms are superb, both in size and appointment, with lots of thoughtful touches. Food in the elegant dining room is presented with the same flair that is evident throughout. The Browns are charming and attentive hosts and make everyone feel like a personal guest.

Open all year.
Rooms: 15 with private facilities
Dining Room/Restaurant Lunch Sun only (d) (other days by arrangement)
Victorian teas in Winter Garden Conservatory 3 - 5 pm
Dinner (f)
Reservations essential
No children
Bed & breakfast £110 - £160
Dinner B & B rates on application
Emphasis on Scottish food and local produce.
Credit cards: 1, 2, 3, 5, 6

Best Overall Excellence 1989

Proprietors: Ian & Audrey Brown

Cairn Lodge
Orchil Road
Auchterarder
Perthshire
PH3 1LX
Tel: 0764 62634

In the village of Auchterarder.

Attractive country house with five comfortable bedrooms each with colour TV offering every opportunity to relax and enjoy an extended stay or just an overnight stop. Elegant restaurant, quiet leisurely atmosphere, a meal of the highest quality complemented by a good selection of fine wines and malt whisky. Enjoy a truly warm welcome at the Cairn Lodge.

Open all year except 26 Dec, 1 + 2 Jan
Rooms: 5 with private facilities
Bar Lunch 12 - 2 pm (a)
Dining Room/Restaurant Lunch 12 - 2 pm (c)
Dinner 7 - 9 pm; 7 - 9.30 pm in Summer
No dogs
Bed & breakfast £45.50 - £75
Dinner B & B rates on application
Seasonal specialities – seafood, game, local produce.
STB 4 Crown Commended
Credit cards: 1, 2, 3
Proprietor: Gilberto Chiodetto

Duchally House Hotel
Duchally
by Auchterarder
Perthshire
PH3 1PN
Tel: 0764 63071
Fax: 0764 62464

Just off A843 Crieff-Dunfermline road, 2 miles south of Auchterarder.

A fine old Victorian country manor house which the proprietors have been refurbishing and decorating with taste and style. The dining room and drawing room are elegant and there is an attractive bar, a beautifully panelled billiard room and a lovely staircase. There are beautiful views of the Ochil Hills from both restaurants, and open log fires throughout the public areas. Menus are interesting with a clear concentration on fresh local produce, and food is very well presented. Our inspector summed it up by saying "a lovely place to stay".

Open all year
Rooms: 15 with private facilities
Bar Lunch 12 - 2.15 pm (a)
Dining Room/Restaurant Lunch 12.15 - 2 pm (b)
Bar Supper 6.30 – 9.30 pm (a)
Dinner 7 - 9.30 pm (c)
Facilities for the disabled
No smoking area in restaurant
Bed & breakfast from £40
Dinner B & B from £60
Wild salmon with mousseline of sole, poached turbot with a whole grain mustard sauce. Fillet of Scotch beef with a Stilton sauce. Baked duck breast with peach or pink peppercorn sauce.
STB 4 Crown Commended
Credit cards: 1, 2, 3, 5, 6
Proprietor: Maureen Raeder

The Gleneagles Hotel
Auchterarder
Perthshire
PH3 1NF
Tel: 0764 62231
Telex: 76105
Fax: 0764 62134

½ mile west of A9, 8 miles north of Dunblane.

A magnificent hotel of international reputation. A resort in itself. A spectacular Scottish 'palace' in rolling Perthshire countryside. Five restaurants, each using the best Scottish produce, range from the relaxed Dormy House Grill (open April to October) to the exquisite Conservatory, while traditional afternoon tea is also served. The Gleneagles Hotel is Britain's

only country hotel to receive the AA's highest accolade of five red stars and they are richly deserved. Few will experience Gleneagles without full enjoyment of the occasion and a wish to return as soon as possible. French and German spoken.

Open all year
Rooms: 236 with private facilities
Dining Room/Restaurant Lunch 12 - 3 pm (f)
Dinner 7 - 10 pm (f)
Country Club Brasserie and Equestrian Centre Restaurant & Bar - residents and members only
Braids Champagne Bar open from 6.30 pm
No smoking area in restaurants
Room Rate £85 - £170
(prices valid until 31/3/91)
Aberdeen Angus and Tay salmon both feature regularly on the menus.
Credit cards: 1, 2, 3, 5, 6 + Carte Blanche

Special Distinction & Merit 1990

AUCHTERMUCHTY
20   F6

Ardchoille Farm Guest House
Dunshalt
Auchtermuchty
KY14 7EY
Tel: 0337 28414

Just outside Dunshalt village on B936, 1½ miles south of Auchtermuchty.

Donald and Isobel Steven welcome you to Ardchoille – a spacious, well appointed centrally heated farmhouse, with superb views of the Lomond hills. Twin-bedrooms have private facilites, colour TV and tea/coffee trays with home-made butter shortbread. Large comfortable lounge. Attractive dining room with elegant china and crystal where delicious freshly prepared meals are presented with flair and imagination. Excellent base for touring, golfing or just relaxing.

Open all year
Rooms: 3 with private facilities
Dinner 7 - 8 pm (d) 4 course set menu
Dinner for non-residents only by prior arrangement
Unlicensed, but guests may take their own wine
No smoking in dining room
No dogs
Bed & breakfast £20 - £25
Dinner B & B from £35.50

▶

Auchtermuchty broth, Pittenweem sole in a sweet green pepper sauce, roast leg of Scotch lamb with apricot and walnut stuffing. Selection of fresh vegetables. Fresh orange souffle – Grand Marnier with home-made vanilla ice-cream.

STB 3 Crown Commended

No credit cards

Proprietors: Donald & Isobel Steven.

AULTBEA
21   **D4**

Drumchork Lodge Hotel
Aultbea
Ross-shire
IV22 2HU
Tel: 044 582 242

Off A832, on hillside above Aultbea.

This quiet, friendly family run hotel is situated on the hillside above the village and commands spectacular views over Loch Ewe. The famous Inverewe Gardens are only six miles away and there are many interesting walks in the area. Welcoming peat, log and coal fires during the winter months.

Open Mar to late Oct

Rooms: 11 with private facilities
Bar Lunch 12 - 2 pm (a)
Bar Supper 5.30 - 8 pm (b)
Dinner 7 - 8 pm (c)
Dogs welcome by arrangement
Bed & breakfast from £27
Dinner B & B from £42

Home-made soups. Locally caught fish and shellfish. Scottish prime meats and venison. Home-made desserts a speciality.

STB 3 Crown Commended

Credit cards: 1, 3.

Proprietors: The Cooper Family

AVIEMORE
22   **E6**

The Old Bridge Inn
Dalfaber Road
Aviemore
Inverness-shire
PH22 1PU
Tel: 0479 811137
Fax: 0479 810116

200 yards from route to Cairngorms from Aviemore.

A popular and cosy licensed restaurant in a rather quaint building by the river with

tables and benches outside, and well patronised by locals and tourists alike. It operates as a conventional bistro and the cooking is good with some innovative touches. The overall atmosphere is pleasing and the whole experience represents value for money. There are Highland evenings every Tuesday and barbecues on good weekends during Summer.

Open all year

Bar Lunch 12 - 2 pm (a)
Bar Supper 6 - 9.30 pm (a)
Facilities for the disabled
No smoking area in restaurant

Home-made soups, buidhe and pates. Local game and poultry, salmon and seafoods. Superb cheeses – and Ecclefechan Tart!

No credit cards

Proprietor: Nigel Reid

Stakis Coylumbridge Resort Hotel
Coylumbridge
Aviemore
PH22 1QN
Tel: 0479 810661
Telex: 75272
Fax: 0479 811309

30 miles south of Inverness and 75 miles north of Perth on A9.

The Coylumbridge Resort Hotel, situated in the heart of the Scottish Highlands is the ideal centre for outdoor leisure and sporting pursuits. There are two indoor heated pools, a sauna, whirlpool, multi-gym and games room. Two tennis courts, putting green, children's adventure play area, clay and pistol shooting and archery.

Open all year

Rooms: 176 with private facilities
All day bistro 12 - 10 pm (a)
Dining Room/Restaurant Lunch 12.30 - 2 pm (b)
Dinner 6.30 - 9.15 pm (c)
Room rate £60
Dinner B & B £31 (min. 2 nights stay)

Medallions of stag in a sloe gin sauce. Baked Scottish sea trout. Woodlands pheasant.

STB 3 Crown Commended

Credit cards: 1, 2, 3, 5

Stakis Four Seasons Hotel
Aviemore
Inverness-shire
PH22 1PF
Tel: 0479 810681
Telex: 75213
Fax: 0479 810862
Country location adjacent to Aviemore Centre.

Stakis Four Seasons Hotel is one of the finest in the scenic Spey Valley. This luxurious hotel provides the ideal base for a visit to Aviemore – Britain's premier leisure resort. Tastefully decorated bedrooms provide the ultimate in comfort; the charming cocktail bar is the perfect place to relax after an active day; and only the best of cuisine can be enjoyed in the elegant Four Seasons Restaurant. Hotel's own first class leisure centre houses a heated indoor pool, spa, sauna, sunbeds and gymnasium.

Open all year

Rooms: 89 with private facilities
Dining Room/Restaurant Lunch 12.30 - 2.30 pm (b)
Dinner 7 - 9.30 pm (d-f)
Bed & breakfast from £61
Dinner B & B from £37 (min. 2 nights stay)
Highland game platter, smoked salmon roulade. Salmon and dill butter, Scottish venison, fillet of Angus beef.

STB 5 Crown Commended

Credit cards: 1, 2, 3, 5

The Winking Owl
Main Road
Aviemore
Inverness-shire PH22 1RH
Tel: 0479 810646
400 yards north of railway station in main street.

Restaurant in converted farm cottage standing in its own grounds, set back from the road in the village's main street. Cosy dining room and cocktail bar with popular pub on first floor (but away from dining room). Friendly, family run business renowned for good food and value for money.

Open all year except mid Nov to mid Dec.

Dinner 6.15 - 9.30 pm except Sun (b-c)

Taste of Scotland applies to restaurant only

Medallions of venison. Scallops Lady Tweedsmuir. Rump Steak Cairngorm. Supreme of Pheasant White Lady.

Credit cards: 1, 2, 3, 5

Proprietor: W McConachie

Burns Byre Restaurant
Mount Oliphant Farm
Alloway
Ayr
KA6 6BU
Tel: 0292 43644

Signposted off A77 south of Ayr – Corton, opposite turn-off to Alloway.

Enjoy Scottish food in the warm and intimate setting of the original byre of Mount Oliphant Farm, with its unspoiled and traditional farmhouse surroundings. Savour the authentic background of Robert Burns' home in his early years (1766-77). Informal atmosphere together with the highest standards of traditional and modern Scottish cuisine.

Open all year
Light lunch 12.15 - 2 pm (a)
Dinner 7 - 9.30 pm (c)
Credit cards: 1, 2, 3, 5
Proprietor: Duncan Baird

Burns Monument Hotel
Alloway
Ayr
KA7 4PQ
Tel: 0292 42466

In Alloway village on B7024, 2 miles south of Ayr town centre.

An elegant and charming historic hotel located in the famous Alloway village. Splendidly situated in its own grounds with landscaped gardens along the banks of the River Doon with the backdrop of Burns Monument and Auld Brig of Doon. Locally renowned restaurant using only the best of fresh local produce. French and German spoken.

Open all year
Rooms: 9, 8 with private facilities
Bar Lunch 12 - 2.15 pm (a)
Dining Room/Restaurant Lunch 1-2 - 2.15 pm (a)
Bar Supper 5 - 9.45 pm (a)
Dinner 7 - 9.45 pm (c)
No smoking area in restaurant
Bed & breakfast £30 - £45
Dinner B & B £43 - £58

Imaginative cuisine featuring locally caught seafood, with meat, game and poultry from the hotel's farm; poached fresh local salmon, medallions of Aberdeen Angus fillet steak. Home-made sweets and cheeses.

STB 4 Crown Commended
Credit cards: 1, 2, 3, 5
Proprietor: Robert Gilmour

Fouters Bistro Restaurant
2A Academy Street
Ayr
Ayrshire
KA7 1HS
Tel: 0292 261391

Town centre, opposite Town Hall and Tourist Information Centre.

Situated in the vaults of an old bank, the place exudes a warm and friendly – almost Provence-like atmosphere. The best available local produce is prepared with the care it deserves, and served with panache. The welcome is genuine, the food is superb. Do reserve in advance.

Open all year.
Dining Room/Restaurant Lunch 12 - 2 pm (a-b)
Dinner 6.30 - 10.30 pm;
7 - 10 pm Sun (b-c)

Ayrshire pheasant with game sauce. Red deer with orange and Glayva butter sauce. Local Guinea fowl with redcurrant and green peppercorn sauce. Smoked chicken and venison. Seafood a speciality.

Credit cards: 1, 2, 3, 5, 6
Proprietors: Laurie & Fran Black

The Hunny Pot
37 Beresford Terrace
Ayr
KA7 2EU
Tel: 0292 263239

In the town centre of Ayr close to Burns' Statue Square.

This is a small but popular and attractive coffee shop and health food restaurant run personally by Felicity Thomson. Pine furniture and a Pooh Bear theme give the place character.

Open all year
Meals served all day from 10 am - 10 pm (a)
Unlicensed
No smoking area in restaurant

All home-made soups, scones, brown sugar meringues, cakes and dish of the day. Puddings include seasonal fruit crumbles, hazelnut meringue cake. Scottish cheeses with oatcakes.

No credit cards
Proprietor: Felicity Thomson

La Nautique
28 New Bridge Street
Ayr
Ayrshire
KA7 1SX
Tel: 0292 269573

In the centre of Ayr opposite Town Hall.

This is a newcomer to the catering scene in this busy west coast town. As the name implies, the restaurant has a strong nautical theme throughout the interior with ships' figureheads and naval memorabilia conveying an 'on board' ambience. It is centrally located adjacent to Ayr Town Hall. Light lunchtime meals and snacks are available and in the evening a more extensive a la carte menu offers a wide range of dishes. There is a light French touch to good quality local Scottish products.

Open all year
Bar Lunch 11.45 am - 2.30 pm (a)
Bar Supper (seasonal) 5.30 - 7 pm (a)
Dinner 7.15 - 10 pm (b)
Closed Sun

Evening a la carte intermingles French haute cuisine with traditional Scottish fare using top quality local produce. Excellent food and service a speciality.

Credit cards: 1, 2, 3
Proprietor: Andrew Kinniburgh

Pickwick Hotel
19 Racecourse Road
Ayr
KA7 2TD
Tel: 0292 260111
Fax: 0292 285348

On A719 Ayr-Dunure road, ½ mile from Ayr town centre.

A magnificent period character building set in its own extensive landscaped gardens and featuring a traditional Dickensian theme characteristic of its name. The hotel is family run and features 15 excellent bedrooms, all with full private facilities. Conveniently close to town centre and all Ayr's amenities, and only a few minutes' walk from the sea front. Large beer garden. French and German spoken.

Open all year
Rooms: 15 with private facilities
Bar Lunch 12 - 2.15 pm (a)
Dining Room/Restaurant Lunch 12 - 2.15 pm (a)
Bar Supper 5 - 9.45 pm (a)
Dinner 7 - 9.45 pm (c)

▶

Dogs accepted by prior arrangement
No smoking area in restaurant
Bed & breakfast from £35
Dinner B & B from £48

Poached local salmon and prawns, locally caught sole fillet stuffed with prawns, supreme of chicken lined with smoked salmon and goats milk cheese, fillets of prime Aberdeen Angus steak stuffed with haggis.

STB   4 Crown Commended

Credit cards: 1, 2, 3, 5, 6

Proprietor: Robert S Gilmour

The Stables Restaurant & Coffee House

Queen's Court
Sandgate
Ayr
KA7 1BD
Tel: 0292 283704

Immediately behind the Tourist Information Centre in the Sandgate.

In the centre of Ayr is a tiny Georgian courtyard which is a haven of little shops with a tea garden. The Stables were built of local stone probably in the late 1760s. The restaurant (evenings only) could best be described as ethnic Scottish. The Coffee House offers lighter fare made on the premises. Special children's menu. In the evenings menus available in French, German, Italian and Spanish.

Open all year except evenings in Nov

Dinner 6.30 - 10 pm except Sun + Mon (b-c)
Coffee House open 10 am - 10 pm (a) but closed all Sun, and Mon evening. No smoking area - daytime only
Smoking discouraged

Mussels in syboe butter, lamb roasted with apricot and rosemary, venison and juniper pie, cranachan and local cheeses. Wines from Moniack Castle and English vineyards. Family owned smokehouse (Craigrossie) provides smoked fish and meats.

Credit cards: 1, 2, 3, 5, 6

Proprietor: Ed Baines

BALLACHULISH
24   **F4**

The Ballachulish Hotel

Ballachulish
Argyll PA39 4JY
Tel: 08552 606

On A828 at the Ballachulish Bridge.

The Ballachulish Hotel commands an inspiring panorama over Loch Linnhe to the peaks of Morvern and Ardgour. In this friendly family owned hotel, careful restoration and refurbishment have ensured a skilful blend of traditional style with modern international standards. Gracious baronial lounges lead to the welcoming Cocktail Bar and the Loch View Restaurant. French and German spoken.

Open all year

Rooms: 30 with private facilities
Bar Lunch 12.30 - 10 pm (a)
Dinner 7 - 10 pm (c)
Bed & breakfast £19.50 - £27
Dinner B & B £36 - £57.50

Smoked Highland goose breast in lemon and lime essence, roast saddle of venison with juniper berry and Scottish wine sauce, Pheasant Glenarthur filled with asparagus forcemeat. Highlander's toffee pudding with whisky butterscotch sauce.

STB 4 Crown Commended

Credit cards: 1, 3

Proprietors: The Young Family

BALLATER
25   **E7**

Craigendarroch Hotel & Country Club

Braemar Road
Ballater
Royal Deeside
AB3 5XA
Tel: 03397 55858
Telex: 739952
Fax: 03397 55447

On A93, 42 miles west of Aberdeen, near Balmoral.

This luxury resort hotel, in the heart of the Scottish mountains, boasts three restaurants with fine cuisine complementing the splendour of the hotel and countryside surrounding Craigendarroch's hillside location. The Oaks and Lochnagar Restaurants are open to non-residents, the other facilities are for members and residents only.

Open all year

Rooms: 50 with private facilities
The Oaks Restaurant Lunch 12.30 - 2.30 pm (c)
Dinner (The Oaks) 7.30 - 10 pm (e-f)
Dinner (Lochnagar) 7 - 10 pm
Cafe Jardin (members and residents only) Lunch 12 - 2.30 pm: Dinner 5.30 - 10 pm
Bed & breakfast from £57.50
Dinner B & B rates on application

STB   5 Crown Highly Commended

Credit cards: 1, 2, 3, 5

The Green Inn

9 Victoria Road
Ballater
AB3 5QQ
Tel: 03397 55701

In centre of Ballater on village green.

Granite-built former temperance hotel now a small licensed restaurant with three letting bedrooms. Emphasis on fresh food and maximum use of local produce. The Chef's specials change every night reflecting the best of what is available to him.

Open all year

Rooms: 3 with private facilities
Dining Room/Restaurant Lunch 12.30 - 1.30 pm (Feb to Oct) (a)
Dinner 7 - 9.30 pm: 7 - 8.30 pm Sun (b)
Bed & breakfast from £18.50
Dinner B & B rates on application

Venison, salmon, game in season, baked crab with a chive and cheese sauce, seafood gateau. Hot strawberries in a Drambuie sauce with home-made vanilla ice-cream. Local dishes.

STB   3 Crown Commended

Credit cards: 1, 3, 6

Proprietors: Carol & Jeffrey Purves

Monaltrie Hotel

5 Bridge Square,
Ballater AB3 5QJ
Tel: 03397 55417
Fax: 03397 55180

On A93, 40 miles west of Aberdeen near Balmoral Castle.

An elegant 19th century Victorian building overlooking the River Dee with its own riverside garden. It has been carefully modernised within without losing any character and is now a pleasant country hotel. The two restaurants have picturesque views over the garden and river and offer a variety of freshly cooked dishes. Convenient for Balmoral Castle, the whisky trail and Aberdeen. Golf, hill-walking, pony trekking, skiing and gliding nearby.   ▶

Open all year
Rooms: 25 with private facilities
Bar Lunch 12 - 2.30 pm (a)
Dining Room/Restaurant Lunch (a) – by arrangement
Bar Supper 6 - 8.45 pm (a)
Dinner 7 - 8.30 pm (c)
No smoking in restaurant
Bed & breakfast from £24 - £29
Dinner B & B £39.50 - £44.50

Smoked salmon crepe, Cullen skink, sole St Nicholas, fillet of pork Auld Alliance, peppered Gaelic steak, Dream of Rob Roy.

STB 4 Crown Commended

Credit cards: 1, 2, 3, 5, 6

Proprietor: James Anderson

PRICE CATEGORIES

(a)	under £10.00
(b)	£10.00 - £15.00
(c)	£15.00 - £20.00
(d)	£20.00 - £25.00
(e)	£25.00 - £30.00
(f)	over £30.00

Moorside House
26 Braemar Road
Ballater AB3 5RI
Tel: 03397 55492

200 yards from centre of village, on main road (A93) leading out of Ballater towards Braemar.

This family run award winning establishment is a former manse built over one hundred years ago, situated in the burgh of Ballater on Royal Deeside. Set in three-quarters of an acre of garden and lawns, it is ideally suited for hill-walking, fishing, golfing or touring the Highlands.

Open mid Mar to mid Nov
Rooms: 9 with private facilities
Dinner from 7 pm except Sun
No smoking in dining room + lounge
Residents only
Bed & breakfast from £14
Dinner B & B from £26

Baked loin of Ayrshire pork in sweet mustard sauce. Grampian chicken in sherry and celery sauce. Grapefruit ceilidh. Wide choice at breakfast.

STB 3 Crown Commended

Credit cards: 1, 3

Proprietors: Ian & Ann Hewitt

BALQUHIDDER
26   F5

Monachyle Mhor Farm
Balquhidder
Lochearnhead
Perthshire
FK19 8PQ
Tel: 08774 622

On A84 north of Callander.

Monachyle Mhor Farmhouse is set in the beautiful Braes o' Balquhidder home of Rob Roy McGregor. Its unique position overlooks Lochs Voil and Doine, whilst the conservatory allows guests to dine and still enjoy the glorious view in the long summer evenings. Your hosts' "fetish" – cuisine and comfort!

Open all year
Rooms: 4 with private facilities
Dining Room/Restaurant Lunch 12 - 2 pm (a)
Dinner 7.30 - 9 pm (b)
No Dogs
Bed & Breakfast from £15
Dinner B & B from £25

Roast quail with Madeira, coriander and cream sauce set on a bed of watercress with fresh fruit.

STB 3 Crown Commended

No credit cards

Proprietors: Rob & Jean Lewis

BANCHORY
27   E8

Horse Mill Restaurant (National Trust for Scotland)
Crathes Castle
Banchory
Kincardineshire
AB3 3QJ
Tel: 033044 634
(out of season: 033044 525)

Royal Deeside A93, 3 miles east of Banchory.

An attractive and colourful restaurant with helpful staff and a friendly atmosphere. Situated in a converted horse mill it is in the grounds of the picturesque 16th century Crathes Castle famous for its painted ceilings, fine furniture and interesting decorations. The walled garden (3¼ acres) is considered to be among the finest in Britain: it includes a notable collection of unusual plants and has its own plant sales centre. A visitor centre contains permanent exhibitions

and a gift shop. The grounds extend to 600 acres, with 15 miles of well marked woodland trails. Frequent events add to the attraction of this charming property.

Open Easter to late Oct
Food service 12 - 5.30 pm (a-b)
Dinner – booked parties only – menu and price negotiable
Private room available
Facilities for the disabled
No smoking in restaurant

Coffee or tea with home-baked scones and cakes. Lunch from an à la carte menu includes home-made soup, traditional dishes and sweets, or freshly made sandwiches and salads – all home-made.

Credit cards: 1, 3

Invery House Hotel
Bridge of Feugh
Banchory
Kincardineshire
AB3 3NJ
Tel: 03302 4782
Telex: 73737
Fax: 03302 4712

B974, 1 mile south of Banchory.

A superb country house hotel set in acres of wooded grounds on the banks of the River Feugh on Royal Deeside. It is furnished tastefully throughout, and to a very high standard. The principal bedrooms are quite exceptional with some of the bathrooms almost as large as an average bedroom. There are thoughtful personal touches. The public rooms feature antiques and paintings. The food lives up to the same excellent standards of the rest of the hotel and is clearly prepared with great care and presented with panache. There are lovely local walks, and golf, fishing and shooting can be arranged for guests. Invery House is very much in the 'exceptional' category.

Open all year
Rooms: 14 with private facilities
Dining Room/Restaurant Lunch 12.30 - 2 pm (c)
Dinner 7.30 - 9.45 pm (e)
No smoking in restaurant
Bed & breakfast from £57.50
Dinner B & B from £85

Venison with brambles, game pie, baked sea trout, lobster, salmon en croute.

STB 5 Crown Highly Commended

Credit cards: 1, 2, 3, 5, 6

Proprietors: Stewart & Sheila Spence

Raemoir House Hotel

Banchory
Kincardineshire
AB3 4ED
Tel: 03302 4884
Telex: 73315
Fax: 03302 2171
On A890 Royal Deeside.

Beautiful historic house set in 3,500 acres of wooded grounds and parkland. Many rooms and suites face south overlooking the nine hole mini golf course and tennis court, and have tapestried walls and antique furniture. This family owned hotel is proud of its Scottish cuisine carefully prepared by award winning chefs.

Open all year

Rooms: 28 with private facilities
Bar Lunch 12.30 - 2 pm (a)
Dining Room/Restaurant Lunch 1 - 2 pm Sun only or by arrangement (b)
Dinner 7.30 - 9 pm (e)
Bed & breakfast from £50
Dinner B & B from £68.50

Cream of pheasant soup, game consommé. Smoked salmon florettes, venison, game, fish pâtés and terrines. Poached Dee salmon, roast venison, grouse, Aberdeen Angus beef, rosetted Scottish lamb.

STB   4 Crown Commended
Credit cards: 1, 2, 3, 5, 6
Proprietor: Kit Sabin

28
BARRHILL
H4

Kildonan Hotel

Barrhill
Ayrshire
KA26 0PU
Tel: 0465 82 292

A714, between Girvan and Newton Stewart.

A splendid Edwardian mansion set in 83 acres of landscaped gardens and woodland. The attached country club offers an indoor pool, sauna, gymnasium, solariums, snooker table, nine hole golf course, tennis and squash courts.

Open all year

Rooms: 31 with private facilities
Bar Lunch 12.30 - 2 pm (b)

Dining Room/Restaurant Lunch 12.30 - 2 pm (b)
Bar Supper 7 - 9.30 pm (b)
Dinner 7 - 9.30 pm (d)
Facilities for the disabled
No smoking area in restaurant
Bed & breakfast from £65
Dinner B & B from £85

Choose from table d'hote or a la carte menus. Locally caught salmon, Scottish game and fresh vegetables and herbs.

STB   4 Crown Highly Commended
Credit cards: 1, 2, 3, 5

29
BEATTOCK
H6

Auchen Castle Hotel & Restaurant

Beattock, Moffat
Dumfriesshire
DG10 9SH
Tel: 06833 407
Fax: 06833 667

Direct access from A74, 1 mile north of Beattock Village, 55 miles south of Edinburgh and Glasgow.

Gracious country house spectacularly situated in 50 acres with fine shrubs and trees. Ten of the 25 bedrooms are in a modern wing. Ideally placed for the Border Country. Located almost mid way between Carlisle and Glasgow or Edinburgh, it has long been a popular place at which to break a journey either for an accommodation stop or meal time break. Children welcome. A little French spoken.

Open all year except Christmas + New Year

Rooms: 25 with private facilities
Bar Lunch 12 - 2 pm (a)
Dinner 7 - 9 pm (b)
Bed & breakfast from £21
Dinner B & B from £30.25

Local lamb, poultry, beef and pork. Game in season. Salmon and shellfish.

STB   4 Crown Commended
Credit cards: 1, 2, 3, 5, 6
Proprietors: Bob & Hazel Beckh

30
BEAULY
D5

Chrialdon Hotel

Station Road, Beauly
Inverness-shire
IV4 7EH
Tel: 0463 782336

On A862, 12 miles from Inverness.

Step through the elegant entrance into a timbered hallway of highland charm. Chrialdon is a very Scottish house – elegant, yet informal, small yet spacious, where comfort and enjoyment of good food are of the utmost importance. Set in the village of Beauly, Chrialdon provides an ideal base for touring the Highlands.

Open all year

Rooms: 7, 3 with private facilities
Dinner 7 - 8.15 pm (b)
No smoking in restaurant
Bed & breakfast £16 - £18.50
Dinner B & B £27 - £30

Home-made soups and rolls. Venison, salmon, trout with complementary sauces. Pecan nut tart, home-made pastries and various rich ices.

STB   2 Crown Commended
No credit cards
Proprietor: Jennifer Bond

Priory Hotel

The Square
Beauly
Inverness-shire
IV4 7BX
Tel: 0463 782309
Fax: 0463 782531

A862, 12 miles north-west of Inverness.

The Priory is a bustling local hotel with a reputation for particularly good food and efficient friendly service. Situated in the main square in Beauly – close to the ancient Priory ruins. The hotel is an ideal base for touring the beautiful north and west of Scotland. Families with children welcome.

Open all year

Rooms: 16 with private facilities
Bar Lunch 12 - 2 pm (a)
Dining Room/Restaurant Lunch 12 - 2 pm (a)
Bar Supper 5.30 - 9 pm (a)
Dinner 5.30 - 9 pm (b)
Selection of food available all day
Bed & breakfast £21.75 - £27.95
Dinner B & B from £28

Haggis, chef's pâté, Orkney herring. Salmon, trout, Scotch lamb, Aberdeen ▶

Angus beef, speciality whisky steaks. Extensive sweet trolley. Vegetarian dishes.

STB 4 Crown Commended
Credit cards: 1, 2, 3, 6
Proprietors: Stuart & Eveline Hutton

BENBECULA ISLE OF

31   D1

Dark Island Hotel
Liniclate
Isle of Benbecula
Western Isles
PA88 5PJ
Tel: 0870 2414/2283
Benbecula lies between North and South Uist (Western Isles).

This unusually named hotel is of modern low ranch style construction and is acclaimed as one of the best hotels in the Hebrides. There is a comfortable and spacious residents' lounge and a dining room which caters for everything from intimate dinners to major functions. An ideal spot for exploring the adjacent islands. Fishing, golf, bird-watching and interesting archaeological sites.

Open all year
Rooms: 42, 35 with private facilities
Bar Lunch 12 - 2 pm (a)
Dining Room/Restaurant Lunch 12 - 2 pm (b)
Dinner 6.30 - 9 pm (c)
Bed & breakfast from £26
Dinner B & B from £39

Lobster, crab, scallops and venison.

STB 4 Crown Commended
Credit cards: 1, 3

BIGGAR

32   G6

Shieldhill Country House Hotel
Quothquan
Biggar
Lanarkshire ML12 6NA
Tel: 0899 20035
Fax: 0899 21092

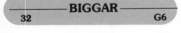

Signposted off main street (A702) in Biggar, 4 miles west taking B7106 for 2 miles then follow signs to hotel.

Christine Dunstan and Jack Greenwald have created a splendid country house hotel from this historic building dating back to 1199, and situated amidst pleasant rolling hills and farmlands. Great care and good taste are evident in every aspect of its furnishings and fittings. Laura Ashley fabrics and wallpapers are much in evidence. Bedrooms are superb some with jacuzzis and four-posters and all with private bathrooms. The same attention to detail has been given to the food which is of a very high standard, thoroughly creative and interesting and demonstrating the skill of a master chef behind the scenes.

Open all year except 1 to 15 Jan
Rooms: 11 with private facilities
Bar Lunch 12 - 2.30 pm (a-b)
Dining Room/Restaurant Lunch 12 - 2.30 pm (d)
Dinner 7 - 10 pm (e)
No children
No dogs
No smoking in restaurant
Bed & breakfast from £86
Dinner B & B from £70

Fillet of veal stuffed with strawberries on a strawberry and sage cream sauce. Roast saddle of venison with a raspberry essence topped with a ginger and cream sauce.

STB 4 Crown Highly Commended
Credit cards: 1, 2, 3, 5, 6

Oustanding Newcomer 1990

Proprietors: C Dunstan & J Greenwald

BLAIR ATHOLL

33   E5

Woodlands
St Andrews Crescent
Blair Atholl
Perthshire PH18 5SX
Tel: 0796 81 403
A9, 7 miles north of Pitlochry.

Cheerful and comfortable, Woodlands was built in 1903 and maintains most original features including service bells. No TV in bedrooms. Good selection of freshly made real teas always available. Guests introduced over a glass before dinner. Leisurely breakfasts with freshly baked bread. Most important house feature – no hurry! All this while gazing at Ben-y-Vrackie!

Open all year
Rooms: 4
Dinner from 7 pm or by arrangement (c)
Residents only
Unlicensed
Bed & breakfast from £15
Dinner B & B from £25

Rannoch venison in red wine and juniper berries. All home-made preserves – including rowan jelly. Lewis salmon, jugged Buckie kippers. Nut soups and vegetarian dishes.

STB Award Pending
No credit cards
Proprietor: Dolina MacLennan (Herdman)

BLAIR DRUMMOND

34   F5

Broughton's Restaurant
Blair Drummond
Stirling
FK9 4XE
Tel: 0786 841897
Less than 1 mile west of Blair Drummond on A873.

Broughton's Country Cottage Restaurant is devoted to the service of good food and wine in a relaxed atmosphere. All dishes are prepared by Chef/Proprietor Helen Broughton and her staff from the finest local produce with most of the vegetables and herbs from the garden. The lunch menu offers a selection of traditional moderately priced dishes such as salmon and haddock fish pie and steak and kidney pudding. There are also some lighter dishes like open smoked salmon sandwiches and vegetarian pancakes. These are complemented by the simple but mouth watering home-made desserts. At dinner the fixed price menu presents all the best ingredients in season in unusual, delectable dishes.

Open all year except last 2 wks Jan + first 2 wks Feb
Dining Room/Restaurant Lunch 12 - 2 pm (a)
Dinner 7 - 10 pm except Sun (d)
Closed Mon
No smoking in restaurant

Local game, jugged hare, ghillies venison, sea trout cooked in sorrel with Hollandaise sauce, duck Gressingham, Arbroath smokie ramekin. Vegetarian dishes always available.

Credit cards: 1, 3

Best Newcomer 1988

Proprietor: Helen Broughton

BLAIRGOWRIE
35   F6

The Old Bank House
Brown Street
Blairgowrie
Perthshire
PH10 6EX
Tel: 0250 2902
Centre of Blairgowrie.

As its name suggests the Old Bank House is a tastefully restored Georgian bank house in a quiet residential part of the town and standing within beautiful gardens. There is an informal and friendly atmosphere about the place and it features log fires, clan bedrooms and an impressive central staircase and gallery.

Open all year
Rooms: 9 with private facilities
Dining Room/Restaurant Lunch on request (a)
Dinner 7 - 8 pm (b)
Residents only
No smoking in restaurant
Bed & breakfast from £22.50
Dinner B & B from £35

Home-made soups, pates and desserts, using fresh local produce – tender Scottish lamb, Tay salmon and Angus beef.
STB   Award Pending
No credit cards
Proprietor: Catherine Pearman

BOAT OF GARTEN
36   E6

Heathbank House
Boat of Garten
Inverness-shire
PH24 3BD
Tel: 0479 83 234
Situated in village of Boat of Garten.

Heathbank House was built around 1900 and is set in large gardens, primarily of heathers (hence the name) and herbs. Each room is decorated in a different colour theme and filled with Victoriana – lace, tapestries, fans, prints, mirrors. The overall effect is very turn-of-the-century, with lots of interesting junk to discover! The dining room is bright with flowers and candle lamps and there is a large comfortable lounge with a log fire and an excellent selection of books. Food is varied, interesting, of unusually high standard and excellent value. There is a

strong commitment to Scottish dishes and produce. There is an obvious anxiety to satisfy guests every needs.
Open Dec to Oct
Rooms: 8, 2 with private facilities
Dinner 7 pm (b)
Unlicensed at time of going to press
Please check when booking whether to take own wine
No smoking in dining room
Bed & Breakfast from £15
Dinner B & B from £25

Scottish lamb steak with mint Hollandaise. Raspberry meringue cheesecake. Home-made ice-creams e.g. Gaelic coffee or banana and cinnamon.
STB   Award Pending
No credit cards
Proprietor: Graham Burge

BONNYBRIDGE
37   G6

Glenskirlie House
Kilsyth Road, Banknock
Bonnybridge
Stirlingshire
FK4 1UF
Tel: 0324 840201
A803 Bonnybridge-Kilsyth road.

Glenskirlie is a small country house set in lovely gardens. Its restaurant has a cosy comfortable atmosphere and has been earning kudos for the standard of its food. Both a la carte and bar lunches are available and when weather permits the bar lunch can be taken outdoors. There is much emphasis on daily fresh specials depending on the availability of produce from the market and there are some intriguing dishes and imaginative sauces. A well presented sweet trolley and a good selection of cheeses round off the menu.
Open all year
Bar Lunch 12 -2 pm (a)
Dining Room/Restaurant Lunch 12 - 2 pm (c)
Dinner 6.30 - 9.30 pm (c)
Closed Mon evening
Facilities for the disabled
Selection of fish and seasonal game
Credit cards: 1, 2, 3, 5, 6
Proprietors: John & Linda MacAloney

BOTHWELL
38   G5

The Grape Vine Restaurant & Lounge Bar
27 Main Street
Bothwell
Lanarkshire
G71 8RW
Tel: 0698 852014
½ mile off M74 (East Kilbride turn-off).

Situated in the centre of a picturesque conservation village, yet within easy access of the motorway. Whether you are looking for a light meal in the bar, or a more leisurely experience in the glass-domed restaurant, both are available all day, with the emphasis on fresh local produce, carefully and creatively prepared under the guidance of chef/patron, Colin Morrison.

Open all year except limited period Christmas + New Year
Food Service 9 am - 10.30 pm (a)
Dinner 5 - 10.30 pm (c)

Local venison, trout, salmon and cheeses featured.
Credit cards: 1, 2, 3
Proprietor: Colin Morrison

BRAEMAR
39   E6

Braemar Lodge
Glenshee Road
Braemar
Aberdeenshire
AB3 5YQ
Tel: 03397 41627
On main A93 Perth-Aberdeen road, on the outskirts of Braemar.

The dining room is the central attraction at this renovated Victorian shooting lodge in the mountains. It is an elegant and relaxing place to enjoy Marian Campbell's much praised innovative and traditional cooking. The best way to guarantee a table is to stay – the relaxed approach means it's yours for the evening. But there is often a - table or two for non-residents – best to check on the night. The bar is unique with massive log fire, oak panelling and Mackintosh furnishings and stained glass. Bedrooms are beautifully furnished and decorated, each one different but all with mountain views.

Open Jan to Oct except from Easter until May Day   ▶

Rooms: 8, 6 with private facilities
Lunch only for pre-arranged parties
Dinner 7 - 8.30 pm (c)
No dogs in public rooms
No smoking in dining room
Bed & breakfast rates on application
Dinner B & B £40 - £49.50

Menu changes daily e.g. fennel and green pepper soup, Aberdeen Angus sirloin steak with Dunsyre blue cheese sauce, trout baked in yoghurt and Drambuie, Marian's bread and butter pudding, all Scottish cheese board.

STB   3 Crown Commended

Credit cards: 1, 3

Proprietors: Trevor & Marian Campbell

BRIDGE OF ALLAN
40   F5

Kiplings
Mine Road
Bridge of Allan
FK9 4DT
Tel: 0786 833617

2 miles off A9.

An interesting old Victorian building in neatly kept grounds. It was built in 1861 as a pump room for the Spa at the time when it was fashionable to take the waters at Bridge of Allan, and was added to in the 1930s. The large semi-circular dining room has been tastefully furnished and the chef/proprietor is usually very much in evidence. The menu shows a lot of imagination, and locals claim that it is the best eating place in Stirling.

Open all year except 2 wks Christmas/New Year

Dining Room/Restaurant Lunch 12.30 - 1.30 pm
Dinner 7 - 9 pm (c)
Closed Sun + Mon

Specialities include fish and game

Credit cards: 1, 2, 3, 6

Proprietor: Peter S Bannister

BRIDGE OF CALLY
41   F6

Bridge of Cally Hotel
Bridge of Cally
by Blairgowrie
Perthshire
PH10 7JJ
Tel: 025 086 231

6 miles north of Blairgowrie, on A93 road to Braemar.

Family owned former coaching inn set in the Perthshire hills. Noted for good food. Full central heating, with a log fire in the bar during the winter months. Free fishing on hotel water, golf, pony trekking and skiing are within easy reach.

Open all year except Nov + first half Dec

Rooms: 9, 6 with private facilities
Bar Lunch 12 - 2 pm (a)
Dining Room/Restaurant Lunch 12 - 2 pm (a)
Dinner 7.15 - 8.45 pm (c)
Bed & breakfast from £19
Dinner B & B from £29.50

STB   3 Crown Commended

Credit cards: 1, 3, 5

Proprietors: Lindsay & Patricia Tolland

BRIDGE OF EARN
42   F6

Rockdale Guest House
Dunning Street
Bridge of Earn
Perth
PH2 9AA
Tel: 0738 812281

A90 – ½ mile from M90 – 4 miles south of Perth.

Bridge of Earn has the best of both worlds. Country surroundings but only four miles from Perth. An ideal situation for touring or a golf break as there are plenty of the well known beautiful courses all within approximately 30 miles. Family run guest house. A caring attitude to guests' comforts. Children and dogs welcome.

Open all year except 26 Dec to 7 Jan

Rooms: 8, 1 with private facilities
Dinner 5.30 - 7 pm set menu – changed daily (b)
Restricted hotel licence
Residents only
Bed & breakfast £12.50 - £15.50
Dinner B & B £20.50 - £23
Reduced winter rates on request

Trout with mushrooms and Pernod sauce, locally caught grilled Tay salmon with creamy orange sauce or lemon and tarragon sauce, chicken cooked with honey, wine and grapes, beef and peppers with orange.

STB   2 Crown Commended

No credit cards

Proprietor: Adele Barrie

BRODIE
43   D6

Brodie Countryfare
Brodie, by Forres
Morayshire
IV36 0TD
Tel: 03094 555

On A96 between Forres and Nairn.

The restaurant seats over 100 people, with farmhouse-style dining furniture indoors and pine picnic benches outdoors. This country style is enhanced by charming conservatory windows and traditional decor. Brodie Countryfare forms part of a shopping complex and diners can find crafts, produce, exclusive fashions and designer knitwear all under the same roof.

Open all year

Food service 9 am - 5.30 pm:
9 am - 7 pm (Summer) (a)
No dogs except guide dogs
Facilities for the disabled
Restaurant is non-smoking with small smoking area.

Salad bar a speciality. Home-cooked dishes using local produce. Home-made soups. Seasonal soft fruit. Selection of home-baking and desserts.

Credit cards: 1, 3

Proprietor: Kathleen Duncan

BUCKIE
44   D7

The Old Monastery Restaurant
Drybridge
Buckie
Banffshire AB5 2JB
Tel: 0542 32660

3 miles south of Buckie, narrow lane above Drybridge.

Approaching the Old Monastery, you will be enchanted first by the views beyond the Moray Firth to distant Sutherland Mountains, then by your immediate ▶

surroundings. The Grays have created an impressively unique restaurant where Douglas produces menus of the kind remembered before the days of convenience foods, guiding his team to prepare dishes of essential flavour, using fresh, mostly local produce – e.g. herbs and some vegetables from the Monastery garden, Highland venison, Spey salmon, Aberdeen Angus beef. Daughter Sandra is responsible for desserts, inheriting her father's instinct for producing wonderful sauces and chocolates. Fine wines complete your meal. Booking preferred for lunch, essential for dinner. No children under eight years old.

Open all year except 2 wks Nov + 3 wks Jan.
Bar Lunch 12 - 2 pm (a)
Dining Room/Restaurant Lunch 12 - 2 pm (b)
Dinner 7 - 9.30 pm (d)
Closed Sun + Mon
No smoking in restaurant
Credit cards: 1, 2, 3
Proprietors: Douglas & Maureen Gray

BURRELTON
45   **F6**

Burrelton Park Hotel
High Street
Burrelton
Perthshire
PH13 9NX
Tel: 08287 206

On A94 Perth-Coupar Angus road, within 10 minutes of Perth and 25 minutes of Dundee.

Not so much an hotel, more a restaurant with attractive rooms, where personal attention and service enhance first class food. Set in the village of Burrelton, a farming community renowned for its soft fruit and potato growing. A perfect centre for daily touring, north, south, east and west. For the sports enthusiast the best golfing, fishing (salmon), shooting, skiing and walking.

Open all year
Rooms: 6 with private facilities
Bar meals served all day 11 am - 11 pm (7 days)
Dinner 6.30 - 10 pm (b)
No smoking area in restaurant
Bed & breakfast from £22.50
Dinner B & B from £30

A multitude of "specials" on the blackboard daily including interesting dishes and the chef's speciality – fresh Tay salmon served in a variety of ways.
STB 3 Crown Commended
Credit card: 3
Proprietors: Malcolm & Karen Weaving

CAIRNDOW
46   **F4**

Loch Fyne Oyster Bar
Cairndow
Argyll PA26 8BH
Tel: 04996 217/264
Head of Loch Fyne A83.

Simple oyster bar in converted old farm building serving local produce including oysters, langoustines, crab, fresh salmon. Own smokehouse provides smoked salmon, trout, eel, mussels, etc. Also seafood shop in smokehouse. Short, very carefully selected, wine list. The restaurant has been expanded to around 80 seats. There is now a bar where customers may sit and enjoy their food and wine.

Open Mar to Oct
Menu available throughout the day: 9 am - 9 pm (b)
Oysters on crushed ice in half shell, baked oysters in parsley and garlic butter, langoustines, poached salmon, sea fish platter, Finnan haddock in milk, Loch Fyne kippers.
Credit cards: 1, 3
Proprietors: Andrew Lane & John Noble

CALLANDER
47   **F5**

Bridgend House Hotel
Bridgend
Callander
Perthshire FK17 8AH
Tel: 0877 30130
On A81 – 200 yards from Callander main street, just over the bridge.

17th century family run hotel, comfortably appointed, with its garden offering a magnificent view of Ben Ledi, yet within three minutes' walk of the town centre. Bedrooms en suite, TVs and tea-makers. Extensive menu in the a la carte restaurant – including a choice of traditional Scottish dishes and game in season. Open fire in lounge, central heating throughout. Children and pets welcome.

Open all year.
Rooms: 7, 5 with private facilities
Bar Lunch 12 - 2 pm (a)
Dinner 7 - 9 pm (c)
Note: pipe and cigars only after 9 pm
Bed & breakfast £14 - £27.50
Dinner B & B £28 - £42.50

A wide range of food from traditional Scottish soup, prime roast beef and lamb to local salmon and Atholl Brose.
STB 3 Crown Commended
Credit cards: 1, 2, 3
Proprietors: Sandy & Maria Park

Highland House Hotel
South Church Street
Callander
Perthshire
FK17 8BN
Tel: 0877 30269
Just off A84 in town centre.

Small Georgian house beautifully furnished offering warm and comfortable accommodation. Intimate bar with wide range of malt whiskies. Tasteful dining room and lounge. Immaculate bedrooms with drink-making facilities. Some rooms with TV and en suite facilities. Full central heating in all rooms. The proprietors strive to offer a warm welcome and personal service to all guests.

Open Mar to Nov
Rooms: 10, 4 with private facilities
Dinner from 7 pm (b)
No smoking in dining room or bedrooms
Dogs accepted at proprietors' discretion
Bed & breakfast from £15
Dinner B & B from £26.50

Home-made soups, pâtés, kippers, herring. Fresh local produce including salmon, trout, venison. Delicious desserts. Children's menu available.
STB 3 Crown Commended
Credit cards: 1, 2, 3
Proprietors: David & Dee Shirley

CREDIT/CHARGE CARDS
1 Access/Mastercard/Eurocard
2 American Express
3 Visa
4 Carte Bleu
5 Diners Club
6 Mastercharge

Roman Camp Hotel
Callander
Perthshire
FK17 8BG
Tel: 0877 30003
Signposted off main route through Callander (A84).

Originally built in 1625 as a hunting lodge, this charming country house hotel on the edge of the Trossachs is a superb centre from which to tour. It is set in 20 acres of beautiful gardens which sweep down to the River Teith. The public rooms are gracious and relaxing, and the dining room enjoys a fine reputation for good food.

Open all year
Rooms: 14 with private facilities
Dining Room/Restaurant Lunch 12 - 2 pm (c)
Dinner 7 - 9 pm (f) 4 course menu
Facilities for the disabled
No smoking in dining room
Bed & breakfast from £40
Dinner B & B from £65
Local fresh fish – salmon, trout – and seafood. Game in season.
STB 4 Crown Commended
Credit cards: 1, 2, 3, 5, 6
Proprietors: Eric & Marion Brown

---

48 — CAMPBELTOWN — H3

Seafield Hotel
Kilkerran Road
Campbeltown
Argyll
PA28 6JL
Tel: 0586 54385
On the shores of Campbeltown Loch – 4 minutes walk from town centre.

Victorian villa built by the founders of Springbank Distillery and reputed to be the first house in Campbeltown fitted with a bath! Has a garden court annexe in the walled garden at the rear of the hotel, offering quiet peaceful accommodation.

Open all year
Rooms: 9 with private facilities
Bar Lunches for non-residents
Dining Room/Restaurant Lunch for non-residents
Dinner 7 - 8 pm (b)
Bed & breakfast £19 - £25
Dinner B & B £29.50 - £35.50
Local fresh seafoods and salmon. Scottish beef, lamb and game.
STB 3 Crown Commended
Credit cards: 1, 3
Proprietors: Alastair & Elizabeth Gilchrist

White Hart Hotel
Main Street
Campbeltown
Argyll
PA28 6AN
Tel: 0586 52440/53356
Fax: 0586 54972
Mull of Kintyre.

Well established town hotel centrally situated in busy fishing port/market town. Ideal base for the famous Machrihanish golf links, the Mull of Kintyre and Campbeltown Loch.

Open all year
Rooms: 20 with private facilities
Bar Lunch 12 - 2 pm (a)
Dining Room/Restaurant Lunch 12 - 2 pm except Sun (a)
Dinner 7 - 9.30 pm: 7 - 8.30 pm Sun (Mar to Oct) (c)
Restaurant closed Sun from Nov to Mar
Bed & breakfast from £25
Dinner B & B rates on application
Serving the best of local fresh seafood, game and meat products.
Credit cards: 1, 3, 6
Proprietors: P Stogdale & B Kennedy

---

49 — CARNOUSTIE — F7

"11 Park Avenue"
11 Park Avenue
Carnoustie
Angus
DD7 7JA
Tel: 0241 53336
On A930 east of Dundee.

A substantial Victorian building with ornate ceilings in the centre of Carnoustie is the setting for this new restaurant. The open fireplace and traditional furnishings combine with the rich colour scheme to create a warm informal atmosphere. The modern style menu makes good use of the best of fresh local produce. Golf courses and the beautiful Angus glens are virtually on the doorstep.

Open all year
Dining Room/Restaurant Lunch 12 - 2 pm (a)
Dinner 7 - 9.30 pm (c)
Closed Sun
Unlicensed – customers may take their own wine

Arbroath smokie and smoked salmon terrine, ragout of seafood, game in season, Heather Honey and Glayva ice cream.
Credit cards: 1, 2, 3, 5
Proprietors: Stephen Collinson & Caroline Mitchell

---

50 — CARRADALE — G3

Carradale Hotel
Carradale
Argyll
PA28 6RY
Tel: 058 33 223
On B842, about 17 miles north of Campbeltown, Argyll.

Sixty years in same family ownership, the hotel is situated in the fishing village of Carradale, and stands in its own gardens above the quaint harbour. The hotel offers squash courts, sauna, solarium. Full central heating. Golf course next to the hotel and safe, sandy beaches nearby.

Open Mar to Oct
Rooms: 20, 18 with private facilities
Bar Lunch 12.30 - 2 pm (a)
Dinner 7 - 8.45 pm (b)
No smoking area in restaurant
Bed & breakfast £17 - £25
Dinner B & B £29 - £37
Kintyre Hill lamb, Carradale oak-smoked salmon, house kippers.
STB 3 Crown Commended
Credit cards: 1, 3, 6
Proprietors: John & Katherine Martin

---

51 — CARRBRIDGE — E6

Dalrachney Lodge Hotel
Carrbridge
Inverness-shire
PH23 3AT
Tel: 047984 252
Fax: 047984 383
Just off A9 south of Inverness and north of Aviemore.

Victorian Hunting Lodge in 14 acres of peaceful surroundings, Dalrachney is a careful blend of old and new. Relax by the log fire in cosy 'Stalkers' Bar or in the à la carte 'Lodge' Restaurant which has gained a reputation for fine food and service. Excellent selection of wines, liqueurs and malts. ▶

Open all year
Rooms: 11 with private facilities
Bar Meals 11 am - 11 pm (a-b)
Dinner 6 - 9 pm (b-c)
No smoking area in restaurant
Bed & breakfast from £25
Dinner B & B from £35

Home-made soups, pates and desserts. Spey Valley salmon, Highland venison, beef, Scotch lamb beautifully prepared and served with fresh vegetables in season.

STB   4 Crown Commended

Credit cards: 1, 2, 3

Proprietor: Helen Swanney

Ecclefechan Bistro
Main Street
Carrbridge
Inverness-shire
PH23 3AJ
Tel: 047 984 374

Main road, Carrbridge, on Carrbridge bypass off A9 north of Aviemore.

Informal family run bistro invoking the best of the Auld Alliance: Scottish food in a French atmosphere, freshly prepared the way you like it, from scones to scallops, steaks to strudel – and coffee that tastes like coffee.

Open all year except last 2 wks Nov + first 2 wks Dec
Open for meals 10 am - 10 pm (a-c)
Closed Tues
Facilities for the disabled

Venison in claret, Hebridean skink, haggis and clapshot, local smoked salmon, Scottish prawns with dill. Ecclefechan tart, Blairgowrie raspberry trifle.

Credit cards: 1, 3

Proprietors: Duncan & Anne Hilditch

Feith Mhor Country House
Beananach
Carrbridge
Inverness-shire
PH23 3AP
Tel: 047 984 621

1 mile west of Carrbridge.

This charming 19th century country house is tastefully furnished, and has a warm friendly atmosphere, set in one acre of delightful gardens and surrounded by peaceful unspoilt countryside. The comfortable well appointed en suite bedrooms enjoy beautiful views. There is a pleasant dining room (non-smoking) and two lovely lounges (non-smoking). Excellent home-cooked fare including local and garden produce in season.

Vegetarian dishes are available by arrangement. This is a wonderful area for those who enjoy walking, bird-watching or touring.

Open Dec to early Nov except 1 to 19 Dec
Rooms: 5 with private facilities
Dinner from 7 pm
No children under 14 years
Bed & breakfast £17 - £18
Dinner B & B £27 - £28

Fruity spiced gammon, roast Scotch lamb and beef, poached fresh salmon. Vegetarian lentil bake, leek and dumpling casserole. Desserts include meringue sunrise, pavlova with raspberries, fresh fruit crumbles.

STB   Award Pending

No credit cards

Proprietor: Penny Rawson

CASTLE DOUGLAS
52   **H5**

Longacre Manor Hotel
Ernespie Road
Castle Douglas
Dumfriesshire
DG7 1LE
Tel: 0556 3576

On A75 on northern boundary of Castle Douglas.

Charming small hotel, personally run, offering warm welcome and service. Situated in 1½ acres of woodland gardens with magnificent views to Screel and Galloway hills. Television, direct dial telephone, radio and tea-making facilities in each room. Premises are fully central heated.

Open all year
Rooms: 4 with private facilities
Dinner 7.30 - 8.30 pm (a)
Bed & breakfast from £19
Dinner B & B from £28

Daily changing menu using locally produced fish, beef, lamb, pork and game with fresh vegetables. Home-made desserts a speciality.

STB   4 Crown Commended

No credit cards

Proprietors: Elizabeth & Walter Meldrum

CLEISH
53   **NEAR KINROSS**   **G6**

Nivingston House
Cleish
Kinross-shire
KY13 7LS
Tel: 05775 216

2 miles from junction 5 on M90. Victorian mansion of 12 acres of gardens commanding superb views over local countryside. Log fires burn in the winter and candles flicker in the evenings. Nivingston House uses the best local produce and their gold award winning chef accompanies these with delightful unusual sauces.

Open all year
Rooms: 17 with private facilities
Bar Lunch 12 - 2 pm (a)
Dining Room/Restaurant Lunch 12 - 2 pm (c)
Dinner 7 - 9 pm (d)
Bed & breakfast from £40
Dinner B & B from £60

STB   4 Crown Commended

Credit cards: 1, 2, 3, 6

Proprietors: Allan & Pat Deeson

COLONSAY
54   **ISLE OF**   **F2**

Isle of Colonsay Hotel
Isle of Colonsay
Argyll
PA61 7YP
Tel: 09512 316

Ferry via Oban (2½ hours), Mon/Wed/Fri only. Additional sailings via Islay in high season.

Probably the most isolated hotel in Great Britain, this 18th century inn is run by Kevin and Christa Byrne on a beautiful Hebridean island which is uniquely rich in wildlife and scenery. Fishing, golf, sailing. Bicycles gratis. Full central heating. French spoken.

Open Mar to early Nov + New Year
Rooms: 11, 8 with private facilities
Dining Room/Restaurant Lunch 12.30 - 1.30 pm (a)
Yacht suppers 7 - 8.30 pm May to Sep
Dinner from 7.30 pm (d)
No smoking in dining room
Bed & breakfast from £37
Dinner B & B from £43

Local wild salmon, local farmed oysters and mussels, local creel caught   ▶

langoustines, local queenies and scallop. Home-made soups, jam, marmalade and bread. Emphasis on fresh local produce with many vegetables from hotel's own garden.

STB 3 Crown Commended

Credit cards: 1, 2, 3, 5

Proprietors: Kevin & Christa Byrne

COLVEND
55   **I6**

Clonyard House Hotel
Colvend
Dalbeattie
Dumfriesshire
DG5 4QW
Tel: 055 663 372
Fax: 055 663 422

4½ miles south of Dalbeattie on A710 Solway coast road. 18 miles west of Dumfries.

Victorian country house hotel in six acres wooded grounds. Typical 19th century dining room overlooking lawns. Also pleasant large cocktail bar for informal meals. Ground floor bedroom wing with full facilities. One room fitted for disabled guests. Safe grounds for children. French and some German spoken. Dogs welcome (small charge).

Open all year

Rooms: 9 with private facilities
Bar Lunch 12 - 2 pm (a)
Dinner 7 - 9 pm (c)
Facilities for the disabled
Bed & breakfast from £25

Solway salmon, Kirkcudbrightshire scallops, Galloway beef and lamb, venison. Luscious home-made sweets of many varieties. Scottish goats cheeses.

STB 4 Crown Commended

Credit cards: 1, 3

Proprietors: N M Thompson & D Thompson

CREDIT/CHARGE CARDS

1 Access/Mastercard/Eurocard
2 American Express
3 Visa
4 Carte Bleu
5 Diners Club
6 Mastercharge

COMRIE
56   **F5**

The Deil's Cauldron Lounge Bar & Restaurant
27 Dundas Street
Comrie
Perthshire
PH6 2LN
Tel: 0764 70352

On A85 west end of Comrie.

The Deil's Cauldron created from a 200 year old Listed building, takes its name from a well known local beauty spot. The attractive black and white exterior leads to a comfortable lounge and two dining rooms (smoking and non-smoking) featuring original stone walls and decorated with fine water colours, old photographs and prints. From the lounge one can enter the garden to find an interesting fish pond and lots of heathers and shrubs. There is a good selection of malt whisky available. Reservations advisable.

Open Feb to Dec

Bar Lunch 12 - 2 pm (a)
Dining Room/Restaurant Lunch 12 - 2 pm (a)
Dinner 6.30 - 8.30 pm (b)
Closed Tues
Separate dining room for non-smokers

The menu features local beef, lamb, fish, home-grown vegetables and game in season. Auld Alliance cooking.

Credit cards: 1, 2, 3

Proprietors: Robert & Judith Shepherd

CONTIN
57   **BY STRATHPEFFER**   **D5**

Coul House Hotel
Contin
by Strathpeffer
Ross-shire IV14 9EY
Tel: 0997 21487
Fax: 0997 21945

On A835 to Ullapool, 17 miles north-west of Inverness.

The ancient Mackenzies of Coul picked an incomparable setting for their secluded Highland country mansion, with fine views over forest and mountain. There are log fires, elegant public rooms and, of course, candlelit "Mackenzie's Taste of Scotland Restaurant". All bedrooms are en suite, equipped with colour teletext TV, radio, direct-dial telephone, hospitality tray, hairdryer and trouser press.

Open all year

Rooms: 21 with private facilities
Bar Lunch 12 - 2 pm (a)
Dinner 7 - 9 pm (c)
Bar Supper 5.30 - 9 pm
Bed & breakfast £23.50 - £33.50
Dinner B & B £41 - £52

Saute of Summer Isles scallops, venison saddle chops, smoked Conon salmon, prawns in Highland garlic butter, escalope of salmon in wine, cream and chive sauce, fillet steaks. Scottish Maiden's Kiss.

STB 4 Crown Commended

Credit cards: 2, 5

Proprietor: Martyn Hill

CORSEMALZIE
58   **I4**

Corsemalzie House Hotel
Corsemalzie, Port William
Newton Stewart
Wigtownshire
DG8 9RL
Tel: 098 886 254

Off A714 Newton Stewart-Port William; take B7005 Wigtown-Glenluce road.

Sporting country house hotel set in 40 acres of woodland and gardens. Extensive game, fishing and shooting rights. Dogs accepted (small charge).

Open Mar to mid Jan

Rooms: 15, 14 with private facilities
Dining Room/Restaurant Lunch 12.30 - 2 pm (a)
Dinner 7.30 - 9 pm (b-c)
Bed & breakfast from £24.50
Dinner B & B rates on application

Fresh and smoked Bladnoch salmon and trout. Game in season, steaks and roasts a speciality; home-grown vegetables. Scottish sweet table and cheese board with oatcakes (Friday and Saturday evenings).

STB 4 Crown Commended

Credit cards: 1, 2, 3, 6

Proprietor: Peter McDougall

COUPAR ANGUS

59   **F7**

Enverdale Hotel
Pleasance Road
Coupar Angus
Perthshire
PH13 9JB
Tel: 0828 27606

Off 2 tourist routes – A94 Perth - Aberdeen, and A923 Dundee - Blairgowrie.

Pleasing 19th century hotel which prides itself on a personal service and a warm and friendly atmosphere. Ideally suited for touring the heart of Scotland – Glamis Castle, Scone Palace, Edinburgh and Glasgow, all within easy driving distance. For the sportsman – skiing, curling, shooting, fishing and golf – 40 courses within one hour's drive including Gleneagles, St Andrews and Carnoustie. Children welcome.

Open mid Jan to Dec

Rooms: 5, 2 with private facilities
Picnic Lunches available
Bar Meals 12 noon - 9.15 pm (a)
Dinner 7.15 - 9 pm except Sun + Mon (b)
Bed & breakfast from £19
Dinner B & B from £28

Fillet steak with cream sauce, mushrooms and Drambuie. Fresh Tay salmon. Home-made soups, pâté, haggis, cakes and pastries. Locally grown raspberries.

STB 2 Crown Commended

Credit cards: 1, 3

Proprietors: Martin & Rosemary Price

CRAIGELLACHIE

60   **D7**

Craigellachie Hotel
Craigellachie
Banffshire
AB3 9SS
Tel: 0340 881204
Fax: 0340 881253

On A941, 12 miles south of Elgin.

New owners and extensive alterations and refurbishment have transformed this famous old hotel into something quite special. The public rooms have been furnished with taste and elegance and the whole place exudes an atmosphere of care and attention. While predominantly in fishing and shooting country it is also very much on the famous Whisky Trail with several nearby distilleries. The excellent quality of food matches, and indeed complements, the high standards elsewhere. French, Swedish and Danish spoken.

Open all year

Rooms: 30 with private facilities
Bar Lunch 12 - 2 pm (a)
Dining Room/Restaurant Lunch 12.30 - 2 pm (b)
Dinner 7.30 - 9.30 pm (d)
Bed & breakfast from £39.50
Dinner B & B from £61

Crayfish chowder with brandy, steamed Spey salmon with apricot and thyme sauce, warm pigeon breast with roast parsnips and claret sauce. Poached strudel with gooseberry compote. Scottish cheese and home-made oatcakes.

STB 4 Crown Highly Commended

Credit cards: 1, 2, 3, 5

Proprietors: Thomas Gronager & Stephen Goodchild

CRAIL

61   **F7**

Caiplie Guest House
53 High Street
Crail
Fife
KY10 3RA
Tel: 0333 50564

High Street, Crail.

A comfortable and neatly maintained guest house in the historic and attractive fishing town of Crail. Small dining room. Guests' sitting room with TV.

Open Mar to Oct

Rooms: 7
Dinner from 7 pm (a)
Residents only
No smoking area in restaurant
Bed & breakfast £10.50 - £13.50
Dinner B & B £19 - £22

Scottish and continental dishes prepared from fresh local produce. Cloutie dumpling, cranachan.

STB 2 Crown Commended

No credit cards

Proprietor: Jayne Hudson

Hazelton Guest House
29 Marketgate
Crail
Fife
KY10 3TH
Tel: 0333 50250

In town centre opposite tourist office and Tolbooth.

The Hazelton is one of an imposing terrace of Victorian merchants houses in the centre of Crail. All rooms have central heating, colour television, tea and coffee-making facilities and wash-hand basin. The relaxed friendly atmosphere and attention to detail ensure a pleasant stay in this charming little fishing town in the East Neuk of Fife.

Open all year

Rooms: 7
Dinner 7 - 7.30 pm (a)
It is requested that guests select their menu by 5 pm
Residents only
No dogs
Bed & breakfast £12.50 - £15.50
Dinner B & B £22.50 - £25.50

Daily changing menu using local produce. Fish, seafood and game featured. Home-smoked specialities. Vegetarians catered for by arrangement.

STB Listed Commended

No credit cards

Proprietors: Alan & Rita Brown

CRIANLARICH

62   **F5**

Allt-Chaorain Country House
Crianlarich
Perthshire
FK20 8RU
Tel: 08383 283

On A82, 1 mile north of Crianlarich.

Roger McDonald bids "welcome to my home" which is situated in an elevated position 500 yards from the roadside, with commanding views of Benmore and Strathfinnan from the south-facing sun lounge. The traditional wood-panelled dining room caters for three tables of six people, while the lounge has a log fire burning throughout the year and considerable antique and reproduction furniture.

Open mid Mar to end Oct

Rooms: 9 with private facilities
Dinner 7 prn - later by arrangement (b)
Residents only

▶

No smoking in dining room, bedrooms and main lounge.
A sun lounge is set aside for those who wish to smoke
Bed & breakfast rates on application
Dinner B & B £33 - £39

Wide range of traditional fresh fare. Game pie, pork fillets, braised steaks, breasts of chicken, beef olives stuffed with haggis. Cloutie dumpling.

STB 3 Crown Commended

Credit cards: 1, 3

Proprietor: Roger McDonald

CRIEFF
63 **F6**

Crieff Visitors Centre
Muthill Road
Crieff
Perthshire
PH7 4AZ
Tel: 0764 4014

On A822 leading out of Crieff to the south.

Quality self-service restaurant, showroom, audio visual room and garden centre complex alongside two rural factories producing thistle pattern Buchan pottery and high quality Perthshire Paperweights. Within one hour of Glasgow, Edinburgh and St Andrews, close by Gleneagles amidst fine Highland scenery. Serves a range of popular dishes and snacks.

Open all year

Self-service restaurant and all facilities open 7 days, 9 am - 6 pm. Closes earlier in the Winter.
Facilities for the disabled

Credit cards: 1, 2, 3, 6

Cultoquhey House Hotel
by Crieff
Perthshire
PH7 3NE
Tel: 0764 3253

On A85, 2 miles east of Crieff.

Distant hills, log fires, wood panelling, loose covers, old gundog, croquet lawns, wild rhododendrons, ancient oaks, bumpy tracks, billiard room, vintage port, hot water bottles, stags' heads, four-poster beds, mountainous stairs, fresh sea trout, elderflower sorbet, family home, weathered sandstone, leaking roof, roe deer, bats at dusk.

Open Apr to Feb

Rooms: 12, 10 with private facilities

Bar Lunch 12 - 2.30 pm (a)
Dining Room/Restaurant Lunch 12 - 2.30 pm (a)
Dinner 7.30 - 9 pm (b-c)
Bed & breakfast from £25
Dinner B & B from £37

Delicious soups. Fresh wild salmon. Grouse and blaeberry sauce. Perthshire venison terrine. Home-made hazelnut and Drambuie ice cream.

STB Award Pending

Credit cards: 1, 2, 3, 5

Proprietors: David & Anna Cooke

Murraypark Hotel
Connaught Terrace
Crieff
Perthshire
PH7 3DJ
Tel: 0764 3731
Fax: 0764 5311

A85 to residential part of town.

Pink-stoned large Victorian house standing in its own grounds in the residential part of town. A comfortable restaurant with uncrowded atmosphere overlooks a pleasant garden. Based on established Scottish foods with many interesting variations. French spoken. Children and dogs welcome.

Open all year

Rooms: 13 with private facilities
Bar Lunch 12 - 2 pm (a)
Dining Room/Restaurant Lunch 12.30 - 2 pm (b)
Dinner 7.30 - 9.30 pm (d)
Guests are requested to refrain from smoking in the dining room
Bed & breakfast from £29
Dinner B & B from £44

Scampi wrapped in bacon and grilled on a skewer with cheese and pineapple. Chicken in a light curry cream with banana and pineapple served on rice. Mushrooms with Stilton, cream and port.

STB 4 Crown Commended

Credit cards: 1, 2, 3, 5

Proprietors: Ann & Noel Scott

Smugglers Restaurant
Glenturret Distillery
The Hosh
Crieff
Perthshire
PH7 4HA
Tel: 0764 2424

On A85 north-west of Crieff.

Self-service restaurant (130 seats) situated in an 18th century converted

whisky warehouse within Scotland's oldest highland malt distillery. Award winning visitors centre. Audio visual presentation and 3-D exhibition. Whisky tasting bar – taste different ages of Glenturret, 8, 12, 15, and 21 years old, and The Glenturret Malt Liqueur. Whisky Shop. Children welcome. New disabled access.

Open Mar to Dec

Bar Lunch 12 - 2.30 pm (b) Smugglers
Dining Room/Restaurant Lunch 12 - 2.30 pm (b) Pagoda Room - exclusive dining room with waitress service
Dinner – group bookings only both Smugglers and Pagoda (f)
Closed Sun
No smoking area in Smugglers Restaurant
No smoking in Pagoda Room

Glenturret flavoured pâté, smoked salmon, venison steak, Hosh haggis and vegetarian haggis. Cranachan and gâteaux.

Credit cards: 1, 2, 3

Best Bar Lunch 1989

Proprietor: Peter Fairlie

CRINAN
64 **G3**

Crinan Hotel
Crinan
Lochgilphead
Argyll
PA31 8SR
Tel: 054 683 261
Fax: 054 683 292

A82 Glasgow-Inveraray. A83 - Lochgilphead. Follow road to Oban – 5 miles out of Lochgilphead.

Magnificent views over Loch Crinan, the sea and islands. Exclusive seafood restaurant enjoys breathtaking sunsets and stunning views.

Open all year

Rooms: 22 with private facilities
Bar Lunch 12.30 - 2 pm (a)
Dinner 7 - 9 pm (d-e)
Bed & breakfast £37 - £45
Dinner B & B rates on application

Jumbo Prawns Corryvreckan, Scottish beef, local wild salmon.

STB 4 Crown Commended

Credit cards: 1, 3

Proprietors: Nick & Frances Ryan

CROMARTY

Royal Hotel
Marine Terrace
Cromarty
Ross-shire
IV11 8YN
Tel: 03817 217

On A832, 20 miles north-east of Inverness.

The hotel is situated overlooking the beach and harbour in the ancient and historic village of Cromarty. All the well appointed bedrooms have views of the sea and Ross-shire mountains. The reputation for excellent food and value for money plus traditional Scottish hospitality is guarded with pride by the staff.

Open all year

Rooms: 10 with private facilities
Bar Lunch 12 - 2 pm (a)
Dining Room/Restaurant Lunch 12 - 2 pm (b)
Bar Supper 5.30 - 9 pm
Dinner 7 - 8.30 pm (c)
No smoking in restaurant
Bed & breakfast from £20
Dinner B & B from £30

Wide range of traditional Scottish fare. Farmhouse crepe. T-bone steaks. Crab salads.

STB 3 Crown Commended

Credit cards: 2, 3

Proprietors: Stewart & Betty Morrison

CULLEN

Bayview Hotel
Seafield Street
Cullen
Banffshire
AB5 2SU
Tel: 0542 41031

A98 between Banff and Fochabers – overlooking Cullen Harbour.

A really charming little hotel splendidly converted to provide interesting public rooms and well equipped bedrooms. Cullen is a pleasant small harbour town and the Bayview commands excellent views over the harbour, the beaches and Moray Firth. David and Frances Evans base their menus on the quality local products most readily available which of course includes fresh seafish and shellfish.

Open Dec to Oct

Rooms: 6, 5 with private facilities
Bar Lunch 12 - 2 pm (a)
Dining Room/Restaurant Lunch 12 - 2 pm Sun only (a)
Bar Supper 6.30 - 9 pm (a)
Dinner 6.30 - 9 pm (b)
No dogs
Bed & breakfast £22 - £30
Dinner B & B £35.50 - £43.50

Cullen skink. Fillet of salmon cooked in vermouth. Trout with horseradish and walnut stuffing. Iced honey and whisky cream.

STB 4 Crown Commended

Credit cards: 1, 3

Proprietors: David & Frances Evans

CULLODEN MOOR

Leanach Farm
Culloden Moor
by Inverness
IV1 2EJ
Tel: 0463 791027

5 miles south of Inverness off B851 to Culloden/Croy.

This attractive farmhouse run by Iain and Rosanne MacKay is beautifully situated in historic surroundings within easy distance of Inverness. Emphasis is placed on a warm welcome combined with good well cooked food and comfortable accommodation.

Open all year

Rooms: 3
Dinner 6.30 pm except Sun + Sat (b)
Residents only
Unlicensed
No smoking in dining room
Dinner B & B from £20

Home-made soups and puddings. Fresh trout and salmon. Scottish meats and fresh vegetables.

STB Listed Commended

No credit cards

Proprietors: Iain & Rosanne MacKay

CREDIT/CHARGE CARDS

1 Access/Mastercard/Eurocard
2 American Express
3 Visa
4 Carte Bleu
5 Diners Club
6 Mastercharge

CUPAR

Ostlers Close
Bonnygate
Cupar
Fife KY15 4BU
Tel: 0334 55574

A92, Cupar town centre.

This is a gem of a place. A small, intimate and entirely unpretentious restaurant situated in a small lane off the main street in Cupar. Jimmy Graham the chef proprietor produces some of the best food in Fife utilising, especially, east coast fish and shellfish with skill and imagination. His wife Amanda presides over the dining room with great charm and friendliness. The combination of the two is irresistible.

Open all year except 1 wk Oct + 1 wk Jun
Dining Room/Restaurant Lunch 12.15 - 2 pm (c)
Dinner 7 - 9.30 pm (e)
Closed Sun + Mon

Cream of Tay salmon soup, Pittenweem seafood, e.g. prawns with garlic and fresh herb butter. Selection of game in season with home-made jellies.

Credit cards: 1, 3

Best Restaurant 1989

Proprietors: Jimmy & Amanda Graham

DALBEATTIE

Auchenskeoch Lodge
by Dalbeattie
Kirkcudbrightshire
DG5 4PG
Tel: 038 778 277

5 miles south-east of Dalbeattie on B793.

Former Victorian shooting lodge personally run by the proprietors. Period furnishings throughout ensure a genuine country house atmosphere, whilst woodlands, formal gardens and rhododendron walks provide privacy and tranquillity. Facilities include fishing on own loch, billiard room and croquet lawn. Great emphasis is put on the quality and freshness of the food. To this end the menu is kept small with a choice of two dishes at each course; it changes daily and makes full use of the excellent meat and fish available locally. Wherever possible the vegetables, salads, herbs and soft fruits are fresh from the garden.

Open Easter to end Oct   ▶

Rooms: 5 with private facilities
Dinner 7.30 - 8 pm (b)
Booking essential for non-residents
Bed & breakfast £19 - £21
Dinner B & B £30 - £32
Small menu, changing daily. Emphasis on fresh local produce.
STB   3 Crown Commended
Credit cards: 1, 3
Proprietors: Christopher & Mary
               Broom-Smith

PRICE CATEGORIES

(a)	under £10.00
(b)	£10.00 - £15.00
(c)	£15.00 - £20.00
(d)	£20.00 - £25.00
(e)	£25.00 - £30.00
(f)	over £30.00

DAVIOT
70   NEAR INVERNESS   D5

Daviot Mains Farm
Daviot
Inverness
IV1 2ER
Tel: 046 385 215
On B851 (B9006) to Culloden/Croy, 5 miles south of Inverness.
Comfortable early 19th century Listed farmhouse in quiet situation five miles from Inverness, under the personal supervision of Margaret and Alex Hutcheson. Relax in the warm atmosphere of this friendly home where delicious meals are thoughtfully prepared for you and where log fires burn in both sitting room and dining room. Children and dogs accepted by arrangement.

Open all year
Rooms: 3
Dinner 6.30 pm except Sun
Unlicensed – guests welcome to take own wine
No smoking in dining room
Bed & breakfast from £12.50
Dinner B & B from £19
According to season – home-made soups, fresh local salmon and trout, Scottish meats, vegetables and cheeses. Local fruits and home-made puddings.
STB   2 Crown Commended
No credit cards
Proprietors: Margaret & Alex Hutcheson

DIRLETON
71   G7

Open Arms Hotel
Dirleton
East Lothian
EH39 5BG
Tel: 0620 85 241
A198 between Gullane and North Berwick.
An up market inn set in one of Scotland's prettiest villages overlooking the 13th century castle village green. In the same family's hands for 40 years, the well known restaurant specialises in a warm welcome complemented by log fires and fresh foods. French and German spoken.
Open all year
Rooms: 7 with private facilities
Bar Lunch 12.30 - 2.30 pm (a)
Dining Room/Restaurant Lunch 12.30 - 2.30 pm (a)
Dinner 7 - 10 pm (c)
Bed & breakfast £43 - £60
Dinner B & B £70 - £75
Mussel and onion stew. Supreme of chicken de Vaux. Cranachan with blackcurrants.
STB   4 Crown Commended
Credit cards: 1, 3
Proprietor: Arthur Neil

DOLPHINTON
72   G6

Dolphinton House Hotel
Dolphinton
nr West Linton
Peeblesshire EH46 7AB
Tel: 0968 82286
On A702, 7 miles east of Biggar and 3 miles west of West Linton.
Imagine the finest natural fare served in a Victorian dining room overlooking the Border hills. Consider the skills of a master chef preparing gourmet food for a limited number. Deliberate over some 125 of the world's best wines – reasonably priced. You've discovered Dolphinton – a 19th century manor in 186 acres of woodland – idyllic!
Open all year
Rooms: 12 with private facilities
Bar Lunch 12 - 2 pm (a)
Dining Room/Restaurant Lunch 12.30 - 2 pm (c)
Dinner 7 - 9 pm (d)
No smoking in dining room
Bed & breakfast from £72
Dinner B & B from £102.50
All Scottish produce – venison, sea trout, grouse, lamb, beef, soft fruits. 'The Scottish Gourmet' food.
STB   4 Crown Highly Commended
Credit cards: 1, 2, 3, 5, 6.

DORNOCH
73   D6

Dornoch Castle Hotel
Castle Street
Dornoch
IV25 3SD
Tel: 0862 810216
In the centre of the cathedral town of Dornoch, 2 miles off A9.
Former Bishop's Palace opposite 13th century cathedral, offering comfortable bedrooms, most of which overlook the sheltered garden. The elegant coffee lounge opens onto the terrace. The panelled bar is welcoming for a pre-dinner drink or guests may simply enjoy relaxing in the comfortable TV lounge. The Bishop's Room Restaurant – once the palace kitchen – is one of the finest in the area, with a wine list to match.
Open mid Apr to end Oct
Rooms: 19, 17 with private facilities
Bar Lunch 12.30 - 2 pm (a)   ▶

Dining Room/Restaurant Lunch 12.30 -
2 pm (a)
Dinner 7.30 - 8.30 pm (b)
No smoking in restaurant
Bed & breakfast £24.50 - £34
Dinner B & B rates on application

*Local venison, salmon, trout and lobster.
Aberdeen Angus steaks. Game birds.
Home-made soups, e.g. Brochan
Buidhe, and chef's pâtés.*

STB 3 Crown Commended

Credit cards: 1, 2, 3, 6

Proprietor: Michael Ketchin

DUFFTOWN
74   **D7**

A Taste of Speyside
10 Balvenie Street
Dufftown
Banffshire
AB5 4AB
Tel: 0340 20860

*50 yards from Tourist Information Centre
on Elgin road.*

Situated in Dufftown, the malt whisky
capital of the world, this small
independent restaurant and whisky
tasting centre aims to promote the best
of Speyside food and fine Speyside
malts, of which there is an unrivalled
selection. Proprietors Joe Thompson
and Ann McLean are on hand to assure a
warm welcome. Group bookings out of
season can be arranged.

Open 1 Mar to 31 Oct

Bar lunch 11 am - 6 pm (a)
Dining Room/Restaurant Lunch 11 am -
6 pm (a)
Dinner 6 - 9 pm (a)
No dogs except guide dogs

*Taste of Speyside platter, roast loin of
Scottish lamb, venison and red wine pie,
home-made pâtés, soups, bread.*

Credit cards: 1, 3

Best Bar Lunch 1988

Proprietors: Joe Thompson &
            Ann McLean

DULNAIN BRIDGE
75   **E6**

Auchendean Lodge Hotel
Dulnain Bridge
Grantown-on-Spey
Morayshire
PH26 3LU
Tel: 047 985 347

On A95, 1 mile south of Dulnain Bridge.

An Edwardian hunting lodge, now a
comfortable country hotel, furnished with
antiques and elegant furnishings, whilst
retaining its homeliness. Relax informally
with Highland hospitality and log fires.
Marvel at some of the finest views across
the River Spey and Abernethy Forest
towards the Cairngorm mountains. Then
enjoy the award winning home-cooked
dinners, with specialities using wild
produce from the woods and countryside.
The extensive cellars have over 100 wines
and 30 malt whiskies. Extensive walks in
the woods behind the hotel. French
spoken.

Open all year except Nov + early Dec

Rooms: 7, 5 with private facilities
Dinner 7.30 - 10.30 pm (c) 4-course menu
No smoking in dining room and one of the
lounges
Bed & breakfast £16 - £30
Dinner B & B £33 - £48.50

*Arbroath smokies in ale and cream,
smoked haddock tartare, shaggy ink cap
soup, wild mushroom pate, venison steak
in rowan jelly sauce, mallard with
blaeberries, black and white chocolate
truffle cake.*

STB 3 Crown Commended
No credit cards

Proprietors: Eric Hart & Ian Kirk

Muckrach Lodge Hotel
Dulnain Bridge
Grantown-on-Spey
Morayshire
PH26 3LY
Tel: 047 985 257

On A938, ½ mile west of Dulnain Bridge.

Former shooting lodge located in ten
secluded acres in the beautiful Dulnain
valley. The Dulnain River is adjacent to the
hotel. This tributary of the Spey is famous
for salmon and sea trout. Frequent visitors
to the hotel grounds are the timid roe deer
and the capricious red squirrel along with
the numerous bird life of the area. Log
fires, fully centrally heated. All rooms have
colour TV, telephones and tea/coffee-
makers. Table d'hôte dinners and
extensive wine cellar.

Open all year
Rooms: 10 with private facilities
Bar lunch 12 - 2 pm (a)
Dining Room/Restaurant Lunch 12 -
2 pm (a) Sun only
Dinner 7.30 - 8.45 pm (c)
Bed & breakfast from £31
Dinner B & B from £46.50

*Aberdeen Angus beef, Morayshire lamb,
Spey salmon and sea trout. Kinlochbervie
shellfish, Aberdeen fresh fish. Scottish
cheese board. Muckrach substantial
sandwiches - lunchtime. Home-made
soups, pâté.*

STB 4 Crown Commended

Credit cards: 1, 2, 3, 5

Proprietors: Roy & Pat Watson

DUMFRIES
76   **H6**

Cairndale Hotel
English Street
Dumfries
Dumfriesshire
DG1 2DF
Tel: 0387 54111
Telex: 777530
Fax: 0387 50555

*Situated close to centre of town, on A75
Dumfries-Carlisle route.*

Privately owned and managed by the
Wallace family, this well established hotel
offers all the comfort expected from one
of the region's leading three star hotels.
Originally three Victorian town houses,
the Cairndale has a total of 60 letting
bedrooms. All rooms in the hotel have
private facilities, TV, radio, direct dial
telephone, hairdryer and hospitality tray as
standard, while executive rooms and
suites have queen size double beds,
mini-bars, trouser presses and jacuzzi
spa baths.

Open all year
Rooms: 60 with private facilities
Bar Lunch 12 - 2 pm (b)
Dining Room/Restaurant Lunch 12 -
2 pm (b)
Dinner 7 - 9.30 pm (d)
Bed & breakfast rates on application
Dinner B & B rates on application

*Smoked salmon mousse with tayberry
cream sauce; noisettes of Border lamb
with apricots and brandy sauce; scampi in
Chef Hoefkens' own style; roast sirloin of
Galloway beef. Hot butterscotch pancake
with pear.*

STB 4 Crown Commended

Credit cards: 1, 2, 3, 5

Station Hotel
Lovers Walk
Dumfries
Dumfriesshire
DG1 1LT
Tel: 0387 54316
Telex: 778654

Just outside town centre opposite railway station.

The hotel offers a delightful combination of modern guest comfort and facilities within the maintained character of a Listed building. It is conveniently situated close to the commercial and shopping centre of this charming historic town, yet is only one mile from the attractive Borders countryside and Burns heritage trail.

Open all year

Rooms: 32 with private facilities
Dinner 7 - 9.30 pm (b-c)
Taste of Scotland applies to main restaurant only
No smoking area in restaurant
Bed & breakfast from £36
Dinner B & B from £25

STB 4 Crown Commended

Credit cards: 1, 2, 3, 5, 6

DUNBAR
77   G8

The Courtyard Hotel & Restaurant
Woodbush Brae
Dunbar
East Lothian
EH42 1HB
Tel: 0368 64169

Overlooking the sea at Dunbar (A1 about 28 miles east of Edinburgh).

The water washes against the walls of these fishermen's cottages which have been sympathetically converted to a small hotel and restaurant and have dramatic seascape views. The Courtyard is set in the heart of golf country and is also ideal for touring the Border country with its wild and beautiful coastline – yet only 28 miles from the Edinburgh city lights. The proprietors have built up a good regular clientele and a sound reputation for interesting, imaginative – and inexpensive – food.

Open all year

Rooms: 6, 1 with private facilities
Dining Room/Restaurant Lunch 12 - 2 pm (a)
Dinner 7 - 9.30 pm (b)
Please note: restaurant closed occasionally Sun evenings

Bed & breakfast from £16.50
Dinner B & B rates on application

Home-made pates, soups; local filleted trout; lamb, Aberdeen Angus with Madeira sauce, chicken breast with wild mushroom sauce, panache of fresh vegetables, home-made desserts, extensive wine list.

STB 2 Crown Commended

Credit cards: 1, 3

Proprietors: Anne-Louise Schauerte & Peter Bramley

DUNBLANE
78   F5

Cromlix House
Kinbuck
Dunblane
Perthshire
FK15 9JT
Tel: 0786 822125

A9 to Dunblane then B8033 to Kinbuck.

Now a superb country house hotel, Cromlix House, built in 1880, stands in 5,000 acres and has four private lochs. Log fires burn in public rooms which still contain original furnishings and fine porcelain and silver. Rooms available for exclusive conferences and private dinner parties. Sports include fishing, shooting, croquet, riding and tennis. In a magnificently recreated Victorian conservatory, non-residents are served lunch, full afternoon tea and dinner.

Open all year

Rooms: 14 with private facilities
Dining Room/Restaurant Lunch 12 - 2 pm (b-c)
Full afternoon tea (a)
Dinner 7 - 10 pm (e) 6 course fully inclusive of canape, petit fours and coffee
No smoking area in dining room
Bed & breakfast from £75
Dinner B & B from £105

Sauted partridge breast with sorrel on braised cabbage in a port wine sauce. Sauted medallions of monkfish on aubergine fondue in rosemary butter sauce. White coffee mousse with toasted hazelnut sauce.

STB 4 Crown Highly Commended

Credit cards: 1, 2, 3

Best Country House Hotel 1989

Stakis Dunblane Hydro Resort
Perth Road
Dunblane
Perthshire FK15 0HG
Tel: 0786 822551
Telex: 776284
Fax: 0786 825403

The Stakis Dunblane Hydro is situated on the fringe of the rural town, from which it takes its name. Set in 44 acres of private mature grounds and commanding a magnificent view; the splendid Victorian façade of this famed hotel is just a foretaste of the luxury to follow. Extensive leisure facilities both indoors and outdoors. Regular entertainment.

Open all year

Rooms: 219 with private facilities
Dining Room/Restaurant Lunch 12.30 - 1.45 pm (b)
Afternoon Tea 3 - 5.30 pm
Dinner 6.30 - 9.30 pm (c)
No smoking area in restaurant
Bed & breakfast rates on application
Room rate from £77
Dinner B & B from £38 (min. 2 nights stay)

Terrine of Perthshire pheasant, pigeon and pistachio. Steamed fillet of Tay salmon with fresh spinach and pine kernels.

STB Award Pending

Credit cards: 1, 2, 3, 5, 6

DUNDEE
79   F7

The Old Mansion House Hotel
Auchterhouse
by Dundee
DD3 0QN
Tel: 082 626 366

On A923, 7 miles west of Dundee, then B954 past Muirhead.

A small luxury hotel converted by the present owners from a 16th century baronial home, within 10 acres of beautiful gardens and woodlands. The lands around the house steeped in Scottish history have been in the ownership of several noted families, namely the Ogilvies, Strathmores, and the Earls of Buchan. Superb dining and excellent wine cellar.

Open all year except Christmas + New Year period

Rooms: 6 with private facilities
Bar Lunch 12 - 2 pm (a)
Dining Room/Restaurant Lunch 12 - 2 pm (b)
Dinner 7 - 9.30 pm (c)   ▶

Bed & breakfast from £35
Dinner B & B from £50

Cullen skink, collops in the pan, venison terrine.

STB 4 Crown Commended

Credit cards: 1, 2, 3, 5

Proprietors: Nigel & Eva Bell

Stakis Earl Grey Hotel
Earl Grey Place
Dundee
DD1 4DE
Tel: 0382 29271
Telex: 76569
Fax: 0382 200072

City location on the waterfront.

Situated on Dundee's waterfront, commanding magnificent views over the River Tay. Only minutes from the city centre, this luxurious hotel promotes the very highest standards of service and accommodation. Leisure interests are well catered for too – the hotel's own leisure suite incorporates a pool, exercise area, whirlpool and sauna.

Open all year

Rooms: 103 with private facilities
Dining Room/Restaurant Lunch 12.30 - 2.30 pm (b-c)
Dinner 6.30 - 10 pm (d)
Bed & breakfast from £57
Dinner B & B from £37 (min. 2 nights stay)

Highland venison in honey and Drambuie sauce, breast of pheasant in whisky sauce. Cranachan, Atholl brose, Drambuie cream.

STB 5 Crown Commended

Credit cards: 1, 2, 3, 5

DUNDONNELL
80   **C4**

Dundonnell Hotel
Dundonnell
by Garve
Ross-shire
IV23 2QR
Tel: 085 483 204

On A832 south of Ullapool.

Set by the shores of Little Loch Broom in the spectacular wilderness of Wester Ross this three star hotel renowned for its quality and comfort has been in the ownership of the Florence family for the past 28 years. Mid-way between Ullapool and Gairloch this is the ideal place from which to explore the

surrounding hills and glens as well as the better known attraction of Inverewe Gardens.

Open Easter to Oct

Rooms: 24 with private facilities
Bar Lunch 12.30 - 2.30 pm (a)
Dining Room/Restaurant Lunch by arrangement only (b)
Dinner 7 - 8.30 pm (c)
Bed & breakfast £26 - £35
Dinner B & B £34.50 - £50

Home-made soups, scallops Moniack, Drambuie prawn, seafood chicken, salmon in dill, cranachan, Scottish flummery, Caledonian cream.

STB 4 Crown Commended

Credit cards: 1, 3, 6

Proprietors: Selbie & Flora Florence

DUNFERMLINE
81   **G6**

Pitfirrane Arms Hotel
Main Street
Crossford
Dunfermline
Fife KY12 8NJ
Tel: 0383 736132

A994 west of Dunfermline i.e. Glasgow road.

The Pitfirrane Arms Hotel is one of the few original coaching inns left in the country which has been restored and extended to meet the modern demand for excellent cuisine and high standards. Situated in the pleasant residential village of Crossford, on the main Dunfermline-Glasgow road (A994), the hotel is within easy access of M90.

Open all year

Rooms: 38 with private facilities
Bar Lunch 12 - 2 pm (a)
Dining Room/Restaurant Lunch 12 - 2 pm (a)
Dinner 6 - 10.15 pm (b)
Bed & breakfast from £33
Dinner B & B from £40

Locally available fresh produce.

STB 4 Crown Commended

Credit cards: 1, 2, 3

Proprietor: M McVicars

DUNKELD
82   **F6**

Stakis Dunkeld House Hotel
Dunkeld
Perthshire
PH8 0HX
Tel: 03502 771
Telex: 76657
Fax: 03502 8924

Dunkeld House stands on the bank of the River Tay, one of Scotland's finest salmon rivers and is set in over 200 acres of gardens and grounds in the magnificent Perthshire countryside. The addition of modern leisure and sporting facilities enhance the attraction of this elegant country house.

Open all year

Rooms: 91 with private facilities
Dining Room/Restaurant Lunch 12.30 - 2.30 pm (d)
Dinner 7 - 10 pm (f)
Bed & breakfast from £60
Dinner B & B from £55 (min. 2 nights stay)

STB 5 Crown Commended

Credit cards: 1, 2, 3, 5, 6

PRICE CATEGORIES

(a)	under £10.00
(b)	£10.00 - £15.00
(c)	£15.00 - £20.00
(d)	£20.00 - £25.00
(e)	£25.00 - £30.00
(f)	over £30.00

Struther Farmhouse
Newmill Road
Dunlop
Ayrshire
KA3 4BA
Tel: 0560 84946

*North Ayrshire – 12 miles Glasgow –
8 miles Kilmarnock.*

Struther is set in a beautiful well
established garden on the edge of a rural
village. Large comfortable rooms, great
food and hospitality combine to make
Struther the perfect place for a home from
home stay or a private dinner party.

Open all year except Mar, but booking
essential
Rooms: 5
Dinner 6.30 - 8.30 pm except Sun + Mon
(b)
Dinner residents only Sun + Mon
Unlicensed – guests welcome to take
own wine
Bed & breakfast from £14
Dinner B & B from £24 - £28
*Roast meats, fresh fruit and vegetables,
poached salmon. Sweets always a
speciality.*
STB 1 Crown Approved
No credit cards
Proprietors: Bob & Peggy Wilson,
　　　　　　Robertha Leggat

Ardfillayne Hotel
Beverley's Restaurant
Bullwood Road
Dunoon
Argyll
PA23 7QJ
Tel: 0369 2267
Fax: 0369 2501

West end of Dunoon (A815).

A fine country house set in 16 acres of
wooded grounds overlooking the old town
of Dunoon and the Clyde estuary. The
hotel is a treasure trove of antique
furniture. Beverley's Restaurant with
fresh flowers, lace, candlelight and silver,
creates an atmosphere of Victorian
sophistication. A large a la carte menu
features some of the most famous French
dishes, using Aberdeen Angus beef,
lobster, fish and shellfish, direct from the

west coast islands. An extensive wine list,
old malts, brandies and ports complete a
memorable meal. Altogether a top class
restaurant, strongly recommended in
many leading guides including AA top 500
restaurants in Great Britain.

Open all year
Rooms: 8 with private facilities
Dining Room/Restaurant Lunch, by prior
arrangement, à la carte only
Dinner 7 - 10 pm (d)
Restaurant closed Sun evening in Winter
No smoking in restaurant
Bed & breakfast rates on application
Dinner B & B rates on application
*Venison Lady Mary of Guise – an old
recipe for dressing venison, with spices,
claret, lemons, butter and walnut ketchup.
Steak Glengoyne – grilled, with smoked
Orkney cheese and flamed with whisky.
Halibut steak poached in milk with a light
lemon and cream sauce. Scallops St
Veronique. Cream of mussel soup. Loch
Fyne oyster and champagne soup. Baked
Loch Fyne crab.*
STB 4 Crown Highly Commended
Credit cards: 1, 2, 3, 5
Proprietors: Bill & Beverley McCaffrey

Enmore Hotel
Marine Parade
Dunoon
Argyll
PA23 8HH
Tel: 0369 2230

*Seafront between Dunoon and Hunters
Quay.*

Charming Georgian country house hotel
situated on the seafront between Dunoon
and Hunters Quay. Lovingly tended and
cared for by the resident proprietors. Local
and own garden produce to provide
superb Scottish fare. Scottish delicacies
from Loch Fyne and Argyll.

Open Mar to Nov
Rooms: 12 with private facilities
Food served throughout the day
Dinner 7.30 - 9 pm (c) 5 course menu
Bed & breakfast from £37
Dinner B & B from £55
*Loch Fyne fish dishes, local venison and
salmon.*
STB 4 Crown Commended
Credit cards: 1, 3, 5
Proprietors: David & Angela Wilson

Barony Castle Hotel
Blackbarony
Eddleston
Peebles EH45 8QW
Tel: 07213 398
Fax: 07213 275

*12 miles south of Edinburgh, 4 miles north
of Peebles.*

The Barony Castle has a truly impressive
appearance – so reminiscent of a French
chateau that one almost looks for the
vineyards. The building goes back to the
early 16th century and it is claimed that
King James VI and Sir Walter Scott have
stayed there. It has been tastefully
restored and furnished. Bedrooms are
large and comfortable with all the modern
accessories one expects. There are 65
acres of grounds and an indoor heated
swimming pool with sauna and jacuzzi.

Open all year
Rooms: 33 with private facilities
Bar Lunch 12 - 2.30 pm (a)
Dining Room/Restaurant Lunch 12 -
2.30 pm (b)
Bar Supper 6 - 9.30 pm (a)
Dinner 7 - 9.30 pm (c)
Facilities for the disabled
No smoking area in restaurant
Bed & breakfast from £35
Dinner B & B rates on application
Credit cards: 1, 2, 3, 5

Abbotsford Restaurant & Bar
3 Rose Street
Edinburgh EH2 2PR
Tel: 031 225 5276
Rose Street, behind Jenners.

This is a good example of a traditional pub
with a separate restaurant upstairs,
serving good honest inexpensive meals in
an atmosphere of Victorian charm. It has
been acclaimed in the United States as
one of the best hostelries in Scotland.
Small parties are catered for, by
arrangement, in the restaurant.

Open all year
Bar Lunch 12 - 2 pm (a)
Dining Room/Restaurant Lunch 12 -
2.15 pm (a)
Dinner 6.30 - 10 pm (a)
Closed Sun
Credit cards: 1, 3
Proprietor: Colin Grant

Caledonian Hotel

Princes Street
Edinburgh
EH1 2AB
Tel: 031 225 2433
Telex: 72179
Fax: 031 225 6632
West end of Princes Street.

The 'Grande Dame' of Edinburgh dominating the west end of Princes Street, this magnficent deluxe hotel offers gracious accommodation and a range of superb food. The elegant Pompadour Restaurant with its subtle colours and delicate murals features Scottish specialities, while the Gazebo Restaurant offers a more informal lunch and an à la carte or table d'hôte dinner menu with many Scottish dishes.

Open all year
Rooms: 237 with private facilities
Bar Lunch (Platform 1) 12 - 2 pm (a)
Lunch (Pompadour) 12.30 - 2 pm except Sun + Sat (c)
Lunch (Gazebo) 12 - 2.30 pm (c)
Afternoon Tea (Lounge) 3 - 5.30 pm
Dinner (Pompadour) 7.30 - 10.30 pm: 7.30 - 10 pm Sun (f)
Dinner (Gazebo) 6 - 10 pm (d)
No smoking area in restaurants
Bed & breakfast from £119.75
Dinner B & B rates on application
Musselburgh pie, mussel and onion brose, asparagus strudel, hot smoked salmon with cinnamon and plum tea, Tobermory smoked sea trout.
STB 5 Crown Highly Commended
Credit cards: 1, 2, 3, 5, 6

Best Hotel 1988

Dubh Prais Restaurant

123B High Street
Edinburgh
EH1 1SG
Tel: 031 557 5732
Edinburgh Royal Mile.

Tucked away in a cavern on the High Street, a block away from John Knox's House – Dubh Prais (Gaelic for cauldron) is an interesting new restaurant on this famous Edinburgh street. James McWilliams, the chef/proprietor, has created a delightful cosy atmosphere which offers fine Scottish cuisine with an interesting international touch.

Open all year
Dining Room/Restaurant Lunch 12 - 2.30 pm (a)
Dinner 6.30 - 10.30 pm (b)
Closed Sun + Mon

Light pheasant and watercress mousse, saddle of hare, duck and bramble sauce, poached wild salmon, Mallaig scallops and Aberdeen Angus steak – just a few of the dishes you could expect to find on the menu.
Credit cards: 1, 2, 3
Proprietor: James McWilliams

George Hotel

George Street
Edinburgh
EH3 2PB
Tel: 031 225 1251
City centre of Edinburgh.

Listed amongst Edinburgh's premier hotels, the George enjoy a fine reputation. There are 195 comfortable bedrooms, with superb views over the city. Le Chambertin Restaurant offers the finest cuisine and the Carvers Table offers traditional roasts. The Clans Bar has a Scottish theme, decorated with artifacts and curios of the whisky trade.

Open all year
Rooms: 195 with private facilities
Dining Room/Restaurant Lunch 12.30 - 2 pm (b-c)
Dinner 7 - 10 pm (c)
No smoking area in restaurant
Bed & breakfast £94 - £138
Dinner B & B rates on application
STB 5 Crown Commended
Credit cards: 1, 2, 3, 5, 6

Henderson's Salad Table

94 Hanover Street
Edinburgh
EH2 1DR
Tel: 031 225 2131
2 minutes from Princes Street under Henderson's wholefood shop.

Established for 25 years, Henderson's is a well known and popular rendezvous for healthy eaters. It offers a continuous buffet of fresh salads and savouries and sweets prepared with care and served in an informal cosmopolitan atmosphere. Seating for up to 200. Live music in the evenings. Innovators of healthy eating.

Open all year
Open Mon to Sat 8 am - 10 pm
Closed Sun except during Festival
No smoking area in restaurant
Wide selection of herb teas, freshly squeezed juice, wines from growers using organic methods, hand-made bakery items made with stoneground flour, free-range eggs.
Credit cards: 1, 2, 3
Proprietors: Henderson Family

The Howtowdie Restaurant

24a Stafford Street
Edinburgh EH3 7BD
Tel: 031 225 6291
Stafford Street is off Shandwick Place at the west end of Princes Street.

In an area of the city's West End rather starved for good restaurants, this is a small intimate and pleasant Scottish restaurant using Scottish produce with French overtones in the sauces. The menu includes many local specialities. Musical evenings when the proprietor entertains his guests on the fiddle are especially popular with visitors. The purple, grey and black colours of the west coast are predominant in the decor and create an attractive ambience.

Open all year except 1 + 2 Jan + 25 + 26 Dec
Dining Room/Restaurant Lunch 12.30 - 2 pm except Sun + Sat (b)
Dinner 7 - 10.30 pm except Sun (d)
Please note: restaurant open Sun from May to Sep
Chicken howtowdie stuffed with haggis. Fillet of beef in Drambuie sauce. Fresh Scottish salmon. Royal rack of lamb. Seafood brochette.
Credit cards: 1, 2, 3, 5, 6
Proprietor: Alan Fairlie

Igg's Restaurant

15 Jeffrey Street
Edinburgh EH1 1DR
Tel: 031 557 8184
Off the Royal Mile.

This is a very interesting newcomer to Jeffrey Street which is just off the Royal Mile and has a reputation for its small interesting shops. The unusual name is derived from the first name of the proprietor, Ignacio Campos, who runs the restaurant personally. He has a wealth of catering experience behind him and this is a dignified yet relatively relaxed restaurant, with a bright interior and good standards of food preparation and presentation. "Specials" on the menu change daily dependent on the availability of produce in the market. Spanish and French spoken.

Open all year
Dining Room/Restaurant Lunch 12 - 2 pm (a)
Dinner 6 - 10 pm (c)
Closed Sun
No smoking area in restaurant
Venison in a berry sauce. Lobster with crayfish sauce.
Credit cards: 1, 2, 3, 5, 6
Proprietor: Ignacio Campos

Jackson's Restaurant

2 Jackson Close
209 High Street, Royal Mile
Edinburgh
EH1 1PL
Tel: 031 225 1793

A small interesting restaurant tucked away down the historic Jackson Close. Popular amongst both Scots and visitors. Jackson's offers excellent Scottish cuisine with a subtle French flair. Friendly service and a relaxing ambience make dinner in Jackson's a night to remember.

Open all year
Dining Room/Restaurant Lunch 12 - 2 pm (a)
Dinner 6 - 10.30 pm (b-c)
Extended hours during Edinburgh Festival
Haggis balls served in a whisky cream sauce, smoked salmon, Aberdeen Angus steaks with speciality sauces, fresh salmon, game and seafoods.
Credit cards: 1, 2, 3, 6
Proprietor: Lynn MacKinnon

Keepers Restaurant

13B Dundas Street
Edinburgh
EH3 6QG
Tel: 031 556 5707

Dundas Street is to north of Princes Street and the continuation of Hanover Street.

Set in a delightful Georgian basement on the site of Scotland's first wine bar, this restaurant comprises three cellar rooms and a wine/coffee bar. The cellar rooms, with their original stone walls and floors, provide a warm, relaxing atmosphere and may be reserved for business meetings and private functions.

Open all year

Bistro bar upstairs open from 10.30 am all day
Bar Lunch 12 - 2.30 pm (a)
Dining Room/Restaurant Lunch 12 - 2.30 pm (a)
Pre-theatre 6 - 7 pm (a) any two courses à la carte
Dinner from 6 pm (b)
Closed Sun except during Festival unless by special arrangement
No smoking area in restaurant
Imaginative game and poultry dishes – duck in wine and honey sauce garnished with grapefruit; venison collops with red wine and cranberry sauce. Extensive range – fish, steak, vegetarian dishes.
Credit cards: 1, 2, 3, 5
Proprietor: Sheena Marshall

Kelly's Restaurant

46 West Richmond Street
Edinburgh
EH6 9DZ
Tel: 031 668 3847

West Richmond Street is off Clerk Street – the continuation of North Bridge from the east end of Princes Street.
Situated in an old bakehouse in an atmosphere which is warm and comfortable. Sociable candlelight dinners are enjoyed amongst old pine, linen napery and antique lace. Patronised by a wide variety of diners – Kelly's aims to give value for money, friendly service and the best of Scottish food, and has earned a fine reputation. Booking essential.

Open all year except 2 wks Jan
Dinner 6.45 - 9.45 pm (c)
Closed Sun + Mon
Diners requested not to smoke until after 9 pm
Smoked Scottish salmon with mushrooms in Pernod sauce. Border lamb cutlets with an orange Grand Marnier and rosemary glaze. Scallops poached in cream, spring onion and whisky sauce. Chocolate box surprise.
Credit cards: 1, 2, 3
Proprietor: Jacque Kelly

King James Thistle Hotel

Leith Street
Edinburgh EH1 3SW
Tel: 031 556 0111
Telex: 727200
Fax: 031 557 5333

East End of Princes Street.
The Restaurant St Jacques is an authentic brasserie serving traditional Scottish food in a distinctly French manner. The limed oak, gleaming marble and glistening brass make it impressive for business lunches or intimate for a special occasion. Italian, French, German and Spanish spoken.

Open all year
Rooms: 147 with private facilities
Bar Lunch (Boston Bean Co) 11.30 am - 2 pm (a)
Dining Room/Restaurant Lunch (St Jacques) 12.30 - 2 pm (b)
Dinner (St Jacques) 6.30 - 10.30 pm (d)
No dogs except guide dogs
Bed & breakfast from £45
Dinner B & B from £59.50
Both the à la carte and cafe menu feature Scottish dishes including west coast oysters, saddle of hare with game sauce, medallions of venison with wild mushrooms and chocolate Glayva pot.
STB 5 Crown Highly Commended
Credit cards: 1, 2, 3, 5, 6 + Trumpcard

Lightbody's Restaurant & Bar

23 Glasgow Road
Edinburgh
EH12 8HW
Tel: 031 334 2300

On the main Corstorphine road out of Edinburgh towards the airport and Glasgow.

Family run business with friendly, warm atmosphere and consistent standards. A popular business rendezvous at lunchtime and light bar meals are also available for lunch and evening (week days only). More leisurely meals chosen from an à la carte menu which changes regularly using the best of fresh Scottish produce.

Open all year
Dining Room/Restaurant Lunch 12 - 2.30 pm (a)
Dinner 6 - 10.30 pm (b)
Closed Sun
Fresh soups made with Scottish seafoods. Salmon, mussels and lobsters (when available), Scotch beef, lamb, venison in a variety of sauces. Duck, freshwater trout, and white fish bought locally.
Credit cards: 1, 2, 3
Proprietors: Malcolm & Norman Lightbody

The Magnum

1 Albany Street
Edinburgh
EH1 3PY
Tel: 031 557 4366

On corner of Dublin Street (continuation of North St Andrew Street) and Albany Street.

There has always been a dearth of good eating places north of St Andrew Square, but now The Magnum fills the void. This is a first class up market restaurant and bar beautifully appointed and drawing on the business and financial centre around it for its lunchtime clientele, but with a wider catchment area in the evenings. The restaurant exudes an atmosphere of elegant relaxation and the food is prepared carefully and presented with appeal.

Open all year except Christmas + Boxing Days + 1 to 4 Jan
Bar Lunch 12 - 2.30 pm (a)
Dining Room/Restaurant Lunch 12 - 2.30 pm except Sat (c)
Bar Supper 6.30 - 9.45 pm (a)
Dinner 6.30 - 10 pm (c)
Closed Sun
Menus change regularly dependent on availability of good fresh fish and shellfish, lamb, beef.
Credit cards: 1, 2, 3, 5

Martins Restaurant

70 Rose Street North Lane
Edinburgh
EH2 3DX
Tel: 031 225 3106

In the north lane off Rose Street between Frederick Street and Castle Street.

Not easy to find, but persist. This is a gem of a restaurant run personally by Martin and Gay Irons. They are superb hosts and are justifiably proud of this delightful intimate restaurant. The table linen is always spotless, the flowers are fresh and the food exceptionally well prepared and imaginatively presented. Chef David McCrae's fine cooking has made this one of Edinburgh's best.

Open all year except from 22 Dec to 21 Jan (incl)
Dining Room/Restaurant Lunch 12 - 2 pm except Sat (b)
Dinner 7 - 10 pm (d-e)
Closed Sun + Mon
No smoking in dining areas

Menus are based on the availability of fresh local produce, are regularly changed and specialise in fresh Scottish seafish, shellfish and game.

Credit cards: 1, 2, 3, 5

Best Welcome/Hospitality 1988

Proprietors: Martin & Gay Irons

The Royal Over-Seas League

Over-Seas House
100 Princes Street
Edinburgh EH2 3AA
Tel: 031 225 1501
Telex: 721654
Fax: 031 226 3936

Over-Seas House Edinburgh is one of the few remaining of the original Princes Street buildings. The bedrooms, however, have all been refurbished in keeping with today's standards. The restaurant, with its spectacular view of Edinburgh Castle, is in the more modern part of the building and has also been refurbished.

Open all year
Rooms: 15 with private facilities
Bar Lunch 12 - 2 pm (a)
Dining Room/Restaurant Lunch 12.30 - 2 pm (a-b)
Dinner 7.30 - 9.30 pm (a-b)
Bed & breakfast from £46 (Temporary membership fee for non-members)
Dinner B & B rates on application

Loch Tay salmon supreme, collops of pork 'Auld Reekie', fillet of beef medallion Cockpen.

STB 3 Crown Commended
Credit cards: 1, 2, 3, 5

Sheraton Edinburgh

1 Festival Square
Edinburgh
EH3 9SR
Tel: 031 229 9131
Telex: 72398
Fax: 031 229 6254

Lothian Road opposite Usher Hall and only 5 minutes from Princes Street.

A superb luxury hotel in the city centre within easy walking distance of theatres and concert halls. It has every amenity to be expected from the Sheraton chain. The elegant Cafe Beaumont restaurant overlooks Festival Square and is noted for the excellence of its food and service. An extensive range of 'Taste of Scotland' dishes is offered. Sunday lunch is a speciality and there is also a 'Taste of Scotland' banqueting menu. For those who wish to relax, there is a leisure centre with swimming pool, sauna, whirlpool and full gymnasium. Children are welcome. French, Italian, German and Spanish spoken.

Open all year

Rooms: 263 with private facilities
Dining Room/Restaurant Lunch 12 - 2.30 pm (c)
Dinner 7 - 10.30 pm (c)
Banqueting for up to 485
Coffee, light lunch and afternoon tea served in Lobby Lounge (no smoking area available)
No smoking area in restaurant
Bed & breakfast rates on application
Dinner B & B rates on application
Weekend rates on application

Specialises in light dining and vegetarian menus.

STB 5 Crown Highly Commended
Credit cards: 2, 3, 5, 6

Skippers Bistro

1A Dock Place
Leith
Edinburgh
EH6 6UY
Tel: 031 554 1018

Leith, Edinburgh.

The historic Port of Leith has always needed a place like this and Allan Corbett has provided it. Very much in the style of a French bistro but with a character all of its own, Skippers has a well earned reputation as a leading fresh seafood restaurant – but it is much more than that. There is a friendliness and conviviality about this informal place that makes a meal there one of those pleasant experiences that one likes to remember.

Open all year
Dining Room/Restaurant Lunch 12.30 - 2 pm (a-b)
Dinner 7.30 - 10 pm (b-c)
Specialises in fresh seafood.
Credit cards: 1, 2, 3, 6
Proprietors: Allan & Jennifer Corbett

Stakis Grosvenor Hotel

7-21 Grosvenor Street
Edinburgh
EH12 5EF
Tel: 031 226 6001
Telex: 72445.
Fax: 031 220 2387

Opposite Haymarket Station in the West End.

Ideally situated in Edinburgh's elegant West End, the Stakis Grosvenor Hotel's style goes beyond its fashionable façade. From the comfortable chesterfields in the hotel's public areas to the fine furnishings you'll find in the private bedrooms, the hotel has a unique ambience.

Open all year
Rooms: 134 with private facilities
Bar Lunch 12 - 3 pm except Sun (a)
Dinner 5 - 9.30 pm (c)
Bed & breakfast from £60
Dinner B & B from £31 (min. 2 nights stay)
Taste of Scotland applies to main restaurant

Specialities include game and shellfish beef Balmoral, trout Rob Roy, cranachan, peach Highland cream, haggis.
STB 4 Crown Commended
Credit cards: 1, 2, 3, 5, 6

The Tattler

23 Commercial Street
Leith
Edinburgh
EH6 6JA
Tel: 031 554 9999

On main road in Leith port area (North Edinburgh).

Cosy Victorian-Style pub and restaurant in the historic Port of Leith, which won the National Pub Caterer of the Year 1985 – first in Scotland, runner-up in Britain, and has featured in a series of awards from various bodies in each year since then. In keeping with its situation, The Tattler offers a wide range of seafoods in addition to an imaginative selection of meat, poultry and vegetarian dishes. French, Italian and German spoken.

Open all year
Bar Lunch 12 -2 pm (a)
Dining Room/Restaurant Lunch 12 - 2 pm (c)
Bar Supper 6 - 10 pm (a)

Dinner 6 - 10 pm (c)

Some dishes unique to The Tattler, on extensive restaurant menu with emphasis on use of first class local produce. Bar menu is particularly interesting.

Credit cards: 1, 2, 3, 5, 6

Proprietors: Alan & Linda Thomson

The Witchery by the Castle
Castlehill
Royal Mile
Edinburgh
EH1 1NE
Tel: 031 225 5613
Fax: 031 220 4392

Situated at the entrance to Edinburgh Castle.

The Witchery survives the tourist crush to remain intimate, friendly and quite unique. Already steeped in eight centuries of history, The Witchery, once the very centre of witchcraft in the Old Town, now offers excellent food prepared under the personal supervision of James Thomson. Seafood specialities change daily – oysters, mussels, meat, fish, sole, etc. The restaurant now offers two dining rooms, each with a highly unique atmosphere – one of which is complemented by an outdoor terrace.

Open all year

Meals served from 12 noon - 11 pm (a-b)
Reservations advisable

Steak 'Auld Reekie' – in a whisky and smoked cheese sauce, duck with honey, salmon with fresh dill Hollandaise, quenelle of trout.

Credit cards: 1, 2, 3, 5, 6

Proprietor: James Thomson

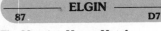

ELGIN

87   D7

The Mansion House Hotel
The Haugh
Elgin
Morayshire
IV30 1AN
Tel: 0343 48811

The charm of the past with the up to date comfort you deserve – all the facilities you would expect in this 19th century old mansion house. The hotel is situated in a quiet location surrounded by mature trees and parkland by the riverside, and yet only minutes walk from Elgin town centre, capital of the whisky trail and in the heart of Scotland's castle and golf trails.

Open all year

Rooms: 18 with private facilities
Bar Lunch 12.15 - 1.45 pm (a)
Dining Room/Restaurant Lunch 12.15 - 1.45 pm (b)
Dinner 7.30 - 9 pm (c-d)
Bed & breakfast from £40
Dinner B & B from £50

Fresh local produce – fish, game, fruit and vegetables, talented presentation and natural flavours of the cuisine match the most demanding expectations.

STB   4 Crown Highly Commended

Credit cards: 1, 2, 3, 5

Proprietor: Fernando de Oliveira

Park House Hotel & Restaurant
South Street
Elgin
IV30 1JB
Tel: 0343 7695

Situated to the west end of Elgin just off A98 and 5 minutes walk from the town centre.

Park House is well placed locally as a base for touring or business. The architecturally Listed building is of classical Georgian design. There is an atmosphere of gracious and practical hospitality within a compact, intimate setting.

Open all year

Rooms: 6 with private facilities
Dining Room/Restaurant Lunch 12 - 2 pm (a)
Dinner 7 - 10 pm (c)
Bed & breakfast from £35
Dinner B & B from £48

Scottish fare is the produce of sea, lochs, rivers and countryside. Try perhaps smoked salmon and avocado souffle, venison casserole, cranachan.

STB   3 Crown Commended

Credit cards: 1, 2, 3, 5, 6

Proprietor: Ken Asher

ELIE

88   F7

Bouquet Garni Restaurant
51 High Street
Elie
Fife KY9 1BZ
Tel: 0333 330374

A delightful little restaurant in the centre of this charming East Neuk town. With ample supplies of fresh fish and seafood on its doorstep the Bouquet Garni naturally specialises in high quality fish dishes but with a complementary range

of other typical Scottish fare. The intimate and cosy candlelit dining room is almost certain to appeal to the connoisseur of good food. Well worth a detour. A little French spoken.

Open all year except closed first wk Nov + first 2 wks Feb
Dinner 7.30 - 9.30 pm except Sun (c-d)
Closed Sun only main season; Sun + Mon out of season
No smoking area in dining room

Rich langoustine and tomato flavoured bisque; fillet of salmon with langoustine mousse, creamed leeks, on Muscadet sauce of potato, chives and cheese. Strawberry shortcake with Glayva liqueur cream and sweet butterscotch cream.

Credit cards: 1, 3

Proprietors: Andrew & Norah Keracher

ERBUSAIG

89   BY KYLE OF LOCHALSH   D3

The Old Schoolhouse Restaurant
"Tigh Fasgaidh"
Erbusaig, Kyle
Ross-shire
IV40 8BB
Tel: 0599 4369

Outskirts of Erbusaig on Kyle-Plockton road.

In an idyllic setting, standing alone, this charming old schoolhouse, built in the 1820s as the main school for the area around Erbusaig, now offers an education of a different sort. You can enjoy seafood to steaks, vineyards to vegetarian, Bach to Beethoven, candlelight to carnations – offered in the comfortable mellow atmosphere of a building where generations of local families have learned the three 'Rs'.

Open Easter to end Oct

Dinner 7 - 10.30 pm (b-c)
Nov to Easter open Fri + Sat by prior arrangement only

Home-made dishes from local seafood and Scottish meats. Scallops with garlic and basil. Chicken and prawns in a spicy Madeira sauce.

Credit cards: 1, 3

Proprietors: Calum & Joanne Cumine

PRICE CATEGORIES

(a)	under £10.00
(b)	£10.00 - £15.00
(c)	£15.00 - £20.00
(d)	£20.00 - £25.00
(e)	£25.00 - £30.00
(f)	over £30.00

FALKIRK
91   **G6**

Inchyra Grange Hotel
Grange Road
Polmont
Falkirk
FK2 0YB
Tel: 0324 711911
Telex: 777693
Fax: 0324 716134

Junction 4 or 5 M9 motorway. Situated on border of Polmont/Grangemouth.

A fine example of a Scottish country house set in eight acres of private grounds and offering every modern amenity. In the restaurant you can choose from the varied à la carte or table d'hôte menus, carefully prepared dishes featuring local favourites.

Open all year
Rooms: 33 with private facilities
Bar Lunch 12 - 2 pm: 12.30 - 2 pm Sun (a)
Dining Room/Restaurant Lunch 12.30 - 2 pm except Sat (b)
Bar Supper 6 - 10 pm (a)
Dinner 7 - 9.30 pm (c)
Dinner Sat - à la carte only
Bed & breakfast from £65
Dinner B & B from £80
STB 4 Crown Commended
Credit cards: 1, 2, 3, 5
Proprietor: K Marwick

Stakis Park Hotel
Camelon Road
Falkirk
FK1 5RY
Tel: 0324 28331
Telex: 776502.
Fax: 0324 611593
On A803 central Falkirk.

The Stakis Park Hotel is ideally located less than one hour from Glasgow and Edinburgh. Its 55 well appointed bedrooms all include private facilities, radio, TV, telephone and hospitality tray. For the business user, function facilities from 5 to 200. The hotel's recently refurbished restaurant boasts à la carte menus specialising in 'Taste of Scotland' dishes.

Open all year
Rooms: 55 with private facilities
Dining Room/Restaurant Lunch 12.30 - 2.30 pm (b)
Dinner 7 - 10 pm (c)
Bed & breakfast from £48
Dinner B & B from £37 (min. 2 nights stay)
STB 4 Crown Commended
Credit cards: 1, 2, 3, 5, 6

FALKLAND
92   **F7**

Covenanter Hotel
The Square
Falkland
Fife
KY7 7BU
Tel: 0337 57224
Fax: 0337 57272
Centre of Falkland.

This 17th century coaching inn – almost opposite Falkland Palace – has been run for the past ten years by George and Margaret Menzies who have established a fine reputation for good food and warm hospitality. There is a choice of the traditional restaurant or informal bistro.

Open all year
Rooms: 4 with private facilities
Bar Lunch 12 - 2 pm (a)
Dining Room/Restaurant Lunch 12 - 2 pm (a)
Bar Supper 6 - 9.30 pm (a)
Dinner 7 - 9 pm (c)
Table d'hôte dinner available as well as à la carte.
Closed Mon
No dogs
Bed & breakfast £20 - £32.50
Dinner B & B rates on application

A selection of made to order dishes with emphasis on home produce. Scampi Falkland, Tay salmon, and Scottish beef dishes.
STB Listed Commended
Credit cards: 1, 2, 3, 5, 6
Proprietors: George & Margaret Menzies

Kind Kyttock's Kitchen
Cross Wynd
Falkland
Fife KY7 7BE
Tel: 0337 57477
Off main street in village.

Situated in the heart of the historic village of Falkland, three minutes' walk from Falkland Palace, this very popular and charming restaurant offers the visitor a chance to sample good wholesome fare.

Open Feb to Dec
Meals available all day (a)
Closed Mon
Separate tearoom for non-smokers

Home-baked pancakes, scones, fruit squares, shortbread, wholemeal bread, stovies, cloutie dumpling. Locally grown vegetables used in Scotch broth and at salad table. Selection of teas available.
No credit cards
Proprietor: Bert Dalrymple

Templelands Farm
Falkland
Fife KY7 7DE
Tel: 0337 57383
On A912 south of Falkland village.

Comfortable modernised farmhouse on small working farm with panoramic views all around. Ideal touring centre. Twenty golf courses within 20 miles including St Andrews. National Trust properties nearby. Swimming pools, tennis, bowling in the area. Abundance of home-made food with soups and sweets a speciality. Coffee/tea facilities, clock radio, hairdryer and electric blanket in bedrooms. Children welcome – reduced rates if sharing with parents. Dogs accepted in bedrooms only.

Open Easter to Oct
Rooms: 2
Dinner 7 pm
Advanced booking preferred
Residents only
Unlicensed – guests welcome to take own wine
No smoking except in lounge
Bed & breakfast from £13
Dinner B & B from £19
STB 2 Crown Commended
No credit cards
Proprietor: Sarah McGregor

FETTERCAIRN

Ramsay Arms Hotel
Fettercairn
Laurencekirk
Kincardineshire
AB30 1XX
Tel: 05614 334/5
Fax: 05614 500
On B966 off A93 north of Perth.
The Ramsay Arms started off life as an
18th century coaching inn and can boast
of Queen Victoria as a guest in 1861. Over
the years it has developed and expanded
its facilities till it is now a thoroughly
comfortable hotel with modern en suite
bedrooms and pleasant public rooms.
There is a gymnasium, sauna and jacuzzi.
The hotel enjoys a good reputation for its
food and this combined with the close
personal supervision of the owners Jeff
and Kate Evans, and a polite attentive
staff, make this a pleasing place to stay.
Open all year
Rooms: 12 with private facilities
Bar Lunch 12 - 2 pm (a)
Dining Room/Restaurant Lunch 12 -
2 pm (b)
Bar Supper 6 - 9 pm (a)
Dinner 6 - 9 pm (b)
Bed & breakfast £20 - £28
Dinner B & B rates on application
*Smoked salmon parcels – smoked
salmon filled with a light smokie pate.
Venison with chestnut sauce. Cloutie
dumpling.*
STB 4 Crown Commended
Credit cards: 1, 3
Proprietors: Jeff & Kate Evans

FOCHABERS

Gordon Arms Hotel
80 High Street
Fochabers
Morayshire
IV32 7DH
Tel: 0343 820508
Fax: 0343 820300
A96 between Inverness and Aberdeen.
The roots of this old coaching inn go back
over 200 years and it is a convenient
location for the whisky trail, golf and of
course fishing in the Spey. Although
extensively modernised the hotel retains a
lot of the character and atmosphere of
bygone days. There is an interesting à la

carte menu complemented by a well
balanced wine list.
Open all year
Rooms: 12 with private facilities
Bar Lunch 12 - 2 pm (a)
Dining Room/Restaurant Lunch 12 -
2 pm (a)
Bar Supper 7 - 9 pm (a)
Dinner 7 - 9.45 pm (b)
Facilities for the disabled
Bed & breakfast from £27.50
STB Award Pending
Credit cards: 1, 2, 3, 6

FORFAR

Idvies House
Letham
by Forfar
Angus
DD8 2QJ
Tel: 030 781 787
Telex: 76252
Fax: 030 781 8933
4 miles east of Forfar.
Victorian country mansion set in spacious
wooded grounds with fine views of the
Angus countryside. Tastefully furnished
public rooms and well appointed en suite
bedrooms offer a high standard of
comfort. A well stocked bar features 150
Scottish malt whiskies and the two dining
rooms have menus which reflect the fine
quality and variety of Scottish produce.
Idvies is personally run by the resident
owners, assisted by friendly local staff.
Open all year
Rooms: 10 with private facilities
Bar Lunch 12 - 2 pm (a)
Dining Room/Restaurant Lunch 12 -
2 pm (b)
Bar Supper 7 - 9.30 pm except Sun +
Sat (a)
Dinner 7 - 9.30 pm except Sun (b-c): 7 -
8 pm Sun - residents only
Bed & breakfast from £25
Dinner B & B rates on application
*Home-smoked Tay salmon, Arbroath
smokie mousse and pate. Isle of Mull
mussels. Local crab and lobster. Orkney
oysters. Local venison, game and Angus
steak dishes with Scottish liqueur and
whisky sauces.*
STB 4 Crown Commended
Credit cards: 1, 2, 3, 5, 6
Proprietors: Pat & Fay Slingsby, Judy Hill

FORRES

Knockomie Hotel
Grantown Road
Forres
Moray
IV36 0SG
Tel: 0309 73146
*On A940 just south of Forres on Grantown
Road.*
Knockomie Hotel stands overlooking the
Royal Burgh of Forres which has an
outstanding reputation for its gardens.
Moray is beautiful and interesting with
castles, distilleries, fishing, sailing, golfing,
activities to suit everyone. The restaurant
endeavours to provide the best of Scottish
produce while the bar has an enviable
selection of malts.
Open all year
Rooms: 7 with private facilities
Bar Lunch 12 - 2.30 pm (a)
Dining Room/Restaurant Lunch 12 -
2 pm by arrangement
Dinner 7 - 9 pm (c)
Bed & breakfast from £30
Dinner B & B from £42.95
*Scottish produce – scallops, salmon, rib of
Aberdeen Angus beef, venison.*
STB 4 Crown Commended
Credit cards: 1, 3
Proprietor: Gavin Ellis

Parkmount House Hotel
St Leonards Road
Forres
Morayshire
IV36 0DW
Tel: 0309 73312
*On B9010 Forres-Dallas road, 400 yards
from town centre.*
Delightful Victorian town house in its own
walled flower garden. Situated in a quiet
secluded area of Forres, minutes from the
award winning 'Britain in Bloom' gardens,
golf courses and town centre, Parkmount
makes an ideal centre for exploring the
delights of Moray. Family run hotel
providing luxury en suite bedrooms and
excellent cooking at affordable prices.
Children sharing parents' room half price.
Dogs may be accepted by prior booking. A
good selection of malt whiskies. Low cost
self-drive car hire available.
Open all year except Christmas week +
New Year
Rooms: 6 with private facilities
Dinner from 7 pm (b-c)   ▶

Special diets and non-residents by prior arrangement
No smoking in restaurant
Bed & breakfast from £20
Dinner B & B from £33

Smoked venison with avocado and juniper dressing; smoked salmon and local seafood cocktail; loin of lamb with kiwi fruit and tomato; pan fried Aberdeen Angus steak; roast rack of Morayshire lamb with fresh herbs and redcurrant pear.

STB 4 Crown Commended

Credit cards: 1, 3

Proprietors: David & Angela Steer

FORT AUGUSTUS
97   **E5**

Lovat Arms Hotel
Fort Augustus
Inverness-shire
PH32 2BE
Tel: 0320 6206/4

On A82 in middle of the village.

The Lovat Arms is situated halfway down the Great Glen in a lovely village through which colourful craft are constantly passing along the Caledonian Canal. It is a traditional spacious Victorian hotel set in grounds of 2½ acres with large lawns to the front overlooking Loch Ness and the Benedictine Monastery in some of Scotland's most beautiful Highland scenery. Easy access to local shops. Ample car parking. All bedrooms are centrally heated with colour TVs, direct dial telephones, tea-making facilities, trouser presses etc. The restaurant has an excellent reputation and after your meal you can relax by the open fire with a coffee, or something stronger and more traditional.

Open all year

Rooms: 23, 22 with private facilities
Bar Lunch 12.30 - 2 pm (a)
Dining Room/Restaurant Lunch 12.30 - 2 pm Sun only (a)
Bar Supper 6.30 - 9 pm (a)
Dinner 7 - 8.30 pm (c)
Bed & breakfast from £26
Dinner B & B from £39

Highland game terrine with cranberries, roast prime Aberdeen Angus beef traditional style, fillet of wild Scottish salmon with Hollandaise and watercress. Cranachan.

Credit cards: 1, 3, 6

Proprietors: Hector & Mary MacLean

FORT WILLIAM
98   **E4**

Crannog Seafood Restaurant
Town Pier
Fort William
Inverness-shire
PH33 7NG
Tel: 0397 5589/3919
Fax: 0397 5026

Fort William town pier – off A82 Fort William town centre bypass.

Crannog is run by fishermen who have built a self-contained community based on the fruits of the sea. The fishing boats, smokehouse and processing base market directly to discerning customers. The marketing ideal was brought to fruition when their fishing store on Fort William town pier was converted to a restaurant where you can enjoy the freshest seafood in a delightful waterfront location.

Open all year except Nov
Dining Room/Restaurant Lunch 12 - 2.30 pm (b)
Dinner 6 - 10 pm (c)
Note: opening times may vary in Winter months
No smoking area in restaurant

Crannog bouillabaisse, smoked mussels and aioli, langoustine with hot garlic butter, salmon en croute with spinach sauce, walnut tart and cream.

Credit cards: 1, 3

Glen Nevis Restaurant
Glen Nevis
Fort William
Inverness-shire
PH33 6SX
Tel: 0397 5459

2½ miles along Glen Nevis from Fort William.

The restaurant is set amidst the scenic splendour of one of Scotland's loveliest glens, at the foot of mighty Ben Nevis. It is situated just outside Fort William and has ample parking. Large windows give every table a view of river and mountains.

Open mid Mar to mid Oct
Dining Room/Restaurant Lunch from 12 noon (a)
High Tea from 2.30 pm
Dinner from 5.30 pm (a-b)

Speciality menu changed each week – always features local produce.

Credit cards: 1, 3

The Moorings Hotel
Banavie
Fort William
Inverness-shire
PH33 7LY
Tel: 0397 772 797
Fax: 0397 772 441

3 miles from Fort William:

The Moorings stands beside the Caledonian Canal at Neptune's Staircase, with splendid views towards Ben Nevis and Aonach Mor. The Jacobean-styled restaurant concentrates on Scottish cuisine using indigenous Scottish produce, complemented by its gracious surroundings.

Open all year except Christmas
Rooms: 24 with private facilities
Dinner 7 - 9 pm (d)
Taste of Scotland applies to main restaurant
Bed & breakfast £24 - £30
Dinner B & B £39 - £49

Lochy smoked salmon parcel, Loch Linnhe prawns, Fassock quail, fillet of wild salmon, monkfish tails in red wine, veal with fresh tarragon, roast haunch of Highland venison.

STB 4 Crown Commended

Credit cards: 1, 2, 3, 5, 6

Proprietor: Norman Sinclair

PRICE CATEGORIES

(a)	under £10.00
(b)	£10.00 - £15.00
(c)	£15.00 - £20.00
(d)	£20.00 - £25.00
(e)	£25.00 - £30.00
(f)	over £30.00

CREDIT/CHARGE CARDS

1 Access/Mastercard/Eurocard
2 American Express
3 Visa
4 Carte Bleu
5 Diners Club
6 Mastercharge

GAIRLOCH

The Steading Restaurant
Achtercairn
Gairloch
Ross-shire
IV21 2BP
Tel: 0445 2449

On A832 at junction with B802 in Gairloch.

Coffee shop/restaurant located in converted 19th century farm buildings retaining their old world peace and charm and adjoining the prize winning Gairloch Museum of West Highland Life. All meals are freshly cooked on the premises from local produce, seafood fresh from the loch, cakes and scones home-baked. Special dishes for children. Self-service by day and waitress service in evenings. As the complete menu is available all day it is possible to choose what is wanted when it is wanted. The price ranges shown are therefore what a smaller (lunch) or a larger (dinner) meal might cost. Some French and German spoken. Dogs not allowed in restaurant but may be tied up outside in courtyard with water and shade.

Open Easter to mid Oct
Bar Lunch (a)
Dining Room/Restaurant Lunch (a)
Dinner (b)
Meals available all day 8.30 am - 9 pm
(5 pm Apr + May) (a-b)
Closed Sun

Seafood platter – at least six varied seafoods presented with salad and a variety of dressings. Venison casseroled with red wine, mushrooms and spices. Haddock thermidor, baked in squat lobster sauce.

No credit cards

GATEHOUSE OF FLEET

Cally Palace Hotel
Gatehouse-of-Fleet
Dumfries & Galloway
DG7 2DL
Tel: 0557 814341
Fax: 0557 814522

30 miles west of Dumfries, 1 mile from A75 (main Dumfries-Stranraer road)

A magnificent and imposing four star hotel in an idyllic setting of 100 acres of forest, parkland and loch. The public rooms are particularly elegant and reflect the grandeur of the original 18th century mansion. The hotel has a core of regular devotees who would not dream of going anywhere else. The 55 bedrooms, suites and family rooms are tastefully furnished all with private facilities, colour TV, trouser press, hairdryer etc. Indoor leisure facilities included a heated swimming pool, jacuzzi, sauna and solarium, and outdoors there is putting, tennis and croquet. The restaurant concentrates on using the best of fresh local produce, attractively presented. The hotel is superbly managed and caring well mannered staff are quick to respond to the guest's every need.

Open Mar to Dec
Rooms: 55 with private facilities
Bar Snacks 12.30 - 2 pm (a)
Dining Room/Restaurant Lunch 12.30 - 2 pm (a)
Dinner 6.30 - 9.30 pm (c)
Facilities for the disabled
Bed & breakfast from £40
Dinner B & B £53 to £58

Menus regularly feature prime Galloway beef, venison, Cree salmon. All dishes are served with fresh vegetables in season.

STB   4 Crown Highly Commended
Credit cards: 1, 3

The 1992 TASTE OF SCOTLAND GUIDE
is scheduled to be published in November 1991.

To reserve a copy at the 1991 price of £2.80 (including post & packaging), complete the coupon on page 157 and send it with your cheque or postal order, made payable to TASTE OF SCOTLAND, to

Taste of Scotland (Guide Sales)
33 Melville Street, Edinburgh EH3 7JF.

You will be placed on the priority list to receive the Guide as soon as it is published.

Murray Arms Hotel
High Street/Ann Street
Gatehouse-of-Fleet
DG7 2HY
Tel: 055 74 207

Off A75, 66 miles west of Carlisle between Dumfries and Stranraer.

Warmth, welcome and good food – where you'll enjoy a drink with the locals. In this inn in July 1793 Robert Burns wrote 'Scots Wha Hae'. In one of Scotland's scenic heritage areas rich historically and with a wide variety of birds and wild flowers. Free golf, fishing and tennis.

Open all year
Rooms: 13 with private facilities
Bar meals served all day
Dining Room/Restaurant Lunch from 12 noon (b)
Dinner 7.30 - 9 pm (c)
Bed & breakfast from £35
Dinner B & B from £45

Galloway beef, locally caught fish including salmon and smoked salmon.

STB   4 Crown Commended
Credit cards: 1, 2, 3, 5, 6

GLAMIS

Castleton House Hotel
Eassie
Glamis
by Forfar
Angus DD8 1SJ
Tel: 030 784 340
Fax: 030 784 506

On A94, 3 miles from Glamis Castle.

A fine old stone-built house going back to the turn of the century on the site of an ancient castle. It is set in 11 acres of gardens and woodland in the heart of the Angus countryside and near Glamis Castle. The public rooms are furnished to a very high standard and there are six luxurious bedrooms, well equipped, and all with private bathrooms. Food is interesting and imaginative and presented attractively. Menus change daily based on the availability of fresh produce. There are vegetables, fruit and herbs, in season, from the hotel garden. Service is polite and attentive. The overall experience is first class.

Open all year
Rooms: 6 with private facilities
Bar Lunch 12 - 3 pm (b)
Dining Room/Restaurant Lunch 12 - 2.30 pm (b)

▶

Dinner 7 - 9.30 pm (c)
No dogs
Facilities for the disabled
No smoking in restaurant
Bed & breakfast from £45
Dinner B & B from £60
STB   4 Crown Highly Commended
Credit cards: 1, 2, 3
Proprietors: William & Maureen Little

102   GLASGOW   G5

The Albany Hotel
Bothwell Street
Glasgow
G2 7EN
Tel: 041 248 2656
M8 inner ring road, exit at junction 18 at Charing Cross.

One of Glasgow's premier hotels, situated in the heart of the city. Modern amenities, courteous service and attention to the smallest detail, a first class international hotel where guests can enjoy comfort and luxury. Voted 'Hotel of the Year 1986' by the travel trade.

Open all year

Rooms: 253, 250 with private facilities
Bar Lunch (a)
Restaurant Lunch (Club House) 12.30 - 2.30 pm except Sat (b-c)
Lunch (Original Carvery) 12 - 2.30 pm
Dinner (Club House) 7 - 11 pm - (Dinner/Dance Sat) : 7 - 10 pm Sun (b-c)
Dinner (Original Carvery) 5.30 - 10 pm
Bed & breakfast rates on application
Dinner B & B rates on application
Lounge service - 24 hours. Scottish afternoon tea. Menus include a selection of traditional Scottish and continental specialities, seafood and meats.
Credit cards: 1, 2, 3, 5, 6

The Buttery
652 Argyle Street
Glasgow
G3 8UF
Tel: 041 221 8188
Junction 19, M8 – approach by St Vincent Street and Elderslie Street.

This is a very unusual and, to its devoted clientele, a very special restaurant. Do not be put off by the stark austere look of the exterior of this segment of an old tenement block. Inside it is a joy. There are lovely touches of Victoriana and a demolished church has obviously contributed its pews and furniture to the

construction of the bar. There is an excellent atmosphere of yesteryear in this quiet oasis of comfort and elegance. The high standards of food and polite and unobtrusive service make this one of Glasgow's very best restaurants.

Open all year except public holidays
Bar lunch 12 - 2.30 pm except Sat (a)
Dining Room/Restaurant Lunch 12 - 2.30 pm except Sat (b-c)
Dinner 7 - 10 pm (d-e)
Closed Sun
Cheese choux pastries on cranberry puree. Supreme of Guinea fowl with almonds and caramelised pears. Drambuie and oatmeal creme brulee.
Credit cards: 1, 2, 3, 5

Holiday Inn
Argyle Street
Glasgow
G3 8RR
Tel: 041 226 5577
Fax: 041 221 9202
Junction 19, M8.

The Holiday Inn, Glasgow, is a splendid city centre hotel, offering all the facilities expected of Holiday Inns and within easy walking distance of the main shopping and entertainment areas. Access to the hotel is offered by motorway (M8), the main railway station which is just five minutes' walk away, and Glasgow Airport is a mere ten minutes' drive. Courtesy coach service can be provided.

Open all year

Rooms: 298 with private facilities
Meals 11 am - 10.30 pm
(Patio Restaurant) (b)
Dinner 7 - 10.30 pm (c)
No smoking area in restaurant
Bed & breakfast rates on application
Dinner B & B rates on application
The buffet table offers a new selection of dishes every day. Specialities are served in L'Academie Restaurant.
Credit cards: 1, 2, 3, 5, 6

Hospitality Inn & Convention Centre
36 Cambridge Street
Glasgow
G2 3HN
Tel: 041 332 3311
¼ mile from Exit 16 Cowcaddens/Exit 17 Dumbarton Road on M8 motorway.

The Hospitality Inn is a modern four star luxury hotel set in the heart of the entertainment and shopping centre of Glasgow. It offers 306 spacious

bedrooms, a choice of two bars, two restaurants and hairdressing salon.

Open all year

Rooms: 306 with private facilities
Bar Lunch 12.30 -2.30 pm (a)
Dining Room/Restaurant Lunch 12.30 - 2.30 pm (a-b)
Captain's Table (a), Garden Cafe (a);
Prince of Wales Restaurant (b))
Dinner 7 - 10.30 pm (b)
(Garden Cafe (a); Prince of Wales (b))
Garden Cafe menu available all day
Bed & breakfast rates on application
Dinner B & B rates on application
STB   5 Crown Commended
Credit cards: 1, 2, 3, 5, 6

Kensington's Restaurant
164 Darnley Street
Glasgow
G41 2LL
Tel: 041 424 3662
On the south side of the city.

Tucked away in a quiet backwater on the south side of the city – but worth looking for – and only minutes from the centre of town. The restaurant is small, intimate with delightful oil paintings and interesting antiques.

Open all year.

Dining Room/Restaurant Lunch 12 - 2 pm except Sat (a)
Dinner 6.30 - 9.30 pm (c-d)
Closed Sun
Scottish seafood, game, beef and lamb are featured on all menus.
Credit cards: 1, 2, 3, 5, 6
Proprietor: Denise Drummond

Killermont House Restaurant
2022 Maryhill Road
Glasgow
G20 0AB
Tel: 041 946 5412
North-west Glasgow.

Killermont House Restaurant is the country house restaurant in the city. The house was built in the 19th century as a manse and was tastefully converted in 1987 into a 50 cover restaurant of distinction using the finest Scottish and continental produce handled with care.

Open all year except 1st wk Jan + 2 wks Jul
Dining Room/Restaurant Lunch 12 - 2.30 pm (b)
Dinner 6.30 - 10.30 pm (c-d)
Facilities for the disabled
►

Scottish game in season, west coast shellfish, Tay salmon, unusual Scottish cheeses and home-made bread.

Credit cards: 1, 2, 3

Proprietors: Paul & Christine Abrami

Moat House International

Congress Road
Glasgow
G3 8QT
Tel: 041 204 0733
Telex: 776244
Fax: 041 221 2022

Situated on the banks of the River Clyde next to the SECC.

The Moat House International has 300 guest rooms including 15 suites, each one offering panoramic views, each one a delightful home away from home, luxuriously equipped for your comfort. Everything you need to unwind at the end of the day is provided, complemented by the superb dining and leisure facilities.

Open all year

Rooms: 300 with private facilities
All day dining 12 noon - 11 pm
Dining Room/Restaurant Lunch 12 - 3 pm (a-d)
Dinner 6.30 - 11 pm (a-d)
24 hour room service
No dogs
Facilities for the disabled
No smoking in restaurant
Bed & breakfast from £58.59
Dinner B & B from £69.84
STB 5 Crown Commended
Credit cards: 1, 2, 3, 5, 6

Rogano

11 Exchange Place
Glasgow
G1 3AN
Tel: 041 248 4055

Glasgow city centre.

Since 1876, Rogano has been famed worldwide for its seafood and ambience. Remodelled in 1935 in similar 'art deco' style to the 'Queen Mary' which was at the time being built on the Clyde. Rogano today maintains the same ambience and high standards on which its reputation was founded. Elegant restaurant on ground floor. Bistro style downstairs.

Open all year except public holidays

Bar Lunch 12 - 2.30 pm
Dining Room/Restaurant Lunch 12 - 2.30 pm
Dinner 7 - 10 pm (f)

Lunch/Dinner 12 noon - 11 pm
downstairs in Cafe Rogano (c): Fri + Sat 12 noon to 12 midnight
Closed Sun
Specialist fish restaurant.

Credit cards: 1, 2, 3, 5

Stakis Grosvenor Hotel

Great Western Road
Glasgow
G12 0TA
Tel: 041 339 8811
Telex: 776247
Fax: 041 334 0710

On A82 Great Western Road.

Discreetly elegant, the Stakis Grosvenor Hotel is without question one of the most impressive buildings in Glasgow's fashionable West End. Directly opposite the City's Botanical Gardens. The Stakis Grosvenor Hotel is one mile from the motorway network, and two miles from the City Centre.

Open all year

Rooms: 95 with private facilities
Bar Lunch 12 - 2.30 pm (a)
Dining Room/Restaurant Lunch 12 - 2.30 pm (b-c)
Dinner 5 - 11 pm (b-f)
Bed & breakfast from £60
Dinner B & B from £38 (min. 2 nights stay)

Arbroath smokie salad. Roast haunch of venison and game sauce.

STB 5 Crown Commended

Credit cards: 1, 2, 3, 5, 6

CREDIT/CHARGE CARDS

1 Access/Mastercard/Eurocard
2 American Express
3 Visa
4 Carte Bleu
5 Diners Club
6 Mastercharge

The Triangle

37 Queen Street
Glasgow
G1 3EF
Tel: 041 221 8758
Fax: 041 204 3189

Halfway down Queen Street, above Tam Shepherd's Trick Shop.

The Triangle is the most cosmopolitan restaurant in Glasgow and must be the best addition to the eating-out scene in a long time. Situated in the very heart of the city it is noted for its exciting decor by leading artists and has a style uniquely its own. The Brasserie is rightly popular and of high standard but in the dining room the chefs demonstrate their skills with food of superb quality and excellent presentation. Fresh bread baked on the premises daily. Table d'hote and executive lunch menus available daily in The Brasserie and in the dining room.

Open all year
Bar Meals 12 - 11 pm (a)
Dining Room/Brasseries Lunch 12 - 3 pm (a-d)
Dinner 7 - 11 pm (b-f)

Guinea fowl and pheasant terrine/ pistachio nuts; poached Loch Fyne oysters with spinach, creme fraiche and parmesan; Islay scallop and langoustine nage; Tay salmon mariniere; west coast lobster; saddle of venison.

Best Restaurant 1990

Credit cards: 1, 2, 3, 5, 6

The Ubiquitous Chip

12 Ashton Lane
Glasgow
G12 8SJ
Tel: 041 334 5007

A secluded lane in the heart of Glasgow's West End.

A white-washed Victorian mews stable is the setting for one of Glasgow's most renowned restaurants. The wealth of local Scottish produce is polished by traditional and original recipes, to make this restaurant "a wee gem".

Open all year
Bar meals 12 - 11 pm
Dining Room/Restaurant Lunch 12 - 2.30 pm except Sun (c-d)
Dinner 5.30 - 11 pm: 6.30 - 11 pm Sun

One of the UK's most celebrated, extensive and modestly priced wine lists.

Credit cards: 1, 2, 3, 5

Proprietor: Ron Clydesdale

GLENCARSE
BY PERTH
103   F7

Newton House Hotel
Glencarse
by Perth
PH2 7LX
Tel: 073 886 250
Fax: 073 886 717
A85 between Perth and Dundee.

This former Dower House is set back from
the A85, four miles from Perth and 13
from Dundee, and an ideal location to
explore the dramatic countryside or visit
the numerous places of interest such as
Glamis Castle, Scone Palace and world
famous golf courses. The Newton House
prides itself on a high standard of "old
fashioned hospitality" with the ten en
suite bedrooms overlooking the gardens.
It is a keen advocate of Taste of Scotland's
aims as fresh local produce is presented in
the Country House Restaurant and bar
menus. Fluent French is spoken as well as
German and Spanish.

Open all year
Rooms: 10 with private facilities
Bar Lunch 12 - 2 pm (a)
Dining Room/Restaurant Lunch 12 -
2 pm (a)
Bar Supper 5 - 9 pm (a)
Dinner 7 - 9.30 pm (d) 4 course menu
Bed & breakfast £32 - £44
Dinner B & B from £44 bargain break (min.
2 nights stay)
*Crowdie cheese and herb pate, Arbroath
smokie soup, chicken Gowrie, Mrs
McLeod's salmon, entrecote Glenisla,
Highland game pie.*
STB 4 Crown Commended
Credit cards: 1, 3, 5
Proprietors: Geoffrey & Carol Tallis

GLENFINNAN
104   E4

The Stage House
Glenfinnan
Inverness-shire
PH37 4LT
Tel: 0397 83 246
Fax: 0397 83 307
*15 miles west of Fort William on A830.
'Road to the Isles' – ½ mile on right past
Glenfinnan monument.*

This is a historic location for Scots – the
place at which Bonnie Prince Charlie
landed from France in 1745 to claim the

Scottish throne. The Stage House dates
back to the 17th century and this old
coaching inn has been tastefully
modernised to provide comfortable
accommodation and an informal relaxed
atmosphere. There is an extensive wine
list, real ale, log fire in winter and scope for
lots of outdoor activities like fishing and
walking. Boats may be hired and there are
beaches nearby.
Open Mar to Oct
Rooms: 9 with private facilities
Bar Lunch 12 - 2.30 pm (a)
Bar Supper 5 - 6.30 pm (a)
Dinner 7.15 - 8.30 pm (c)
No smoking in restaurant or rooms
Bed & breakfast £20 - £30
Dinner B & B £35.50 - £45.50
*Fresh and smoked local seafood a
speciality. Home-made soups, local game,
interesting and varied vegetables.
Scottish cheeseboard, cafetiere coffee.*
STB 3 Crown Commended
Credit cards: 1, 2
Proprietors: Robert & Carole Hawkes,
Peggy Mills

GLENLIVET
105   D6

Minmore House
Glenlivet
Ballindalloch
Banffshire
AB3 9DB
Tel: 08073 378
Adjacent to The Glenlivet Distillery.
Minmore House was the home of the
founder of The Glenlivet Distillery.
Situated amidst four acres of gardens with
glorious views. Ten en suite bedrooms.
Log and peat fires. Specialises in the best
of Scottish produce, the menu changing
daily. Marvellous walking, bird-watching,
ideally situated for whisky and castle trails.
Open Easter to Nov
Rooms: 10 with private facilities
Bar and Picnic Lunches can be arranged
for residents
Dinner from 8 pm (c)
No smoking in restaurant
Bed & breakfast from £22
Dinner B & B £37 - £40
*Fresh Lossiemouth langoustine, roast
Highland rack of lamb with fresh mint and
honey glaze, Cullen skink, venison and
game, Lochin Ora burnt cream.*
STB 3 Crown Commended
Credit cards: 1, 3
Proprietor: Belinda Luxmoore

GLENROTHES
106   F7

Balbirnie House Hotel
Balbirnie Park
Markinch, by Glenrothes
Fife KY7 6NE
Tel: 0592 610066
Fax: 0592 610529
*On A92, 1½ miles north-east of
Glenrothes.*

Balbirnie is a most impressive building, set
in a magnificent 416 acre park with a par
71 golf course, deluxe accommodation,
memorable public rooms and outstanding
cuisine. It is only 20 minutes by dual
carriageway from the Forth Road Bridge
and Edinburgh. Clay pigeon shooting, off-
track driving and quad biking available.
Open all year
Rooms: 30 with private facilities
Bar Lunch 12 - 2.30 pm (a)
Dining Room/Restaurant Lunch 12 -
2 pm (a)
Dinner 7 - 9.30 pm (d)
Room Rate from £79 (double)
Bed & breakfast from £49
Dinner B & B from £73
*Fillet of halibut coated with mixed herbs
and grain mustard, set on a tomato and
basil sauce.*
STB 5 Crown Highly Commended
Credit cards: 1, 2, 3, 6

Balgeddie House Hotel
Balgeddie Way
Glenrothes
Fife KY6 3ET
Tel: 0592 742511
Fax: 0592 621702
Just off A911 (north) Glenrothes.
Balgeddie House Hotel is set in acres of
manicured gardens with a panoramic view
over Glenrothes. Guests may relax in the
elegant cocktail bar before sampling the
culinary delights of the head chef in the
well appointed restaurant.
Open all year. Closed 1 + 2 Jan
Rooms: 18 with private facilities
Bar Lunch 12 - 2 pm (a)
Dining Room/Restaurant Lunch 12 -
2 pm (b)
Bar Supper 7 - 10 pm (a)
Dinner 7 - 9.30 pm (b-c)
No dogs
Bed & breakfast from £47.85
Dinner B & B from £58.85
*A wide variety of fresh local produce is
used.*
STB 4 Crown Commended
Credit cards: 1, 2, 3
Proprietor: J Crombie

Rescobie Hotel & Restaurant
Valley Drive
Leslie
Fife KY6 3BQ
Tel: 0592 742143

8 miles from M90 – just of A911 in the village of Leslie.

Rescobie is a country house converted to a small hotel. The owners and staff are welcoming and the atmosphere is relaxed and friendly. There are two comfortable and uncrowded dining rooms and a beautiful lounge with deep armchairs and a log fire. Food is freshly prepared by the chefs from the best of Scottish produce. The table d'hôte menu changes daily and offers four choices of starter and main course. The à la carte menu is small but selective and there is always a full vegetarian menu. Sweets are freshly prepared to order. Children very welcome, appropriate reductions. French and German spoken.

Open all year except Christmas + Boxing Days
Rooms: 8 with private facilities
Bar Lunch 12 - 2 pm: 12.30 - 2.30 pm Sun (a)
Dining Room/Restaurant Lunch 12 - 2 pm: 12.30 - 2.30 pm Sun (a)
Dinner 7 - 9 pm (c)
No dogs
Bed & breakfast £30 - £43
Dinner B & B £25 - £42 (min. 3 day stay)

Seafood salad – scallops, prawns and avocado pear served with lemon vinaigrette; Scottish steak – fillet cooked with mushrooms and onions, flamed with whisky and finished with cream; raspberry shortcake, fruit or toffee basket, cranachan.

STB 4 Crown Commended
Credit cards: 1, 2, 3, 5
Proprietors: Tony & Wendy
            Hughes-Lewis

GOUROCK
107   **G4**

Stakis Gantock Hotel
Cloch Road
Gourock
PA19 1AR
Tel: 0475 34671
Telex: 778584
Fax: 0475 32490

2 miles west of Gourock.

The hotel, which has been recently modernised and considerably extended, has 101 bedrooms, a full leisure club complex including indoor pool, whirlpool bath, sauna and two all weather floodlit tennis courts. On the outskirts of Gourock and set against a woodland backdrop. This hotel is ideal for tourists and business clients alike. The three conference and banqueting suites are suitable for functions up to 200. The Chandlers Restaurant commands magnificent views over the Firth of Clyde to the mountains of Argyll.

Open all year
Rooms: 101 with private facilities
Bar Lunch 12.30 - 2.30 pm (a)
Dining Room/Restaurant Lunch 12.30 - 2.30 pm: 1 - 3 pm Sun (a)
Dinner 6.30 - 9.30 pm (b)
Bed & breakfast rates on application
Dinner B & B from £35 (min. 2 nights stay)

Medallions of venison 'Auld Reekie'; supreme of pheasant Lochiel; fillets of trout Loch Orr.

STB 5 Crown Commended
Credit cards: 1, 2, 3, 5, 6

GRANTOWN ON SPEY
108   **D6**

The Ardlarig
Woodlands Terrace
Grantown-on-Spey
Moray
PH26 3JU
Tel: 0479 3245

On A95 as it enters Grantown-on-Spey.

Unique among the hotels and guest houses of the Spey Valley is the Ardlarig – a tastefully decorated Victorian house set amidst its own gardens. Guests return time after time to enjoy the welcoming and relaxing atmosphere, the high standards of service and, above all, the quality cuisine based mostly on traditional Scottish recipes, freshly prepared on the premises, nothing from the freezer here! The herb garden is a chef's delight and an extensive range of wines and spirits will complement your meal in the elegant candlelit dining room. Leisure events include short cookery courses, painting weekends, champagne breaks in the four poster bedroom to say nothing of impromptu musical evenings! French, German and Italian spoken. Well behaved children and pets are welcome.

Open all year
Rooms: 7
Picnic Lunches by arrangement

Dinner 7 - 8 pm (b) - later by arrangement
Non-residents welcome – reservation essential
No smoking throughout
Bed & breakfast from £18
Dinner B & B from £30

Own pastries, breads and preserves. Prime Highland beef with fresh oranges and Courvoisier; local venison steaks with wild cherry sauce; fresh Speyside salmon poached in cream and Drambuie. Quality vegetarian dishes.

STB 2 Crown Commended
No credit cards
Proprietors: Kevin W Gee &
            Andrew Hunter

Culdearn House
Woodlands Terrace
Grantown-on-Spey
Moray, PH26 3JU
Tel: 0479 2106

On A95, south-west entry to Grantown-on-Spey.

This Victorian house combines character with tastefully appointed modern amenities to provide a high degree of comfort and a distinctly Scottish atmosphere. It is ideally situated for touring the Highlands as well as having interest for golfers, anglers, walkers and bird-watchers. Log and peat fires blaze in the public rooms.

Open Mar to Oct
Rooms: 9 with private facilities
Picnic Lunches to order
Dinner 7 - 7.30 pm (b)
Residents only
No dogs
No smoking in dining room
Bed & breakfast £20 - £25
Dinner B & B £30 - £35

Traditional Scottish fare using lamb, beef, venison and trout, is complemented by a modestly priced wine list and range of malt whiskies.

STB 3 Crown Commended
Credit cards: 1, 3, 6
Proprietors: Alasdair & Isobel Little

Garth Hotel
The Square
Grantown-on-Spey
PH26 3HN
Tel: 0479 2836/2162

On the Square of Grantown-on-Spey.

Set amidst four acres of landscaped garden, the Garth Hotel commands a view of the picturesque Square of Grantown-on-Spey. This three star hotel dates ▶

from the 17th century and offers old world charm with every modern comfort and convenience. Seventeen individually furnished bedrooms – all en suite – with direct dial telephone, colour TV and tea/coffee-making facilities. French and German spoken.

Open all year
Rooms: 17 with private facilities
Bar Lunch 12 - 2 pm (a)
Dining Room/Restaurant Lunch 12 - 2 pm (b)
Dinner 7.30 - 8.30 pm (c)
No dogs
No smoking in restaurant
Bed & breakfast from £28
Dinner B & B from £44
Extensive and selective menu specialising in Taste of Scotland dishes with an accent on fresh local produce, e.g. salmon, trout, venison, game.
STB 4 Crown Commended
Credit cards: 1, 3, 5, 6
Proprietor: Gordon McLaughlan

Ravenscourt House Hotel
Seafield Avenue
Grantown-on-Spey
Moray, PH26 3JG
Tel: 0479 3260
Leave A9 at Carrbridge. 10 miles north-east on A938. Ravenscourt just off main Square.

A country house hotel which exudes an atmosphere of quality and elegance. Dining is in the conservatory with tasteful decor and beautiful table appointments. The drawing room has been furnished sumptuously and there are fine original oil paintings and water colours. Menus are well balanced, the standard of cooking and presentation is high and service is described by our inspector as faultless. Judging by the remarks in the visitors book there is a very satisfied clientele. There is excellent value house wine and generally a wine list catering for all tastes and pockets.

Open all year
Rooms: 9 with private facilities
Dinner 7 - 9.30 pm (c) – set 4 course table d'hote
No dogs
No smoking area in conservatory
Bed & breakfast from £24
Dinner B & B £43
Fresh fish daily. Scottish and French dishes feature equally. Menu changes every third day, with a traditional roast meal on Sunday. Sirloin steaks 'New York' cut. Rack of lamb for two.
STB 3 Crown Commended
No credit cards

Ardvourlie Castle
Aird A Mhulaidh
Isle of Harris
Western Isles
PA85 3AB
Tel: 0859 2307
On A859, 10 miles north of Tarbert.

Ardvourlie Castle is a Victorian hunting lodge built by the Earl of Dunmore in a beautiful setting on the shores of Loch Seaforth in the mountains of North Harris. Carefully restored, it is now a guest house of unusual elegance and charm.

Open all year
Rooms: 4
Dining Room/Restaurant Lunch (d) by arrangement
Dinner (d)
Restricted licence – residents only
Bed & breakfast £22 - £32.45
Dinner B & B £39 - £49.45
Food based on blend of traditional Scottish and innovation, using local and free-range ingredients when available.
No credit cards
Proprietors: Paul & Derek Martin

Kirklands Hotel
West Stewart Place
Hawick
Roxburghshire
TD9 8BH
Tel: 0450 72263
200 yards off A7, ½ mile north of Hawick High Street.

Charming Victorian house hotel with a fine outlook across the town and surrounding hills. Impressive public rooms and spacious, well furnished bedrooms all with radio, colour TV, tea-making facilities and telephone. Excellent cuisine and friendly, efficient service under the personal supervision of the proprietor. Very large garden, children's play area. Ideal place for touring the beautiful Scottish Borders.

Open all year except Christmas, Boxing + New Year's Days
Rooms: 13, 10 with private facilities
Bar Lunch 12 - 2 pm (a)
Dining Room/Restaurant Lunch 12 - 2 pm (a)
Dinner 7 - 9.30 pm (c)

Bed & breakfast from £27.50
Dinner B & B from £40
Tournedos 'Queen o' Scots', Salmon Teviotdale, Trout Belle Meuniere.
STB 4 Crown Commended
Credit cards: 1, 2, 3, 5, 6
Proprietor: Barrie Newland

Mansfield House Hotel
Weensland Road
Hawick
Roxburghshire
TD9 9EL
Tel: 0450 73988
Fax: 0450 72007
On A698 approximately 1 mile from centre of Hawick.

The Mackinnon family own and run this Victorian country house hotel in 10 acres of grounds. Large public rooms with high ornately plastered ceilings, magnificent fireplaces of Italian marble and elegant brass chandeliers. Bedrooms en suite with TV and tea/coffee-making facilities.

Open all year
Rooms: 10 with private facilities
Bar Lunch 12 - 2 pm (a)
Dining Room/Restaurant Lunch 12 - 2 pm except Sun, Sat (b)
Dinner 7 - 9.15 pm (c)
No smoking area in restaurant
Bed & breakfast £26
Dinner B & B from £39.50
All meals individually prepared by prize winning chef using the best local produce. Home-made desserts a speciality. Extensive range of Scottish cheeses, malt whiskies and liqueurs.
Credit cards: 1, 2, 3, 5
Proprietors: Sheila & Ian MacKinnon

The Old Forge Restaurant
Newmill on Teviot
by Hawick
TD9 0JU
Tel: 0450 85298
4 miles south of Hawick on A7.

The Old Forge was formerly the village smiddy which retains the original forge, bellows, stone walls and beamed ceiling. Bill and Margaret Irving run a relaxed and unassuming restaurant usually full of appreciative locals who come to take advantage of the marvellous value for money that the menu offers. Advance booking advisable. Try, perhaps, cheese souffle with spinach and sorrel filling, followed by chestnut, mushroom and orange soup accompanied by a loaf of home-made granary bread. Enjoy wild ▶

rabbit cooked in a parcel with port and herbs, or main course or vegetarian dish of the day – aubergine stuffed with apricots and nuts – followed by black coffee water-ice with whipped cream. There is an award winning cheese list consisting of an amazing number of Scottish farmhouse cheeses including four local Border cheeses. To complement the meal there is an extensive wine list at ungreedy prices. Enquire about the self-catering accommodation. Children welcome. French is spoken.

Open all year except first 2 wks May + first 2 wks Nov
Dinner 7 - 9.30 pm (b)
Closed Sun + Mon
No dogs except guide dogs
Credit cards: 1, 3
Proprietors: Bill & Margaret Irving

The Penny Black
2-6 North Bridge Street
Hawick
Roxburghshire, TD9 9QW
Tel: 0450 76492
Fax: 0450 77877
Near the horse statue at the end of the main street. Next door to the Post Office.
A tasteful refurbishment of the old postal sorting office for Hawick and now a bar/bistro in one section and a formal restaurant in the other. Many of the original features of the building have been retained such as a telephone box, pillar box, original sorters stools etc. The menu, which changes every five or six weeks is fairly extensive. The emphasis is on presenting good quality food at reasonable prices. Children welcome. Well behaved dogs welcome in the bar/bistro but not in the restaurant.

Open all year
Bar Lunch 12 - 2 pm (a)
Bar Supper 6 - 9.30 pm (a)
Dinner 7 - 9.30 pm (b)
Closed Sun + Mon
No dogs in restaurant
Facilities for the disabled
No smoking area
Local fish and best Border beef
Credit cards: 1, 3, 5
Proprietor: Robin Black

Whitchester Christian Guest House
Borthaugh
Hawick
Roxburghshire, TD9 7LN
Tel: 0450 77477
2 miles south of Hawick on A7, ¼ mile off on B711 to Roberton.
A former Dower House of the Buccleuch Estate set in 3½ acres of garden. David and Doreen Maybury have relocated

from Duns to this quiet beautiful spot. The house has been refurbished in a comfortable and relaxing style. All food including the bread is cooked on the premises and local produce is widely used. Full board includes a traditional Scottish afternoon tea. A wide range of soups are made such as carrot and coriander and lemon and yoghurt, sweets include brulees, pavlovas, sorbet concoctions and many others, a large Scottish cheese board is kept.

Open all year from mid March 1991
Rooms: 9, 3 with private facilities
Dining Room/Restaurant Lunch 12.45 - 1.15 pm (a)
Tea 4.30 pm - 5 pm
Dinner 7 - 8 pm (a)
Note: Sun – main meal at lunchtime, light evening meal only
Unlicensed
Bed & breakfast from £13
Dinner B & B from £19
Rowan poached trout, Border beef steak in black pepper sauce, blackcurrant nut meringue gateau, cranachan, syllabubs, home-made soups and bread.
No credit cards
Proprietors: David & Doreen Maybury

HELMSDALE
111   C6

Bunillidh Restaurant
2-4 Dunrobin Street
Helmsdale
Sutherland
KW8 6JX
Tel: 043 12 457
Just off A9 in centre of Helmsdale, next to Timespan Heritage Centre.
Bunillidh – pronounced "Buneely" – is a family run restaurant situated in a modern building forming a corner of an attractive square, looking over the Strath of Kildonan and near the River Helmsdale. In the spacious dining area guests may enjoy a coffee, home-made sweets from the trolley, or partake of one of the many seafood specialities.

Open Mar to Nov
Menu available all day 10 am - 9 pm (a-b)
Open 7 days Jun to end Sep, otherwise closed Mon
Chef/patron's harbour kettle, local lobster and salmon, langoustines in garlic butter. Ocean symphony - a platter of local cold fish.
Credit cards: 1, 3
Proprietors: Malcolm & Linda Holden

Navidale House Hotel
Helmsdale
Sutherland
KW8 6JS
Tel: 043 12 258
½ mile north of Helmsdale on A9.
A former Victorian shooting lodge of the Dukes of Sutherland, Navidale is now a comfortable country house hotel. It stands in seven acres of garden on a cliff top overlooking the Moray Firth. There is an air of spacious elegance about the public rooms which have superb panoramic views and open fires. There are fine sea views from most of the bedrooms. The kitchen makes good use of the fine supply of local seafish and shellfish.

Open Feb to mid Nov
Rooms: 18, 12 with private facilities
Bar Lunch 12 - 1.45 pm (a)
Dinner 7 - 8.45 pm (c)
No smoking in restaurant
Bed & breakfast £20 - £30
Dinner B & B £35.50 - £46
Fresh Skye oysters. Steamed mussels with garlic butter. Wing of skate with prawn and caper butter. Caithness rack of lamb with garlic and red wine sauce.
Credit cards: 1, 2, 3
Proprietor: Marcus Blackwell

Johnstounburn House Hotel
Humbie
East Lothian
EH36 5PL
Tel: 087533 696
Fax: 087533 626

From A68 to Jedburgh, turn at Fala, 2 miles on right.

Surrounded by acres of lawns, gardens and picturesque farmland at the foot of the Lammermuir Hills, the visitor to Johnstounburn could hardly imagine that he or she is only 15 miles away from bustling Edinburgh. And once inside the 17th century stone walls, warmed by the open fires and treated to an outstanding menu made with fresh local produce, one begins to appreciate the depth of Scotland's heritage. Johnstounburn has 20 well appointed bedrooms, conference rooms for as many delegates, an exquisite pine-panelled dining room, and a singularly relaxing wood-panelled lounge.

Open all year

Rooms 20 with private facilities
Bar Lunch 12 - 2 pm (a)
Dining Room/Restaurant Lunch 12 - 2 pm (b)
Dinner 7 - 9 pm (c)
Bed & breakfast from £55
Dinner B & B rates on application

Seafood terrine wrapped in smoked salmon, roast saddle of venison and peppered duck breast.

STB 4 Crown Commended

Credit cards: 1, 2, 3, 5, 6

The Old Manse of Marnoch
Bridge of Marnoch
Huntly
AB5 5RS
Tel: 0466 780873

On B9117, one mile off Huntly-Banff A97 route.

The Old Manse of Marnoch is a Georgian country house set in five acres of mature gardens on the River Deveron. Well appointed bedrooms, elegant lounges and dining room set with silver and crystal, combine to provide an experience of true Scottish hospitality where guests are encouraged to feel genuinely at home. The set dinner menu changes daily and absolutely everything is prepared in The Old Manse kitchen, whilst the herb parterre and walled kitchen garden supply organic produce in season. This is definitely not the place for butter portions or plastic jam! Fluent German spoken. Dogs welcome, but not in the dining room.

Open all year

Rooms: 4, 2 with private facilities
Packed Lunch - as requested
Dining Room/Restaurant Lunch (a) as requested
Dinner 7 - 10 pm (b)
Residents and their guests only. Private parties by arrangement
No smoking in dining room
Bed & breakfast from £16.50
Dinner B & B from £29

Fine Scots cooking, traditional and contemporary. Extensive breakfast menu includes spiced beef, devilled ham, home-baked breads, own jams and marmalades.

STB 3 Crown Highly Commended

No credit cards

Proprietors: Patrick & Keren Carter

Glenmoriston Arms Hotel
Invermoriston
Glenmoriston
Inverness-shire
IV3 6YA
Tel: 0320 51206

At junction of A82 and A887 in Invermoriston.

This 200 year old coaching inn nestles at the foot of Glenmoriston, one of Scotland's loveliest glens, a few minutes from world famous Loch Ness. An ideal base for touring the West Highlands and Skye. An acclaimed restaurant serving local venison, Angus steaks and wild salmon in season. There is a superb selection of malt whiskies to complement your meal.

Open all year

Rooms: 8 with private facilities
Bar Lunch 12 - 2 pm (a)
Dining Room/Restaurant Lunch 12 - 2 pm Sun only (a)
Bar Supper 5.30 - 8.30 pm (a)
Dinner 6.30 - 8.30 pm (b)
Bed & breakfast from £25
Dinner B & B from £38

Sauteed fillets of venison in a black cherry and ginger sauce; poached darne of local salmon served with an orange and herb butter.

STB 4 Crown Commended

Credit cards: 1, 3

Proprietor: Alan Draper

Culloden House Hotel
Culloden
nr Inverness
IV1 2NZ
Tel: 0463 790461

3 miles from Inverness, 5 miles from Inverness Airport.

Culloden House is an architectural gem with an historic and romantic association with Bonnie Prince Charlie and the Battle of Culloden which was fought nearby. It has acres of parkland, fine lawns and trees, and is an oasis of exceptional quiet. Magnificent public rooms and exceptionally well furnished, luxurious bedrooms.

Open all year

Rooms: 20 with private facilities
Dining Room/Restaurant Lunch 12.30 - 2 pm (d)
Dinner 7 - 9 pm (f)
Bed & breakfast from £62.50
Dinner B & B rates on application

Aberdeen Angus steaks and salmon specialities, game in season.

STB 5 Crown Highly Commended

Credit cards: 1, 2, 3, 5, 6

Proprietors: Ian & Marjory McKenzie

Dunain Park Hotel
Dunain Park
Inverness
IV3 6JN
Tel: 0463 230512

A82, one mile from Inverness.

Ann and Edward Nicoll give a warm welcome and offer fine food in this beautiful small hotel, secluded in six acres of gardens and woodland. They maintain high standards of cuisine, comfort and service while retaining the aura of a country house. An atmosphere enhanced by log fires, antiques and oil paintings. Centrally heated throughout. Two acres vegetable garden. Indoor heated swimming pool and sauna. Egon Ronay recommended. Macallan Scottish ▶

Restaurant of the Year 1989. New extension with six further rooms opened during 1990.

Open all year except 3rd wk Nov, Christmas Day + 2 wks Jan/Feb

Rooms: 14 with private facilities
Light Lunch 12.30 - 2 pm (a)
Dinner 7 - 9 pm (c)
No smoking area in restaurant
Bed & breakfast £35 - £45
Dinner B & B £54 - £64

Saddle of venison, lamb, Highland cattle steaks, Guinea fowl, duck, quail, salmon, seafood and extensive sweet buffet.

STB 4 Crown Highly Commended

Credit cards: 1, 2, 3, 5

Proprietors: Ann & Edward Nicoll

Glen Mhor Hotel & Restaurant
Ness Bank
Inverness
IV2 4SG
Tel: 0463 234308

On river bank below castle.

Superbly situated on the south bank of the River Ness near the town centre. Most bedrooms have en suite facilities. Freshly prepared local produce is featured in modern Taste of Scotland menus in the up market Riverview Restaurant which is open for dinner and Sunday lunch. Nico's Bistro Bar is an interesting alternative and informal venue for traditional Highland dishes and snacks, day and night.

Open all year except 31 Dec to 3 Jan

Rooms: 30, 27 with private facilities
Bar Lunch 12 - 2.15 pm (a)
Dinner 6.30 - 9.30 pm (b)
Bed & breakfast from £31.50
Dinner B & B from £40 (min. 3 nights stay)

Salmon in various styles, langoustines, oysters, mussels, fresh fish, beef, lamb – all prepared to order.

STB 4 Crown Commended

Credit cards: 1, 2, 3, 5

Proprietor: J Nicol Manson

Invermoy House Private Hotel & Carriages of Moy Restaurant
Moy
nr Tomatin
Inverness-shire
IV13 7YE
Tel: 080 82 271

On B9154, 11 miles south of Inverness.

Family run hotel of unusual charm. Former Highland railway station. Ideally situated for touring Highlands. All rooms on ground level. Two restored railway carriages,

furnished in Edwardian style form a separate unique restaurant (in addition to the hotel dining room) serving à la carte meals. Special diets by arrangement.

Open all year

Rooms: 7, 1 with private facilities
Dinner 7 - 9 pm (c-e)
No smoking area in dining room
Bed & breakfast from £14
Dinner B & B from £26

Home-made soups and pâtés. Local salmon, trout and game in season. Scottish meats and vegetables with home-grown herbs. Scottish cheeses.

STB 2 Crown Commended

Credit cards: 1, 3

Proprietors: D & V Simpson, H & T Pascoe

Kingsmills Hotel
Culcabock Road
Inverness
IV2 3LP
Tel: 0463 237166
Telex: 75566
Fax: 0463 225208

Leave A9 at 'Crown and Kingsmills'. Follow Kingsmills sign, right at first roundabout and left at second – just past golf course.

A fine hotel in the Highlands. Kingsmills Hotel nestles in four acres of beautiful gardens, only one mile from town centre. Large garden rooms and luxury villas prove ideal for families – children free sharing parents' room. Also indoor heated swimming pool and leisure club. New luxury bedrooms and conservatory completed by Easter 1991.

Open all year

Rooms: 85 with private facilities
Bar Lunch 12.15 - 2 pm; 12.30 - 2 pm Sun (a-b)
Dining Room/Restaurant Lunch 12.15 - 2 pm; 12.30 - 2 pm Sun (c)
Dinner 7 - 9 pm (d)
Bed & breakfast from £68
Special weekend breaks available

STB 4 Crown Commended

Credit cards: 1, 2, 3, 5, 6

Moniack Restaurant and Bar
Highland Wineries
Kirkhill
Inverness
IV5 7PQ
Tel: 046 383 336

Situated 7 miles from Inverness on the Beauly road.

The Castle Wine Bar Restaurant lies within 15 minutes of Loch Ness. The

restaurant is an adjunct to the winery which makes an interesting range of Scottish wines. It is a traditional stone-built restaurant enhanced in the evening by candlelit tables and an open fire.

Open late May to mid Sep 11 am - 11 pm

Dining Room/Restaurant Lunch 12 - 2.30 pm (a)
Dinner 7 - 9.30 pm except Sun, Mon (a-b)
In Winter months, open Fri + Sat (dinner only) and Sun (lunch), but closed Jan

Salmon en croute with dill cream sauce. Lobster in season. Fillet Rossini.

Credit cards: 1, 3

Proprietor: Kit Fraser

Station Hotel
Academy Street
Inverness
IV1 1LG
Tel: 0463 231926

In town centre of Inverness adjacent to the railway station.

This traditional town centre hotel has been at the hub of the business and social life of Inverness for over a century. The Strathconon Restaurant has been consistently acclaimed for the standard of its cuisine and service. Table d'hôte and à la carte menus.

Open all year

Rooms: 67, 53 with private facilities
Bar Lunch 11.30 am - 2.15 pm (a)
Dining Room/Restaurant Lunch 11.30 am - 2.15 pm
Dinner 7 - 9.15 pm (b)
Bed & breakfast from £35
Dinner B & B from £48.50

Fresh local mussels with white wine and cream. Medallions of venison lightly cooked in honey and whisky with julienne of apricots.

STB 4 Crown Approved

Credit cards: 1, 2, 3, 5, 6

Whinpark Hotel
17 Ardross Street
Inverness
IV3 5NS
Tel: 0463 232549

By Eden Court Theatre.

The restaurant with rooms. Within easy walking distance of the town centre and near to Eden Court Theatre on the River Ness. The restaurant offers 'something special' to the discerning diner. Using local produce such as Ness salmon, game and Aberdeen Angus steak. A relaxed house-party atmosphere with a truly Highland welcome.

▶

Open all year

Rooms: 8, 4 with private facilities
Dining Room/Restaurant Lunch 12 -
2 pm except Sun, Sat (a)
Dinner 6.30 - 9.30 pm (b)
Bed & breakfast from £20
Dinner B & B from £30

*Collops of venison, finished in lemon
thyme and whisky sauce, stuffed fillets of
rock turbot with a smoked salmon and
shrimp mousse.*

STB 3 Crown Commended

Credit card: 3

Proprietor: Stephen MacKenzie

INVERURIE

116   E8

Thainstone House Hotel
Thainstone Estate
Inverurie
Aberdeenshire
AB5 9NT
Tel: 0467 21643
Fax: 0467 25084

*On A96 north of Aberdeen (8 miles from
airport).*

Situated at the gateway to the castle
country, this palladian mansion house is
set in 14 acres of the woodlands and
rolling pastures of Donside. King Robert
the Bruce, who camped nearby before his
debacle with the Comyns of Buchan at the
Battle of Barra in 1308, would no doubt
have appreciated the chance to select fine
wine from the cellars. And James Wilson,
a signatory of the American Declaration of
Independence who hailed from
Thainstone, would certainly have
approved of the gourmet menu. The
present mansion was reconstructed in
1759 after sacking by Jacobite forces in
the '45 rebellion. Over the next year, the
hotel is expanding and once the extension
is completed it will have 50 bedrooms,
extended restaurant facilities and a new
leisure complex. It is the owners' aim to
retain as far as possible the original
character of this period country house.
French spoken.

Open all year

Rooms: 8 with private facilities
Bar Lunch 12 - 2 pm: 12.30 - 2.30 pm
Sun (a)
Dining Room/Restaurant Lunch 12 - 2 pm:
12.30 - 2.30 pm Sun (b)
Bar Supper 6.30 - 9.30 pm (b)
Dinner 6.45 - 9.30 pm (e)
Bed & breakfast £25 - £37.50

Dinner B & B £40 - £50

*Fillet of salmon with white crab meat
bound in a delicate white wine sauce and
held in a light flaky pastry case. Highland
spring lamb gently baked with fresh
tarragon and sauted strips of cucumber.*

STB 4 Crown Commended

Credit cards: 1, 2, 3, 5

Proprietors: Edith & Michael Lovie

PRICE CATEGORIES

(a)	under £10.00
(b)	£10.00 - £15.00
(c)	£15.00 - £20.00
(d)	£20.00 - £25.00
(e)	£25.00 - £30.00
(f)	over £30.00

IRVINE

117   G4

Hospitality Inn, Irvine
46 Annick Road
Irvine
Ayrshire
KA11 4LD
Tel: 0294 74272
Telex: 777097
Fax: 0294 77287

*On outskirts of Irvine on A71 to
Kilmarnock.*

The hotel is luxurious. The palm-
festooned Hawaiian Lagoon is one of the
most spectacular features with a myriad
of tropical plants and rocks, an exquisitely-
styled à la carte restaurant and a
Moroccan-style bar. A conference and
banqueting facility for up to 250. French
and German spoken. Special children's
menu available.

Open all year

Rooms: 128 with private facilities
Dining Room/Restaurant Lunch 12.30 -
2 pm (c)
Lunch (Lagoon) 12.30 - 6 pm (b)
Dinner 7.30 - 10 pm (e)
Dinner (Lagoon) 6 - 11 pm (c)
Bed & breakfast rates on application
Dinner B & B rates on application

*The Chef prepares a new à la carte menu
each season to offer the best of seasonal
specialities.*

STB 5 Crown Commended

Credit cards: 1, 2, 3, 5, 6

ISLAY
118   ISLE OF   G2

Harbour Inn
Bowmore
Isle of Islay
Argyll
PA43 7JR
Tel: 049 681 330

Isle of Islay's most central village.

A small traditional village inn overlooking
the harbour in the island's most central
village. It has a comfortable cosy feel to it
and our inspector concluded that "when
the renovations have been finished, this
will be a great place to go". Joy and
Douglas Law are an enthusiastic couple
and are intent on establishing a reputation
for good food. Presentation is good and
service is friendly and efficient. Four day
package stays are available with the ferry
fare included.

Open all year

Rooms: 4, 2 with private facilities
Bar Lunch 12 - 2 pm (a)
Bar Supper 5 - 6.30 pm (a)
Dinner 7 - 9 pm (b)
No meals served on Sun except for
residents
Bed & breakfast from £17.50
Dinner B & B from £25.50

*The best local produce freshly cooked,
lobster, scallops, oysters, mussels,
salmon, venison, lamb and beef.*

Credit cards: 1, 3

Proprietors: Douglas & Joy Law

Kilchoman House Restaurant
by Bruichladdich
Isle of Islay
Argyll
PA49 7UY
Tel: 049 685 382

Off B8018 on the Atlantic coast.

Stuart and Lesley Taylor offer you
magnificent crags, wild goats, historic
site, peat fires, island hospitality, crack
with mine host, great food from his
'missus', unspoilt island, 3 night off-
season breaks in five adjacent self-
catering cottages. Kilchoman House is a
former manse said to occupy the site of
the Summer Palace of the Lords of the
Isles. The 18 seat restaurant which is the
dining room of the Taylors' house is
popular with locals and visitors alike. A
lovely 20 minute drive from the nearest
village, there is no possibility of 'passing
trade' and reservations are essential. The
self-catering cottages (open all year) ▶

also require advance booking at the most popular times of year.

Cottages open all year.
Restaurant limited opening Nov to Mar
Dinner from 7.30 pm except Sun (c)
Reservations essential
Closed Sun

Drunken bullock, chicken with Islay cheese, wild venison with rowan jelly, Islay scallops with mushrooms and parsley, lobster thermidor, Kilchoman mist.

No credit cards
Proprietors: Stuart & Lesley Taylor

ISLE OF WHITHORN
119　　　**I5**

Queen's Arms Hotel
22 Main Street
Isle of Whithorn
Wigtownshire
DG8 8LF
Tel: 09885 369

A750 south of Newton Stewart.

A small country hotel with a homely atmosphere at the entrance to a small fishing village. Family run, it offers a personal and friendly service. Food is of good Scottish produce prepared in the traditional manner. The atmosphere is relaxed and informal.

Open all year
Rooms: 10, 4 with private facilities
Bar Lunch 12.30 - 2 pm (a)
·Bar Supper 9 - 10 pm
Dinner 7.30 - 9.30 pm (c)
No smoking area in restaurant
Bed & breakfast from £16.50
Dinner B & B rates on application

Lobster, Galloway steaks and local fresh fish.

Credit cards: 1, 3, 5
Proprietor: Donald Niven

KELSO
120　　　**G8**

Floors Castle
Kelso
Roxburghshire
TD5 7RW
Tel: 0573 23333

A699 west of Kelso.

Floors is the magnificent and imposing Border home of the Duke of Roxburghe much of which is open to the public. The self-service restaurant which caters for visitors is plainly but comfortably furnished and has a well sheltered open courtyard in which you may eat out in good weather. The restaurant makes good use of available fresh produce from the castle gardens, salmon from the River Tweed and, there is some good home-baking.

Open May to Sep except Fri + Sat
Also open Easter, and Fri during Jul + Aug
Dining Room/Restaurant Lunch (a)

Floors kitchen pheasant pâté, Tweed salmon, smoked Tweed salmon, home baking from Floors Castle kitchens.

Credit cards: 1, 3

Sunlaws House Hotel
Heiton
Kelso
Roxburghshire
TD5 8JZ
Tel: 05735 331

On A698, Kelso-Jedburgh road in the village of Heiton.

The 18th century Scottish baronial gentleman's home, converted only five years ago and owned by the Duke of Roxburghe. It offers the charm and comfort of a stylish period and luxurious country house, whether fishing, shooting, relaxing or enjoying the countryside.

Open all year
Rooms: 21 with private facilities
Bar Lunch 12.30 - 2 pm (b)
Dining Room/Restaurant Lunch 12.30 - 2 pm except Sun + Sat (c)
Dinner 7.30 - 9.30 pm (d)
Bed & breakfast from £62
Dinner B & B rates on application

Special children's menu.

STB 4 Crown Commended
Credit cards: 1, 2, 3, 5

KENTALLEN
121　　OF APPIN　　**F4**

Ardsheal House
Kentallen of Appin
Argyll
PA38 4BX
Tel: 063 174 227

On A828, 4 miles south of Ballachulish Bridge.

Set in 900 acres of woods and meadows overlooking Loch Linnhe, this 1760 house has oak panelling, open fires and is furnished with antiques. The relaxed, congenial atmosphere is conducive to enjoying the superb meals and fine wines, and offers a true taste of the best of Scotland.

Open Easter to Nov
Rooms: 13 with private facilities
Dining Room/Restaurant Lunch 12 - 2 pm (b)
Dinner 8.30 pm (f)
No smoking in restaurant
Dinner B & B £55 - £74

Ramekin of Loch Linnhe prawns and Colonsay oysters in rose jelly with garden herbs; mangetout and ginger soup; medallions of venison with blackcurrant vinegar. Rosette of beef with sage butter, chestnut puree and thyme.

Credit cards: 1, 3
Proprietors: Bob & Jane Taylor

KILCHRENAN
122　　　**F4**

Ardanaiseig Hotel
Kilchrenan, by Taynuilt
Argyll PA35 1HE
Tel: 086 63 333
Fax: 086 63 222

3½ miles off B845 at Kilchrenan.

It is easy to fall in love with a place like Ardanaiseig. Everything about it seems just right. It is set in a renowned shrub and woodland garden on the shores of Loch Awe with really magnificent views. But superlatives do not stop with the scenery. This is a country house hotel that is beautifully appointed, in which the staff are exceptionally courteous and good mannered and give the clear impression that looking after the needs of guests is a genuine pleasure. The kitchen reflects the same high standards that prevail throughout this peaceful haven, food is imaginative and prepared and presented with panache.

Open mid Apr to late Oct
Rooms: 14 with private facilities
Dining Room/Restaurant Lunch 12.30 - 2 pm (c)
Dinner 7.30 - 9 pm (f)
No smoking in dining room
Dinner B & B £60 - £100

Warm home-smoked scallops with snow peas and chives. A symphony of west coast shellfish pan-fried and accompanied by a saffron butter sauce. Crisp brandy snap basket filled with fresh garden fruits.

Credit cards: 1, 2, 3, 5

Best Hospitality & Welcome 1990

Proprietors: Jonathan & Jane Brown

Taychreggan Hotel
Kilchrenan
by Taynuilt
Argyll
PA35 1HQ
Tel: 086 63 211

Leave A85 at Taynuilt on to B845 on loch side past Kilchrenan.

There was a time when sturdy Highland cattle going to market were made to swim across Loch Awe and land at Taychreggan where they rested for the night. It is not surprising therefore, that this hotel started off as a drovers' inn. It is now a very comfortable, delightful small hotel in a most peaceful and secluded site with splendid views across the loch. There are still echoes of the past in the cobbled courtyard – a pleasant place in which to sit out and enjoy a cool drink, and there are three well equipped public rooms. The dining room is attractively laid out and there is a strong emphasis on fresh local products, well presented and served. Various theme weekends in Autumn and Winter.

Open Mar to Dec
Rooms: 16 with private facilities
Bar Lunch 12.15 - 2.15 pm (a)
Dining Room/Restaurant Lunch 12.15 -
2.15 pm (c)
Dinner 7.30 - 9.15 pm (e)
Bed & breakfast – special rate £35 per person, Nov to Dec + Mar
Dinner B & B from £55

Local fresh fish, prawns, turbot, halibut, salmon, venison, roast beef, etc. Served in an enterprising and interesting manner.
STB 4 Crown Commended
Credit cards: 1, 2, 3, 5
Proprietors: John & Monika Tyrrell

KILDRUMMY
123   E7

Kildrummy Castle Hotel
Kildrummy
by Alford
Aberdeenshire
AB3 8RA
Tel: 09755 71288

On A97 Ballater-Huntly road, 35 miles west of Aberdeen.

A converted mansion house overlooking the ruins of the original 13th century castle amidst acres of planted gardens and woodland. The interior features the original turn-of-the-century wall tapestries and oak panelling. Full central heating and all modern facilities have not detracted from the original atmosphere or character of the house.

Open Mar to Dec
Rooms: 16 with private facilities
Dining Room/Restaurant Lunch 12.30 -
1.45 pm (c)
Dinner 7 - 9 pm (d)
No smoking in dining room
Bed & breakfast £42 - £49
Dinner B & B £45 - £69

Salmon terrine on a saffron sauce lightly laced with Scotch whisky. Warm salad of Kildrummy game. Loin of veal with a light almond and rosemary sauce with a timbale of wild rice.
STB 4 Crown Highly Commended
Credit cards: 1, 2, 3, 6
Proprietor: Thomas Hanna

KILFINAN
124   G4

Kilfinan Hotel
Kilfinan
nr Tighnabruaich
Argyll
PA21 2AP
Tel: 070 082 201

On the eastern shores of Loch Fyne.

Ancient coaching inn, modernised to very high standards without losing any of its traditional character, set in breathtaking beautiful countryside on the eastern shores of Loch Fyne.

Open all year
Rooms: 11, 10 with private facilities
Dining Room/Restaurant Lunch 12 -
2 pm (a)
Dinner 7.30 - 9.30 pm (c)
Bed & breakfast rates on application
Dinner B & B rates on application

Fresh local produce including scallops, mussels, prawns and salmon from Loch Fyne, pheasant, wild duck and venison from adjoining Otter Estate form the basis for a variety of memorable meals.
STB 3 Crown Commended
Credit cards: 2, 3, 5
Proprietor: T Wignell

KILLIECRANKIE
125   E6

Killiecrankie Hotel
by Pitlochry
Perthshire PH16 5LG
Tel: 0796 3220
Fax: 0796 2451

On old A9, 3 miles north of Pitlochry.

A converted Dower House, set in four acres of well kept gardens overlooking the historic Pass of Killiecrankie. Furnished to a high standard to reflect the expected small country house atmosphere and comfort requirements of the most fastidious guest.

Open late Feb to mid Nov
Rooms: 12 with private facilities
Bar Lunch 12.30 - 2 pm (a)
Bar Supper 6.30 - 9.30 pm (b)
Dinner 7 - 8.30 pm (d)
No smoking in dining room
Bed & breakfast £31.50 - £37.50
Dinner B & B £49 - £56.95

Traditional Scottish menu featuring speciality soups, Tay salmon, fresh Buckie fish, Angus beef, Scotch lamb, venison, game and cheeses.
STB Award Pending
Credit cards: 1, 3
Proprietors: Colin & Carole Anderson

KILLIN
126   F5

The Ardeonaig Hotel
South Loch Tay
nr Killin
Perthshire FK21 8SU
Tel: 05672 400

On the south side of Loch Tay (Edinburgh 1½ hours).

Set in 20 acres on the banks of Loch Tay, this 17th century coaching inn offers good food in an informal atmosphere, superb salmon and trout fishing on the loch, rough shooting over 5,000 acres and clay pigeon facility in grounds. Golf, riding, hill-walking and watersports available in area.

Open Mar to Nov
Rooms: 12 with private facilities
Bar Lunch 12 - 2 pm (b)
Dinner 7 - 8.30 pm (d)
Bed & breakfast from £25
Dinner B & B from £37

Fresh Tay salmon, local game, fresh brown trout, best of local fruits and vegetables and Scottish cheeses.
STB 3 Crown Commended
Credit cards: 1, 2, 3, 5
Proprietors: Stephen & Sian Brown

KILMARNOCK
127   G5

The Coffee Club
30 Bank Street
Kilmarnock
Ayrshire, KA1 1HA
Tel: 0563 22048

On A77 between Glasgow and Ayr.

Situated in one of the oldest streets in
Kilmarnock opposite the Laigh Kirk.
Offering something for everyone – quick
service, snack meals and large varied
menu including grills and vegetarian
dishes and dinner by candlelight. All food
is produced to order using fresh produce
where practicable and bakery items are a
speciality. You may take your own wine.

Open all year
All meals served from 10 am - 10 pm (a)
Closed Sun
Unlicensed – guests welcome to take
own wine
No smoking area in restaurant
*Fish, omelettes, chicken dishes and grills.
Slimmers special. Vegetarian dishes.
Children's menu. Sandwiches and salads
etc.*
Credit cards: 1, 3
Proprietors: Svend Kamming &
                      William MacDonald

KILMUN
128   G4

Fern Grove
Kilmun
Argyll
PA23 8SB
Tel: 036984 334

*6 miles from Dunoon on A880 on the side
of the Holy Loch.*

The former family home of the 'Campbells
of Kilmun' is on a site overlooking the Holy
Loch. The welcoming warm hospitality of
hosts Ian and Estralita Murray creates a
very comforting and friendly atmosphere
in this attractive Victorian house. It is not a
large building and it emanates an air of
relaxation and cosy family living. Estralita
presides in the kitchen and prepares daily
menus using only fresh local and home-
grown produce and creates interesting
and appealing meals. There is a sensibly
priced wine list.

Open all year
Rooms: 4 with private facilities
Lunch 12 - 2.30 pm (a)
Dinner from 7 pm (c)

No dogs
No smoking in restaurant
Bed & breakfast £19 - £23
Dinner B & B £32 - £36
STB   3 Crown Commended
Credit cards: 1, 3
Proprietors: Ian & Estralita Murray

KINCLAVEN
129   F6

Ballathie House Hotel
Kinclaven
by Stanley
Perthshire
PH1 4QN
Tel: 025 083 268
Telex: 76216

*Off A9 north of Perth through Stanley or
off A93 south of Blairgowrie-Kinclaven.*

A superior country house within its own
estate overlooking the River Tay (salmon).
Totally refurbished to a high standard.
Very comfortable, informal and relaxed.
Attentive and friendly staff. Four-poster
and canopied beds. Sportsman's lodge
available.

Open Mar to Jan
Rooms: 22 with private facilities
Dining Room/Restaurant Lunch 12.30 -
2 pm (a-b)
Dinner 7 - 8.30 pm (c-d)
Bed & breakfast £40 - £50
Dinner B & B £57 - £68

*Local salmon and game. Soft fruits in
season.*
STB   4 Crown Highly Commended
Credit cards: 1, 2, 3, 5

KINCRAIG
130   E6

Invereshie House
Kincraig
Kingussie
Inverness-shire
PH21 1NA
Tel: 05404 332
Fax: 05404 260

Off A9, 5 miles south of Aviemore.

Country house dating from 1680,
furnished with the care and attention such
a beautiful building deserves. Situated in
40 acres of parkland, Invereshie House is a
haven of tranquillity.

Open all year

Rooms: 9 with private facilities
Lunch available on request to residents
only
Dinner 7.15 - 10 pm (b-c)
Bed & breakfast from £24.50
Dinner B & B from £39.50

*Start the day "18 choice" breakfast –
finish it with prime halibut, turbot,
lobsters, prawns, grouse, wigeon,
mallard, venison or Aberdeen Angus beef.*
STB   Award Pending
Credit cards: 1, 3
Proprietors: A & P Methven-Hamilton

KINGUSSIE
131   E6

The Cross
High Street
Kingussie
Inverness-shire
PH21 1HX
Tel: 0540 661166

*2 hours north of Edinburgh, in centre of
Kingussie.*

Relax in front of a blazing log fire; ponder
over the delicious offerings on the menu;
sip a glass of chilled dry sherry while
perusing the award winning wine list; take
your seat at a candlelit table in the smoke-
free dining room; then savour a meal
"long to be cherished".

Open all year except 2 wks May +
3 wks Dec
Rooms: 3 with private facilities
Private party luncheons by arrangement
Dinner 6.30 - 9.30 pm except Sun +
Mon (c-d)
No smoking in dining room
Bed & breakfast rates on application
Dinner B & B from £42

*Hramsa mushrooms, mousseline of pike,
chanterelle soup, fillet of wild roe deer
"Francatelli", chocolate whisky laird or
raspberry fantasy.*
No credit cards

Best Restaurant 1989

Proprietors: Tony & Ruth Hadley

The Osprey Hotel
Ruthven Road
Kingussie
Inverness-shire
PH21 1EN
Tel: 0540 661510

In Kingussie village.

Scottish Taste of Britain winner 1985. A gem of a small Highland hotel where only the best of everything is served. A warm, hospitable place where guests enjoy one another's company and the conversation flows. The proprietor was described by the Consumers Association in 1987 as one of life's great hosts. Great food and outstanding cellar.

Open Jan to Oct

Rooms: 8, 4 with private facilities
Dinner 7.30 - 8 pm (c)
No smoking in restaurant
Bed & breakfast £16 - £30
Dinner B & B £32 - £48

Wild mushrooms, North Sea bake, peat-smoked salmon. Venison with chanterelles, noisettes of lamb, chicken with wild mushrooms. Highland casserole. Chocolate meringue gateau, blackcurrant pie.

STB 2 Crown Commended

Credit cards: 1, 2, 3, 5, 6

Proprietors: Duncan & Pauline Reeves

---

132 KINLOCHBERVIE C4

Kinlochbervie Hotel
Kinlochbervie
by Lairg
Sutherland
IV27 4RP
Tel: 097 182 275
Fax: 097 182 438

On B801, via A838 from Lairg.

An imposing modern three star family hotel with superb views of Kinlochbervie harbour and Loch Clash. Recently refurbished to a high standard. Candlelit dining room. Personally supervised by Rex and Kate Neame whose confidence in the service they provide leaves you free to enjoy Kinlochbervie and the surrounding area.

Open all year

Rooms: 14 with private facilities
Bar Lunch 12 - 1.45 pm (a)
Dining Room/Restaurant Lunch 12 - 1.45 pm (a)
Bar Supper 6.30 - 8.30 pm (a)

Dinner 7.30 - 8.30 pm (d-e)
Note: restricted services Nov to Mar
No smoking in dining room
Bed & breakfast £35 - £45
Dinner B & B from £45

Locally caught white fish, king prawns, salmon and lobster are prepared and cooked with skill and pride.

STB 4 Crown Commended

Credit cards: 1, 2, 3, 5, 6

Proprietors: Rex & Kate Neame

---

133 KINLOCH RANNOCH F5

Bunrannoch House
Kinloch Rannoch
Perthshire
PH16 5QB
Tel: 08822 407

Turn right after 500 yards on Schiehallion road from Kinloch Rannoch off B846.

Bunrannoch is a former hunting lodge nestled at the foot of the 'sleeping giant' mountain close by Loch Rannoch. The cosy lounge, log fires and uninterrupted Highland views complement the delicious aromas from the kitchen. Walk the mountain glens, ramble on Rannoch Moor or catch a trout in the loch, then return to Bunrannoch House to relax and savour the delights of Highland cooking.

Open all year

Rooms: 7, 2 with private facilities
Dinner 7.30 - 9.30 pm (b)
No smoking in dining room
Bed & breakfast £12 - £14
Dinner B & B £22 - £24

Fillet of venison in redcurrant and port. Best Scotch fillet cooked to your taste in whisky cream sauce. Apple and walnut cake with butterscotch and rum sauce.

STB Listed Approved

Credit cards: 1, 3

Proprietor: Jennifer Skeaping

Cuilmore Cottage
Kinloch Rannoch
Perthshire
PH16 5QB
Tel: 08822 218

100 yards from east corner of Loch Rannoch.

Cosy 18th century croft in secluded surroundings. Traditionally decorated and cheery log fires. The cooking covers high class Scottish fare, organically grown fruits and vegetables from the cottage

garden. Breakfasts feature free-range eggs and freshly baked bread and pastries. Guests have the complimentary use of mountain bikes, dinghy and canoe to explore the splendid locality.

Open all year except Christmas + New Year

Rooms: 3
Dinner 7 - 8.30 pm (c)
Prior booking essential for dinner for non-residents
Unlicensed – guests welcome to take own wine
No smoking in dining room
Bed & breakfast from £14
Dinner B & B from £29

Filo pastry basket filled with prawns, gigot of Scottish lamb in rosemary, garlic and mint sauce, grilled Tay salmon with cucumber cream, supreme of wild mallard duck served with apricot and nut stuffing. Whisky and coffee parfait.

STB Listed Commended

No credit cards

Small is Beautiful Award 1990

Proprietor: Anita Steffen

---

134 KINNESSWOOD F6

The Lomond Country Inn & Restaurant
Main Street
Kinnesswood
nr Kinross
KY13 7HN
Tel: 0592 84 317

4 miles from Kinross. From south, M90 junction 5, B9097 via Scotlandwell. From north, M90 junction 7, A911 via Milnathort.

The historical hotel, which overlooks Loch Leven, has long since been the focal point of the area. Now with the addition of the modest annexe it provides accommodation for visitors in 12 en suite rooms, thus adding to the attraction of the well established and renowned restaurant, where game dishes, local caught fish and Scottish produce adorn the à la carte menu. Bar lunches and suppers are served. Open fires and friendly atmosphere.

Open all year

Rooms: 12 with private facilities
Bar Lunch 12 - 2 pm (a)
Dining Room/Restaurant Lunch 12 - 2 pm (a)

▶

Bar Supper 6.30 - 9 pm: 6.30 -
9.30 pm Fri + Sat (a)
Dinner 6.30 - 9 pm: 6.30 - 9.30 pm
Fri + Sat (c-d)
Light snacks (scones, sandwiches and
tea) served on request all day.
Bed & breakfast from £16
Dinner B & B from £25

*Loch Leven trout – this distinctive local
trout is simply grilled in butter to retain its
special flavour and served with fresh local
vegetables.*
Credit card: 3

KINROSS
135   F6

Croftbank House Hotel
30 Station Road
Kinross
Fife, KY13 7TG
Tel: 0577 63819

Junction 6, M90, on approach to Kinross.
Chef/patron Bill Kerr and his wife Diane
run this old Victorian house as a small and
friendly hotel and restaurant, serving
creative and imaginative food. Ideally
situated for shooting, fishing and golf –
surrounded by world famous golf courses
– and with good access to Edinburgh,
Perth, Stirling and St Andrews. Chef
appointed to Master Chef Institute of UK.

Open all year
Rooms: 3 with private facilities
Bar Lunch and Executive Lunch 12 -
2 pm (a)
Supper Grill Room 6 - 9 pm Tue to Fri
+ Sun
Dinner 7 - 9 pm (e)
Closed Mon
No smoking in restaurant
Bed & breakfast rates on application
Dinner B & B rates on application
*Seafood parcel, beef and oyster pie, warm
monkfish salad, breast of wild pigeon.*
STB   Award Pending
Credit cards: 1, 3
Proprietors: Bill & Diane Kerr

CREDIT/CHARGE CARDS	
1	Access/Mastercard/Eurocard
2	American Express
3	Visa
4	Carte Bleu
5	Diners Club
6	Masterchage

KIPPEN
136   G5

Cross Keys Hotel
Main Street
Kippen
by Stirling
FK8 3DN
Tel: 078 687 293

*On B822 Callander-Fintry road and just off
A811 Stirling-Erskine Bridge road, only 8
miles west of Stirling.*
A small family run 18th century hotel set in
the peaceful and picturesque village of
Kippen, near Stirling. The hotel has old
world character augmented by log fires in
the bars during winter, a cosy stone-
walled restaurant and family room.

Open all year except evening 25 Dec +
New Year's Day
Rooms: 3
Bar Lunch 12 - 2 pm (a)
Dinner 7 - 8.45 pm (b)
Bed & breakfast £15 - £18
Dinner B & B rates on application
*Home-made soups and pâtés. Roast
venison and fresh raspberry and red wine
sauce. Athole brose with Kippen honey.*
Credit card: 1
Proprietors: Angus & Sandra Watt

KIRKCUDBRIGHT
137   I5

Auld Alliance Restaurant
5 Castle Street
Kirkcudbright
DG6 4JA
Tel: 0557 30569

Kirkcudbright town, opposite the castle.
Black and gold fronted Listed building with
a display of shells and other seaside
paraphernalia in the bay window. In this
small restaurant Anne serves and Alistair
cooks the quality produce of Scotland
prepared in the French culinary style. The
menu features local seafood and
Galloway beef.

Open Easter to late Oct
Dining Room/Restaurant Lunch 12 -
2 pm Sun only
Dinner 6.30 - 9 pm (b)
*Kirkcudbright queen scallops fried in garlic
butter with smoked Ayrshire bacon,
finished in Galloway cream.*
No credit cards
Proprietors: Alistair & Anne Crawford

Selkirk Arms Hotel
High Street
Kirkcudbright
Kirkcudbrightshire, DG6 4JG
Tel: 0557 30402
Fax: 0557 31639

Off A75, 27 miles west of Dumfries.
Historic 18th century hotel with Burns
connection in picturesque harbour town.
Newly refurbished but still retaining the
character of the hotel. Extensive à la carte
and daily changing table d'hôte menus.
Marvellous walking, fishing, bird-
watching. Nearby beaches. Large
secluded garden.

Open all year
Rooms: 15 with private facilities
Bar Lunch 12 - 2 pm (a)
Dining Room/Restaurant Lunch 12 -
2 pm (c)
Bar Supper 6.30 - 9 pm (a)
Dinner 7 - 9.30 pm (c)
Bed & breakfast £32.50 - £36.50
Dinner B & B £46.25 - £50.25
*Seafood, scallops, salmon, Dover sole,
plaice, lobster. Galloway beef and lamb.
Pheasant in a cream and lemon sauce.
Duck breast in an orange and brandy
sauce.*
STB   4 Crown Commended
Credit cards: 1, 2, 3, 5
Proprietor: John Morris

KIRKINTILLOCH
138   G5

The Lady Margaret Canalboat
c/o Scotland in View Ltd
10 Bankhead Road, Waterside
Kirkintilloch
Glasgow G66 3LH
Tel: 041 776 6996 or 0836 607755

*Canal boat based at Glasgow Road
Bridge Jetty, on A803 between
Bishopbriggs and Kirkintilloch.*

Calm water canal cruises on the northern
outskirts of Glasgow, in country scenery,
with floodlights and central heating for all
year-round operation. The purpose-built
canalboat is tastefully appointed. Crystal
glasses and Wedgwood crockery
enhance attractive table settings, with
pink linen and fresh flowers. A relaxing
experience, unrivalled in Scotland.
Available for group bookings at any time,
any day. The boat provides a quality venue
which is especially suitable for business
entertainment, family gatherings and
weddings – as well as for individual ▶

table bookings or weekend cruises for that special occasion.

Operates all year
Lunch (Sun only) sailing at 1 pm from Cadder Jetty (c)
Dinner sailing at 7.30 pm Thu, Fri + Sat only (d) from Glasgow Road Bridge Jetty
Advance booking essential

Imaginative set menus incorporating the best in fresh Scottish produce and dishes with an emphasis on quality and presentation.

Credit cards: 1, 2, 3, 5

Proprietor: Patrick Le Pla

PRICE CATEGORIES

(a)	under £10.00
(b)	£10.00 - £15.00
(c)	£15.00 - £20.00
(d)	£20.00 - £25.00
(e)	£25.00 - £30.00
(f)	over £30.00

KIRKMICHAEL
139   E6

The Log Cabin Hotel
Kirkmichael
by Blairgowrie
Perthshire
PH10 7NB
Tel: 025 081 288

Signposted off A924 in Kirkmichael.

Uniquely built of whole Norwegian pine logs, nestles high in Glen Derby with panoramic views. The hotel is centrally heated and double glazed so you are assured of a warm welcome and a memorable meal in the restaurant. An ideal centre for touring Perthshire and for skiing in Glenshee.

Open all year
Rooms: 13 with private facilities
Bar Lunch 12 - 2 pm (a)
Dinner 7.30 - 9 pm (b-c)
Bed & breakfast from £18.15
Dinner B & B from £30.95

Home-produced dishes including Edinburgh club special, game dishes, collops, lamb Lady Lucy, and delicious sweets – chocolate whisky gâteau, hazelnut and cinnamon tart with Blair raspberries.

Credit cards: 1, 3, 5

Proprietor: A F Finch

KYLE OF LOCHALSH
140   E3

The Lochalsh Hotel
Kyle of Lochalsh
Ross-shire
IV40 8AF
Tel: 0599 4202
Telex: 75318
Fax: 0599 4881

At the ferry terminal for Skye.

A fine Highland hotel with uninterrupted views of the Isle of Skye. A haven of comfort and hospitality. The popular restaurant faces the picturesque island and makes good use of the wide range of fresh local produce.

Open all year except Christmas wk
Rooms: 38 with private facilities
Dinner 7.30 - 9 pm (d)
Bed & breakfast rates on application
Dinner B & B rates on application

Local game, seafood, collops of beef with wild mushrooms, Scottish salmon in many different dishes.

Credit cards: 2, 3, 5, 6

Wholefood Cafe, Highland Designworks
Plockton Road
Kyle of Lochalsh
IV40 8DA
Tel: 0599 4388

On Kyle/Plockton road.

Situated on the outskirts of Kyle, in the old village school. Snacks or complete meals served from 12 noon till closing time. All food cooked on the premises using only fresh and natural ingredients.

Open Easter to Oct 10 am - 9.30 pm
Morning coffee 10 - 12 noon
Dining Room/Restaurant Lunch 12 - 6 pm
Dinner 6 - 9.30 pm (a-b)
Note: also open during Winter + early Spring, telephone to check opening times
No smoking in restaurant

Home-made soups: potato and chive, celery and cashew nut; herring in oatmeal, walnut and celery quiche, wild Loch Duich salmon, fresh spinach and cashew bake, buckwheat pancakes with broccoli and cream cheese.

Credit cards: 1, 3

Proprietor: Fiona Begg

KYLESKU
141   C4

Linne Mhuirich
Unapool Croft Road
Kylesku, by Lairg
Sutherland
IV27 4HW
Tel: 0971 2227

¾ mile south of the new Kylesku Bridge on A894.

Fiona and Diarmid MacAulay welcome non-smokers to their modern crofthouse. Panoramic views of hills and lochs, quietly situated overlooking Loch Glencoul. RSPB Handa Island, and lovely, lonely sandy beaches nearby. Directions and maps for many local walks provided. Dinner menus discussed with guests after breakfast. Vegetarian food available. Recommended in "Complete Healthy Holiday Guide". Menu changes daily. Guests welcome to take their own wine as premises not licensed to provide alcoholic beverages. French spoken.

Open May to Oct
Rooms: 3, 1 with private facilities
Dinner from 7.30 pm
No smoking throughout
Bed & breakfast £13 - £16
Dinner B & B £20 - £23

Local fish and seafood – Kylesku prawn vol au vents; smoked haddock au gratin; salmon baked with lemon and herbs. Home-made quiches and pates. Casseroles. Vegetarian dishes. Tempting desserts and home-baking. Filter coffee. Scottish honey and cheeses.

STB 2 Crown Commended

No credit cards

Proprietors: Fiona & Diarmid MacAulay

LAGGAN
142   NEAR NEWTONMORE   E5

Gaskmore House Hotel
Laggan
nr Newtonmore
Inverness-shire
PH10 1BS
Tel: 052 84 250
Fax: 052 84 207

On A86 Newtonmore-Fort William road, 8 miles from Newtonmore.

This award winning restaurant commands spectacular views over the Upper Spey Valley. All bedrooms fully en suite – an ideal choice to stay in comfort and enjoy excellent meals. ▶

Open Dec to Oct

Rooms: 11 with private facilities
Bar Lunch 12 - 2 pm (a)
Dinner 7 - 9 pm (c)
Bed & breakfast from £27.50
Dinner B & B from £45

Specialising in freshness of food with an emphasis on local game, fish, meat and vegetables – complemented by a superb cellar.

STB 4 Crown Commended

Credit cards: 1, 2, 3

Proprietors: James & Jacqueline
Glendinning

LANGBANK
143   G5

Gleddoch House
Langbank
Renfrewshire
PA14 6YE
Tel: 0475 54 711
Telex: 779801

Off M8 Glasgow-Greenock at Langbank.

Beautifully situated in 250 acres overlooking the River Clyde and Loch Lomond hills the hotel offers all the advantages of gracious living and distinctive cuisine. Amenities include free use of the 18 hole golf course within the grounds and Clubhouse facilities of squash, sauna, snooker and horse-riding. Formerly a family residence, the hotel has been tastefully converted, yet retains the features of a private home with service and accommodation of the highest standard.

Open all year

Rooms: 33 with private facilities
Bar Lunch (Clubhouse) 12.30 - 2.30 pm
Dining Room/Restaurant Lunch 12.30 - 2.30 pm except Sat (b)
Dinner 7.30 - 9 pm (d-e)
Bed & breakfast from £54
Dinner B & B from £55 (weekend break)

West coast seafood, scallops etc. Seasonal game dishes. Regional Scottish traditional dishes.

STB 4 Crown Commended

Credit cards: 1, 2, 3, 5, 6

LARGS
144   G4

Wham's & The Platter
80 Main Street
Largs
KA30 8DH
Tel: 0475 672074

A78 west coast route between Ardrossan and Greenock.

Situated in a building dating from 1887, these two restaurants operate similar self-service menus over lunchtime, but in the evening the style changes to a more relaxed table service – Wham's offering seafood as its speciality while The Platter specialises in steaks. Dine in the conservatory-style Wham's, or in The Platter's Victorian ambience.

Open all year

Dining Room/Restaurant Lunch 11.45 am - 2.45 pm
Dinner 5 - 8.45 pm (c)
Closed Sun

Menu and seasonal daily specials including Cullen skink, Arbroath smokies, Loch Fyne kippers, mussels, oysters, crayfish, lobster. Platter fillet of beef, Scottish lamb chops, home-made steak pie.

Credit cards: 1, 3

LETHAM
145   F7

Fernie Castle Hotel
Letham
Cupar
Fife
KY7 7RU
Tel: 033 781 381

On A914, 1 mile north of A91 intersection.

Fernie Castle, built as a 16th century fortified hunting tower and set in 30 acres of secluded grounds, is now a beautifully refurbished country house hotel. Situated in central Fife, it is an ideal base for golfing, shooting and fishing or those wishing to explore the considerable historic attractions of this ancient county.

Open all year

Rooms: 16 with private facilities
Bar Lunch 12.30 - 2 pm (a)
Dining Room/Restaurant Lunch 12.30 - 2 pm (d)
Dinner 7.30 - 9.30 pm (e)
Bed & breakfast £50 - £90
Dinner B & B rates on application

Mallard and grouse terrine served on redcurrant jelly; poached salmon stuffed with lobster pate; grilled honey-marinated venison fillet in wild mushroom and brandy port sauce. Fruit meringue – redcurrants, raspberries, blackcurrants, strawberries in a whisky sabayon.

Credit cards: 1, 2, 3, 5

Proprietors: Norman & Sheila Cinnamond

ISLE OF LEWIS
146   C2

Handa
18 Keose Glebe
Lochs
Isle of Lewis
PA86 9JX
Tel: 0851 83334

1½ miles off A859, 12 miles south of Stornoway.

This is a delightful modern home on a hilltop which seems hundreds of miles from anywhere but of course is not. It is a convenient spot for exploring Lewis and Harris but much nearer at hand – virtually on the doorstep – there is hill-walking, bird-watching, fishing, and otter sighting if you are lucky. In this small comfortable haven, island hospitality and personal attention are very much to the fore. Alongside traditional recipes there is innovative home-cooking using fresh herbs and vegetables from the kitchen garden. Vegetarian and individual dietary requirements are catered for. There is brown trout fishing on the private loch 100 yards from the house and a boat and equipment can be hired.

Open Mar to Oct

Rooms: 3, 1 with private facilities
Dinner 6.30 - 8 pm (a)
Unlicensed
No smoking in restaurant
Bed & breakfast £12 - £15
Dinner B & B £18 - £21

Home-made breads, soups; lamb and dill hotpot, lemon sole with walnut stuffed mushrooms; shellfish plattter, salmon in orange and vermouth, wild brown trout with mint, fillet steak in port and mushrooms.

STB 2 Crown Commended

No credit cards

Proprietors: Murdo & Christine Morrison

Park Guest House

30 James Street
Stornoway
Isle of Lewis
PA87 2QN
Tel: 0851 2485

½ mile from ferry terminal. At junction of Matheson Road, James Street and A866 to airport and Eye peninsula.

A substantial stone-built house dating to around 1883, centrally located in the town of Stornoway. The old wood of the interior has been refurbished and the public rooms and bedrooms are tastefully decorated. The dining room, featuring a Glasgow style fireplace, has a warm, homely atmosphere. Fresh local produce – shellfish, game, venison, Lewis lamb – feature on the menu prepared with care and presented by chef/proprietor, Roddy Afrin. Ideal base for touring, golf, bird-watching, fishing etc. or just exploring some of the lunar-like landscapes of Lewis and Harris.

Open all year except 24 Dec to 5 Jan

Rooms: 5
Packed Lunches available (a)
Dining Room/Restaurant Lunch 12 - 1.45 pm except Sat (a)
Dinner 6 pm (table d'hote) – residents only
Dinner 7.30 - 8.30 pm (à la carte) (c-d)
Closed to non-residents Sun + Mon
No dogs
Bed & breakfast from £16
Dinner B & B from £25

Home-made soups, pâtés, desserts. Smoked trout mousse wrapped in oak-smoked salmon. Hebridean scallops and crowdie in puff pastry. Noisettes of local venison in port wine sauce with blackcurrants.

STB 2 Crown Commended

No credit cards

Proprietors: Catherine & Roddy Afrin

---

147 LIVINGSTON VILLAGE **G6**

The Village Bistro

15/17 Main Street
Livingston Village
West Lothian
EH54 7AF
Tel: 0506 411226

Original village of Livingston New Town.

Picturesque former Victorian post office and one time 17th century coaching inn, now a delightful restaurant with an interesting ambience. Situated in the original village of Livingston New Town, just off the M8 motorway, on the banks of the River Almond. Children welcome.

Open all year

Meals served 11 am - 3 pm except Sun + Sat (a-c)
Dinner 5 - 11 pm (c)
Facilities for the disabled
No smoking area in restaurant

Pick your own fresh lobster from the tank. Fillet of beef Bonnie Prince Charlie. Saute of chicken 'Ecosse'. Hot peaches with black cherries and Cointreau.

Credit cards: 1, 2, 3, 5

Proprietors: Peter & Ally Fildes

---

148 LOCH EARN ST FILLANS **F5**

Achray House Hotel

Loch Earn, St Fillans
Perthshire
PH6 2NF
Tel: 076485 231

Loch Earn, St Fillans.

Beautifully situated overlooking Loch Earn and mountains beyond. Twelve miles west of Crieff (A85). Richly furnished, small hotel owned and run by husband and wife.

Open Mar to Nov

Rooms: 5, 2 with private facilities
Bar Lunch 12 - 2 pm (b)
Bar Supper 6.30 - 9.30 pm
Dinner 6.30 - 9.30 pm (c)
Bed & breakfast from £19.50
Dinner B & B from £26

Game, steaks, seafood and outstanding sweet menu.

STB 3 Crown Commended

Credit cards: 1, 2, 3

Proprietors: Tony & Jane Ross

---

149 LOCHEARNHEAD **F5**

Golden Larches Restaurant

Balquhidder Station
Lochearnhead
Perthshire FK19 8NX
Tel: 05673 262

Situated on A84, 2 miles south of Lochearnhead.

This is a very attractive little restaurant on the main route between Strathyre and Lochearnhead, catering mainly for the passing motorist and tourists. There are usually colourful window boxes and hanging baskets. The interior is crisp and clean, with pine furniture. It is family run and specialises in home-made scones, cakes and fruit pies. Meals are simple but cooked to order and feature traditional Scottish soups and good Angus steaks and steak pies, but local Tay trout and fresh vegetables are also available.

Open Easter to Oct

Meals and snacks served all day
Open till 7 pm low season; 9.30 pm high season (a-b)

Home baking of sweets and cakes. Scottish high tea.

No credit cards

Proprietors: James & Loraine Telfer

Lochearnhead Hotel

Lochearnhead
Perthshire FK19 8HP
Tel: 056 73 229

On A84 at the side of Loch Earn.

Small friendly hotel and restaurant at the west end of Loch Earn and with lovely views across the loch in a popular water skiing and windsurfing area. Seven golf courses within 20 miles. Ample hill-walking and organised walks. Traditional fare and cordon bleu dishes served in the candlelit dining room. Bar meals are also popular in the Bistro Bar with its magnificent views over the loch. Children are warmly welcomed and there is a special menu available.

Open Mar to Nov

Rooms: 14, 5 with private facilities
Bar meals served all day 11 am - 9.30 pm
Dining Room/Restaurant Lunch 12 - 2.30 pm (a)
Dinner 7.30 - 9.30 pm (b)
Bed & breakfast from £19.05
Dinner B & B rates on application

Venison and salmon in season. Special vegetarian menu.

STB 2 Crown Approved

Credit cards: 1, 2, 3, 5

Proprietor: Angus Cameron

LOCHGILPHEAD
150   G4

Stag Hotel
Argyll Street
Lochgilphead
Argyll PA31 8NE
Tel: 0546 2496

On A83 between Oban and Inveraray.

Central for Oban, Inveraray and Mull of
Kintyre. Family run hotel – furnished to the
highest standard throughout. All rooms
with colour TV, telephone, tea/coffee-
making facilities. Residents' lounge,
sauna and solarium available. Free golf
available for guests at the local nine hole
course.

Open all year
Rooms: 17 with private facilities
Bar Lunch 12 - 2 pm (a-b)
Bar Supper 6 - 8.30 pm
Dinner 7 - 9 pm (c)
Bed & breakfast from £25
Dinner B & B from £37.50

*Loch Fyne salmon, venison steak, Sound
of Jura clams, Islay malt whisky syllabub.*

STB 4 Crown Commended

Credit cards: 1, 3

Proprietor: Joyce Ross

LOCH GOIL
151   F4

**Eversley Private Country House
& Restaurant**
Carrick Castle
Loch Goil
Argyll
PA24 8AF
Tel: 03013 535

A charming Victorian country house
overlooking Loch Goil in one of the most
beautiful unspoilt scenic areas of Argyll.
Ideal for touring, walking and water
sports. Eversley offers comfortable guest
rooms individually styled to suit the period
and with most commanding a magnificent
view of the loch. With plentiful supplies of
good local produce great care is taken with
the preparation and imaginative
presentation of dishes, which are served
by candlelight in the elegant dining room
overlooking the loch.

Open all year except 2 wks Feb
Rooms: 5, 4 with private facilities
Lunch by prior arrangement
Dinner 7 - 9 pm (c)
No smoking in dining room

Restricted licence
Bed & breakfast from £19
Dinner B & B from £30

*Freshly cooked local produce including
home-made pasta, pâté, terrines,
mousselines, venison, salmon and
Scottish beef and lamb. Vegetarian and
special diets catered for.*

No credit cards

Proprietors: Howard & Lynden Taylor

LOCHINVER
152   C4

Macphail's
216 Clashmore, Stoer
by Lochinver
Sutherland IV27 4JQ
Tel: 057 15 295

*B869, 10 miles from Lochinver, West
Sutherland.*

A traditional croft house, modernised to a
high standard, but retaining much of the
original character, including roof beams
and peat/log fires. The atmosphere is
welcoming, warm and friendly. A lochside
situation overlooking the sea to the
Hebrides. Sandy beaches nearby.
Peaceful with no passing traffic.

Open Easter to Oct
Rooms: 3, 1 with private facilities
Dinner from 7 pm (b)
Prior booking essential (24 hours in
advance) for non-residents
No dogs
Facilities for the disabled
No smoking area in dining room
Unlicensed – guests welcome to take
own wine
Bed & breakfast from £11
Dinner B & B from £20

*Home-made bread and oatcakes. A
variety of interesting menus, including
traditional Scottish dishes using local
salmon, venison and seafoods. Vegetarian
by request. Freshly ground coffee.*

No credit cards

Proprietors: Pat & Madeline Macphail

LOCH LOMOND
153   G5

Cameron House Hotel
Loch Lomond
Alexandria
Dumbartonshire
G83 8QZ
Tel: 0389 55565
Fax: 0389 59522

*On A82 near Balloch, on the banks of Loch
Lomond.*

This most impressive location has been
developed carefully and skilfully with due
regard to the aesthetics of the site and is
now a superb luxury resort hotel set in 108
wooded acres on the south west shore of
Loch Lomond. There are excellent leisure
facilities and a choice of three restaurants.
You can choose the elegance of the
Georgian Room or the Grill Room with its
emphasis on local produce and you can
enjoy afternoon tea overlooking the loch in
the tranquility of the Drawing Room. The
hotel restaurants are open to non-
residents but leisure facilities are for
members and residents only.

Open all year
Rooms: 68 with private facilities
Dining Room/Restaurant Lunch 12.30 -
2 pm (c)
Dinner 7 - 10.30 pm (d)
No dogs
Facilities for the disabled
No smoking area in restaurant
Bed & breakfast £100 - £125
Dinner B & B rates on application
Credit cards: 1, 2, 3, 5, 6

LOCKERBIE
154   H6

Somerton House Hotel
Carlisle Road
Lockerbie
Dumfriesshire
DG11 2DR
Tel: 05762 2583

*Outskirts of Lockerbie approx 300 yards
from main A74.*

A robust Victorian mansion standing in its
own grounds, with interesting
architectural aspects especially the
unusual Kauri timber panelling and plaster
cornices. All bedrooms en suite, TV,
central heating and direct dial telephone.

Open all year except 1 Jan
Rooms: 7 with private facilities   ▶

Bar Lunch 12 - 2 pm (a) à la carte
Bar Supper 6 - 9.30 pm
Dinner 7 - 9 pm (c) à la carte
No smoking in restaurant
Bed & breakfast from £28
Dinner B & B rates on application

Whole grilled sardines and garlic bread. Devil's Beeftub soup. Local lamb cooked in yoghurt with apricots. Collops in the pan. Galloway pork and beef. Local salmon and trout (in season).

Credit cards: 1, 2, 3

Proprietors: Sam & Patricia Ferguson

LYBSTER
155   C6

Portland Arms Hotel
Lybster
Caithness
KW3 6BS
Tel: 059 32 208

On A9, 12 miles south of Wick.

The Portland was built to serve as a staging post early last century. There have been many changes, but the quality of personal service established then has been maintained. Fully central heated and double glazed. All rooms have private facilities including colour TV, telephone, tea-making facilities. Four-poster beds available. Executive rooms with jacuzzi baths also available.

Open all year
Rooms: 20 with private facilities
Bar Lunch 12 - 2.30 pm (a)
Dining Room/Restaurant Lunch 12 - 2.30 pm (a)
Dinner 7 - 9.30 pm (a-b)
Bed & breakfast from £25
Dinner B & B from £36.90

Succulent Aberdeen Angus steaks, seafood platters, game dishes, fresh cream sweets.

Credit cards: 1, 2, 3, 5, 6

CREDIT/CHARGE CARDS

1   Access/Mastercard/Eurocard
2   American Express
3   Visa
4   Carte Bleu
5   Diners Club
6   Mastercharge

MACHRIHANISH
156   H3

Ardell House
Machrihanish
by Campbeltown
Argyll
PA28 6PT
Tel: 0586 81 235

Situated on the south-west coast of Kintyre.

Ardell house is a stone-built Victorian villa overlooking Machrihanish Golf Course and miles of sandy beaches with magnificent views over Islay, Jura and Gigha. There are three golf courses in the area and pony-trekking, windsurfing and angling can be arranged nearby. All rooms en suite with tea/coffee-making facilities and colour TV. AA award winner – Guest House of the Year for Scotland.

Open Apr to Oct except for advance bookings in Winter
Rooms: 10, 9 with private facilities
Dinner from 7 pm (c)
Residents only
Bed & breakfast £18 - £27
Dinner B & B £30 - £40

Local seafood, Scottish beef and cheeses (including Campbeltown Cheddar), home-made soups using fresh vegetables, home-grown herbs, delicious sweet dishes using fresh fruit in season – pavlovas, syllabubs.

STB 2 Crown Commended

No credit cards

Proprietors: David & Jill Baxter

MELROSE
157   G7

Burts Hotel
Market Square
Melrose
Roxburghshire
TD6 9PN
Tel: 089 682 2285
Fax: 089 682 2870

B6361, 2 miles from A68, 38 miles south of Edinburgh.

A delightful hotel situated in this historic town in the heart of the Border country. Ideally situated for walking, horse-riding, golf, game shooting and salmon fishing. Much of the hotel has recently been refurbished to a high standard. The elegant restaurant offers a choice of Scottish and international cuisine.

An extensive lunch and supper menu is also available in the popular lounge bar. Mini-break terms available from November to May.

Open all year
Rooms: 21 with private facilities
Bar Lunch 12 - 2 pm (a)
Dining Room/Restaurant Lunch 12.30 - 2 pm (c)
Bar Supper 6 - 9.30 pm : 6 - 10.30 pm Fri + Sat
Dinner 7 - 9.30 pm (d)
Bed & breakfast from £32
Dinner B & B from £44

Specialities include Tweed salmon, chicken howtowdie, venison and Scottish beef, complemented by an excellent wine list.

STB 4 Crown Commended

Credit cards: 1, 2, 3, 5, 6

Proprietors: Graham & Anne Henderson

MOFFAT
158   H6

Corehead Farm
Annanwater
Moffat
Dumfriesshire DG10 9LT
Tel: 0683 20973

"Devil's Beef Tub", 4½ miles from Moffat.

Picturesque farmhouse on large hill farm. Situated in the "Devil's Beef Tub", amidst the beautiful Moffat hills. A secluded and wooded site at the head of the Annan Valley, just 4½ miles from Moffat. An ideal base for hill-walking – the farm includes Hart Fell at 2651 feet, one of the highest peaks in southern Scotland – or touring the many attractions of Dumfries and Galloway. Fine golf course and excellent tennis courts in the area with fishing and riding available locally.

Open May to Oct or by arrangement
Rooms: 3, 1 with private facilities
Dinner 6.30 - 7 pm except Wed (b)
Residents only
Unlicensed – guests welcome to take own wine
No smoking in dining room
Bed & breakfast from £14 - £19
Dinner B & B from £22 - £27

Own naturally reared lamb and beef with locally produced fish and game used with home-grown vegetables. Fruits from own garden included in mouth-watering desserts. Home-made soups a speciality.

STB 2 Crown Commended

No credit cards

Proprietor: Berenice Williams

Hartfell House

Moffat
Dumfriesshire
DG10 9AL
Tel: 0683 20153

One mile off A74.

A delightful, small family run hotel. 19th century Listed building in rural setting overlooking the surrounding hills and only a few minutes from the town centre. Beautiful woodwork and spacious rooms, four of which now have en suite facilities. Very comfortable homely atmosphere. Ideal for visiting Borders and south-west. Large garden to relax in with putting green.

Open Mar to Nov

Rooms: 9, 4 with private facilities
Dinner 6 - 7 pm (b)
Non-residents by prior booking
No smoking in dining room
Bed & breakfast from £14
Dinner B & B from £24.50

Home-made soups. Scotch lamb Wellington, wild salmon, fillet steak in a Drambuie sauce, fresh fruit and vegetables in season. Gaelic pudding with Heather Cream sauce.

STB   3 Crown Commended

No credit cards

Proprietors: Andrea & Alan Daniel

Well View Hotel

Ballplay Road
Moffat
Dumfriesshire
DG10 9JU
Tel: 0683 20184

Set in half an acre of garden overlooking hills and town, this 19th century country house has been extensively converted and refurbished to make this a small comfortable privately run hotel. Rooms are furnished to an excellent standard and are all supplied with fresh fruit, hand-made biscuits and sherry. Deluxe rooms have many additional extras. To complete the experience, enjoy the creative table d'hôte menus prepared by the kitchen brigade and choose from the extensive wine list to complement your meal. German spoken and also a little French. Children welcome. Dogs accepted by prior arrangement.

Open all year

Rooms: 7, 5 with private facilities
Dining Room/Restaurant Lunch 12.30 - 1.30 pm (b)
Dinner 7 - 8.30 pm (c)
Prior reservation essential for both lunch and dinner

Facilities for the disabled
No smoking in restaurant
Bed & breakfast £19 - £34
Dinner B & B £32 - £48

Smoked haddock souffle, mousseline of turbot, cauliflower and blue cheese soup, fillet of Galloway beef with Kelso mustard sauce, escalope of venison with a blaeberry and mushroom sauce. Carse of Gowrie raspberry and Armagnac brulee.

STB   3 Crown Highly Commended

Credit cards: 1, 3

Proprietors: Janet & John Schuckardt

159 MONTROSE **E8**

Park Hotel

61 John Street
Montrose
Angus
DD10 8RJ
Tel: 0674 73415
Fax: 0674 77091

Midway between town centre and beach.

A very comfortable privately owned hotel, managed by the resident proprietors, Nigel and Norma Henderson. The main building dates from Victorian times. Tasteful alterations and additions have been effected during recent years, so the hotel now offers over 50 bedrooms with private facilities, conference and function suites for up to 200 people and a very attractive cedar-arched restaurant. Set in two acres of well-tended, landscaped gardens overlooking the town's mid links.

Open all year

Rooms: 59, 53 with private facilities
Bar Lunch 12 - 2 pm (a)
Dining Room/Restaurant Lunch 12 - 2 pm (c)
Dinner 7 - 9.30 pm (c)
Bed & breakfast from £50
Dinner B & B rates on application

Ham and haddie for breakfast, Musselburgh kail, fillets of sole, prime Aberdeen Angus beef and Highland coffee.

Credit cards: 1, 2, 3, 5, 6

Proprietors: Nigel & Norma Henderson

160 MUIR OF ORD **D5**

Gilchrist Farm

Muir of Ord
Ross-shire
IV6 7RS
Tel: 0463 870243

From Tore roundabout on A9 take A832 for 4½ miles. Left turn to B862 (Beauly) and Gilchrist signposted first left.

Ann Fraser assures you of a warm welcome to this comfortable farmhouse set in an attractive garden. This working farm is ideally situated for touring the Highlands. 18 hole golf course less than a mile away. Inverness 20 minutes away by car.

Open Apr to Oct – advance booking preferred

Rooms: 2
Dinner 6.30 - 7.30 pm (b)
Residents only
No smoking in dining room
Bed & breakfast from £12
Dinner B & B from £18

Good home-cooking from fresh local produce. Home-made soups and desserts a speciality. Salmon, trout, venison, Scottish beef, lamb, etc in season.

STB   Listed Commended

No credit cards

Proprietor: Ann Fraser

Ord House Hotel

Muir of Ord
Ross-shire
IV6 7UH
Tel: 0463 870492

½ mile west of Muir of Ord on A832 Ullapool-Marybank road.

John and Eliza Allen offer you at Ord House a stay which will be comfortable, relaxed and enjoyable. Table d'hôte and à la carte menus are made up from their own garden produce and local meat, game and fish. Fifty acres of woodlands and beautiful formal gardens, combined with a 17th century laird's house, make Ord something special. All bedrooms have private facilities and many have been recently refurbished. Downstairs, there are log fires in the bar and drawing rooms to enjoy and in the grounds there are croquet and clay-pigeon shooting. Fluent French spoken. Children and dogs are very welcome.

Open May to mid Oct

Rooms: 12 with private facilities ▶

Bar Lunch 12.30 - 2 pm (a)
Dinner 7.30 - 9 pm (c)
Bed & breakfast £24 - £29
Dinner B & B £37 - £44

Ord pigeon pâté; west coast scallops in the shell; chargrilled quail with hazelnut and basil dressing. Fillet of fresh wild salmon en papillote with crepes and cream. Baked ham, heather honey glazed crust.

STB 3 Crown Commended

Credit cards: 1, 2, 3

Proprietors: John & Eliza Allen

MULL ISLE OF

161   **F3**

Ardrioch
Ardrioch Farm
Dervaig
Isle of Mull
PA75 6QR
Tel: 06884 264

1 mile from Dervaig on Calgary road.

Ardrioch – a comfortable cedar wood farmhouse, traditionally furnished. Relax in the mellow wood-panelled sitting room with peat fire and extensively filled bookshelves, and enjoy the view of the sea, loch and surrounding hills. All bedrooms have tea-making facilities, wash-basins and room heaters; en suite facilities available. The house is a short stroll to the loch side and two miles from the harbour, where Ardrioch's own sea sailing is available. Ideal for walking, bird-watching and fishing. Multi-activity holidays also available. Working farm – sheep, cows, friendly collies, lambs and calves, enjoyed by children.

Open May to Oct

Rooms: 4, 1 with private facilities
Dinner 6.30 - 8 pm (a)
Unlicensed – guests welcome to take own wine
No dogs
No smoking throughout
Bed & breakfast from £15
Dinner B & B from £22

Home-smoked mackerel pâté; salmon steaks baked in a cream, lemon and dill sauce; venison casseroled with cider, rowan jelly and mushrooms. Home-made ice-creams – gooseberry and ginger, blackcurrant and cassis, apricot and almond. STB 2 Crown Commended

No credit cards

Proprietors: Jenny & Jeremy Matthew

Craig Hotel
Tobermory Road
Salen
Isle of Mull
PA72 6JG
Tel: 0680 300347

In Salen Village – on Tobermory-Craignure Road.

More home than hotel and situated by the Sound of Mull – ideal for exploring the beauties of Mull, Iona and Staffa – the Craig is a typical 19th century Scottish family house with 20th century comforts, including attractive lounge with log fire, magazines and board games.

Open mid Mar to mid Oct

Rooms: 6
Dinner from 7.15 pm
Residents only
No smoking in dining room
Bed & breakfast £19 - £22
Dinner B & B £26 - £30

Local seafood and Scottish meats cooked with fresh garden herbs. Home-made soups, pâtés, puddings and conserves. Interesting cheese board, cafetiere coffee.

STB 2 Crown Commended

Credit cards: 1, 3

Proprietors: James & Lorna McIntyre

Druimard Country House & Theatre Restaurant
Dervaig
Isle of Mull
PA75 6QW
Tel: 06884 345

On B8073, 8 miles west of Tobermory.

Peaceful family run small country house hotel just outside village overlooking glen, river and sea loch. Well situated for touring, boat trips, fishing, walking, with sandy beaches nearby. Elegant restaurant with well balanced menu specialising in fresh local produce, well appointed bedrooms (colour TVs etc), and Britain's smallest professional theatre.

Open Feb to Dec except Christmas
Rooms: 5, 3 with private facilities
Dinner 6 - 9 pm; 7 - 8 pm Sun (c)
Bed & breakfast £25 - £32.50
Dinner B & B rates on application

Freshly cooked local produce, wild salmon, scallops, crab, venison. Scottish roasts and vegetarian dishes. Home-made soups, individual starters and sweets. Menu changed daily according to availability.

STB 3 Crown Highly Commended

Credit cards: 1, 3

Proprietors: Clive & Jenny Murray

Druimnacroish
Dervaig
Isle of Mull
Argyll
PA75 6QW
Tel: 06884 274

Via ferry from Oban to Craignure. On Salen-Dervaig road, 1½ miles south of Dervaig.

Druimnacroish is an interesting place to stay. Donald McLean virtually converted the buildings himself into an unusual country house hotel in this delightful part of Mull. His wife, Wendy, presides in the kitchen and produces a varied selection of dishes, complemented by vegetables and fruit culled from the hotel's own six acre garden. There is a carefully selected wine cellar. To discover the subtle values of tranquillity and perhaps a new slant on life, it can be a most rewarding experience to join the McLeans in their home at Druimnacroish.

Open May to Oct

Rooms: 6 with private facilities
Packed Lunches to order
Dinner from 8 pm (d)
No smoking in restaurant
Bed & breakfast from £45
Dinner B & B from £65

Specialities include scampi marinated in malt whisky, rib of Aberdeen Angus beef carved at table off the bone. Wild salmon.

STB 4 Crown Commended

Credit cards: 1, 2, 3, 5

Proprietors: Donald & Wendy McLean

The Glenforsa Hotel
Salen
by Aros
Isle of Mull
PA75 6JW
Tel: 0680 300377
Fax: 0680 300535

Signed off A849 Craignure-Tobermory road, 2 miles east of Salen.

An unusual ranch style Norwegian log hotel set in six acres of grounds in a splendidly secluded spot. Public rooms, corridors and bedrooms are all timber-lined and give the hotel a unique character. There is a delightful and comfortable observation lounge on the first floor, a pleasant place to relax with after-dinner coffee and enjoy the view across the Sound of Mull. Jean and Paul Price are genial hosts anxious to make their guests feel welcome. There is good fishing, climbing and walking nearby. Neat and efficient local girls staff the dining room where the owner makes full use of the range of local fresh fish. ▶

Open all year
Rooms: 16 with private facilities
Bar Lunch 12 - 2.30 pm (a)
Bar Supper 5.30 - 9 pm (a)
Dinner 7 - 9 pm (b)
Facilities for the disabled
No smoking in dining room
Bed & breakfast from £26.50
Dinner B & B from £40
Accent entirely on local fish and produce.
STB 2 Crown Approved
Credit cards: 1, 2, 3, 6
Proprietors: Jean & Paul Price

Linndhu House
Tobermory
Isle of Mull, PA75 6QB
Tel: 0688 2425
On A848 south of Tobermory.
A most comfortable, traditional Highland hotel set in 35 acres of glorious woodland two miles south of Tobermory and offering superb cuisine, spacious accommodation and outstanding views, with a trout stream in the grounds. Fishing, walking, bird-watching, golf, deerstalking and pony-trekking can be arranged.
Open all year
Rooms: 8, 5 with private facilities
Light Luncheon 12.30 - 2.30 pm (a)
Dinner 8 - 10 pm (c)
Bed & breakfast £28 - £55
Dinner B & B £48 - £75
Scallops in saffron sauce, carbonade venison, cranachan.
STB 3 Crown Commended
No credit cards
Proprietors: Ian & Jennifer McLean

The Puffer Aground
Main Road, Salen, Aros
Isle of Mull, PA72 6JB
Tel: 068 03 389
On Craignure-Tobermory road.
The quaint name of this restaurant derives from the old days when the 'puffer' – the local steamboat – ran right on to the shore to unload its cargo and went off on the next high tide. The restaurant has a maritime theme and usually features an exhibition of oil paintings during July and August.
Open mid Apr to mid Oct
Dining Room/Restaurant Lunch 12 - 2.30 pm (a)
Dinner 7 - 9 pm (a-b)
Closed Oct
Scottish and Mull produce used whenever possible to create 'home-type' cooking in a friendly atmosphere.
No credit cards
Proprietors: Graham & Elizabeth Ellis

Tiroran House
Tiroran
Isle of Mull
Argyll
PA69 6ES
Tel: 06815 232
From Craignure, A849 towards Iona, turn right onto B8035 at head of Loch Scridain until signposted to Tiroran.

A remote and enchanting country house hotel, beautifully situated on Loch Scridain, offering the highest standards of comfort for those seeking to explore the lovely islands of Mull, Iona and Staffa. Set in over 50 acres of grounds, the lovely gardens include lawns, shrubberies and woodlands which slope down to the loch. Dinners are elegantly served by candlelight in the dining room overlooking gardens and sea loch.

Open Jun to early Oct
Rooms: 9 with private facilities
Lunch as required – residents only
Dinner from 7.45 pm (e)
No smoking in dining room
Bed & breakfast £50 - £70
Dinner B & B £77 - £96
Fresh seafood, including scallops and crab, Hebridean smoked trout and own gravadlax are regular starters. Main courses using lamb and beef from the estate and island venison, with fresh vegetables.
No credit cards

Best Picnic Lunch 1988

Proprietors: Robin & Susan Blockey

Western Isles Hotel
Tobermory
Isle of Mull
PA75 6PR
Tel: 0688 2012
Fax: 0688 2297
40 minute drive from Oban-Craignure ferry.
A magnificent Gothic style building enjoying a truly remarkable situation on the cliff overlooking Tobermory Bay. The views from the dining room, terrace lounge and many of the bedrooms are breathtaking and must surely be regarded as some of the best in Scotland. Bedrooms have been extensively refurbished and are now more in keeping with the general standard of the hotel. All have private bathrooms, TV, tea/coffee-making facilities. Dogs are accepted by prior arrangement, at a small charge.
Open Mar to Jan
Rooms: 28 with private facilities

Bar Lunch 12 - 1.45 pm (a)
Dinner 7 - 8.30 pm (d)
No smoking in dining room
Bed & breakfast £30 - £41.50
Dinner B & B £45 - £55
Home-made soups – menu features many specialities using local products including trout, venison, salmon, prawns, scallops and lobster.
STB 4 Crown Commended
Credit cards: 1, 3
Proprietors: Sue & Michael Fink

Golf View Hotel
Seabank Road
Nairn
IV12 4HD
Tel: 0667 52301
Telex: 75134

An imposing Victorian hotel overlooking the sea and the Black Isle Hills. A full range of leisure centre facilities and a heated outdoor pool. Near to the championship golf course. The chef has earned renown for the standard of preparation and presentation of food.

Open all year
Rooms: 40 with private facilities
Dining Room/Restaurant Lunch 12.30 - 2 pm (a)
Dinner 7 - 9.30 pm (b-c)
Bed & breakfast rates on application
Dinner B & B rates on application
Locally smoked or chef's dill-cured salmon, carved from trolley, served with wholemeal toast. Highland game terrine – rich terrine of pheasant, duck and hare flavoured with whisky and berries in jelly.
STB 5 Crown Commended
Credit cards: 2, 3, 5, 6

The Longhouse
8 Harbour Street
Nairn, IV12 4HU
Tel: 0667 55532
On corner of A96 and Harbour Street, Nairn – 16 miles from Inverness.
Window boxes of flowers in summer give a colourful appearance to this traditional old white-washed building on the edge of Nairn's fishertown. The restaurant is comfortable but not fussy, and there is usually a background of soft music. The menu, on a portable blackboard, is interesting and a lot of thought and care appears to have gone into ▶

its compilation. The food has earned high praise and the staff are courteous and friendly.

Open all year
Dining Room/Restaurant Lunch 12 - 2 pm: 12.30 - 4 pm Sun (a)
Dinner 6.30 - 9.30 pm except Sun (b)
Closed Sun evening + Mon
No smoking area in restaurant
Frequently changing menu with emphasis on local produce, freshly prepared and carefully presented.
Credit cards: 1, 3
Proprietors: Arthur & Aileen Paterson

Taste Bud Restaurant & Bar
44 Harbour Street
Nairn
IV12 4HU
Tel: 0667 52743

A traditional restaurant/bar of high reputation with pine and stone walls, the main theme of the premises, with log fires and comfortable seating. This restaurant is in easy walking distance of Nairn's harbour and fine beaches.

Open all year
Bar Lunch 12 - 2 pm (a)
Bar Snacks 2 - 6 pm (a)
Bar Supper 5 - 10 pm (a)
Dinner 7 - 10 pm (b)
Prime Scottish meat. Local seafood speciality. Selection of game in season and traditional Scottish fare.
Credit cards: 1, 2, 3, 5, 6
Proprietors: William MacLeod & Karen Charman

Ard-na-Coille Hotel
Kingussie Road
Newtonmore
Inverness-shire
PH20 1AY
Tel: 054 03 214

At northern end of Newtonmore village.

Ard-na-Coille is an Edwardian shooting lodge situated on an elevated position in two acres of woodland. Each room, individually and tastefully furnished to retain the period features, has a spectacular view of the Spey Valley and surrounding mountains. The informal and relaxing atmosphere encourages guests to enjoy the widely acclaimed high

standard of cuisine. Menus are based on the finest regional produce and are complemented by an extensive cellar.

Open Jan to mid Nov except 1 wk Apr
Rooms: 7 with private facilities
Dinner from 7.45 pm (d)
No smoking in dining room
Dogs accepted by prior arrangement
Bed & breakfast £19.50 - £37.50
Dinner B & B £35 - £59.50

Crab ravioli in a tarragon sauce. Carrot, ginger and coriander soup. Loin of Highland Spring lamb in a garlic and rosemary sauce. Creme fraiche mousse with orange caramel sauce.
Credit cards: 1, 3
Proprietors: Nancy Ferrier & Barry Cottam

Anchor & Chain Restaurant
Coulmore Bay
North Kessock
Ross-shire
IV1 1XB
Tel: 0463 73313

2 miles from North Kessock village.

Superb location on the water edge with magnificent views of the Beauly Firth. Fresh local produce is used in the preparation of meals and the same care and attention is taken be it for a bar meal or an à la carte dinner. The site of the restaurant is such that there is not too much "passing traffic", and for survival it is necessary to ensure that customers go away completely satisfied and willing to recommend it to their friends. What better basis for a successful restaurant.

Open Feb to Dec
Bar Lunch 12 - 2 pm (a)
Dining Room/Restaurant Lunch 12 - 2 pm (a)
Bar Supper 5.30 - 7.30 pm (a-b)
Dinner 5.30 - 8.30 pm (c)
Mid Oct to May, closed Mon + Tue
Varied à la carte menu at dinner
Credit cards: 1, 3, 6
Proprietor: Iain MacPherson

Esplanade Restaurant
Esplanade
Oban
PA34 5PW
Tel: 0631 66594

Situated on Oban's waterfront with a view of the island of Kerrera, this cosy à la carte restaurant offers the very best of local seafood and prime Scottish meat.

Open all year
Dinner 6 - 10 pm (a-b)
Credit cards: 1, 3
Proprietor: Colin A Felgate

Manor House Hotel
Gallanach Road
Oban
Argyll
PA34 4LS
Tel: 0631 62087
Fax: via 0680 300438

From south side of Oban follow signs to Gallanach and Kerrera Ferry. Past car ferry terminal.

Set in an enviable position in its own grounds on a commanding promontory above Oban Bay, the Manor House has long held the reputation for high quality in the comfort of its accommodation and the excellence of Scottish and French cuisine. All bedrooms have en suite facilities, television, direct dial telephone and central heating. German and French spoken.

Open all year - Feb. to Dec.
Rooms: 11 with private facilities
Bar Lunch 12.30 - 2 pm (a)
Dining Room/Restaurant Lunch 12.30 - 2 pm (a)
Dinner 7 - 8.30 pm (c)
No smoking in restaurant
Dinner B & B from £33 (min. 2 night stay)
Fresh west coast oysters with fennel and honey. Scampi Laphroaig. Parfait Flora MacDonald.
Credit cards: 1, 3
Proprietor: J L Leroy

STB 4 Crown
Commended

Sea Life Centre - Shoreline Restaurant

Barcaldine
Oban
Argyll
PA37 1SE
Tel: 063 172 386

On A828 Oban-Fort William road, 10 miles north of Oban.

Seafood and home-baking fare are specialities in the self-service restaurant with a full range of meals and snacks including a salad table. You'll also be enjoying your meal in comfortable surroundings which give you the best possible vantage point to appreciate fully the majestic splendour of the glorious views over Loch Creran to the mountains beyond.

Open Mar to Nov

Meals served from 10 am - 5 pm: 10 am - 6.30 pm Jul + Aug (a).
Table licence only
No smoking area in restaurant

Seafood lasagne, salmon pie, seafood pie. Local seafood – oysters (fresh), smoked salmon and trout. Coffee shop – with freshly ground coffee and home-baked fare.

No credit cards

Soroba House Hotel

Soroba Road
Oban
PA34 4SB
Tel: 0631 62628

A816 to Oban.

The hotel with its sumptuously appointed dining room stands in a dominant and beautiful site of nine acres above the town, yet close enough to the town facilities, ferry terminal etc.

Open all year

Rooms: 25
Bar Lunch 12 - 2.15 pm (a)
Dining Room/Restaurant Lunch 12 - 2.15 pm (a)
Dinner 7 - 10.15 pm (a-b)
Bed & breakfast from £20
Dinner B & B from £30

Lunches, dinners, suppers are served from an extensive menu which includes local seafood, Scotch beef etc.

Credit cards: 1, 5, 6

Proprietor: David Hutchison

The Waterfront Restaurant

No 1 The Waterfront
The Pier
Oban
Argyll
PA34
Tel: 0631 63110

The waterfront, Oban.

It would be difficult to get closer to the main source of supply than this. The Waterfront Restaurant has built up its reputation by concentrating on the local seafood arriving at the pier at Oban and likes to boast that it gets it "from the pier to the pan as fast as we can". Lovers of fish and shellfish go here to savour the daily catch at remarkably moderate prices.

Open all year

Dining Room/Restaurant Lunch 12 - 3 pm (a)
Dinner 6 - 10 pm (b)

Local seafood.

Credit cards: 1, 3

Proprietor: Stuart Walker

Willowburn Hotel

Clachan Seil
Isle of Seil
by Oban
PA34 4TJ
Tel: 08523 276

11 miles south of Oban, via A816 and B844, signposted Easdale, over Atlantic Bridge.

Welcome to the Willowburn, a small modern privately owned hotel set in two acres of ground on the sheltered north-east shore of the beautiful unspoilt Hebridean island of Seil – linked to the mainland by the only single span bridge to cross the Atlantic. All bedrooms have full amenities and the restaurant, overlooking Seil Sound, offers table d'hôte and à la carte menus for a relaxing end to your day.

Open Easter to late Oct

Rooms: 6 with private facilities
Bar Lunch 12.30 - 2 pm (a)
Bar Supper 6 - 8.30 pm
Dinner 7 - 8 pm (b)
Bed & breakfast rates on application
Dinner B & B from £30

Locally caught Atlantic salmon, squat lobsters, prawns, mussels etc. Herb roast chicken with Drambuie stuffing. Prime Scottish roast beef and steak. Willowburn pâté with whisky and oatmeal.

STB 3 Crown Commended

Credit cards: 1, 3

Proprietors: Archie & Maureen Todd

---

166   OLD DEER   D8
BY MINTLAW

Saplinbrae House Hotel

Old Deer
by Mintlaw
Aberdeenshire
AB4 8PL
Tel: 0771 23515
Telex: 739032

A950, 10 miles west of Peterhead and 30 miles from Aberdeen.

Welcoming country hotel, set in its own estate, originally the Dower House for the Pitfour Estate. The two bars offer substantial bar suppers, or there is a wide choice on the Stag Restaurant menu. Only top quality local meat is used, plus game (duck, pheasant, grouse, partridge) in season from the estate. Comfortable, modernised bedrooms, and friendly personal service ensure a loyal following.

Open all year

Rooms: 14, 12 with private facilities
Dining Room/Restaurant Lunch 12 - 2 pm (a)
Bar Supper 6 - 9.30 pm
Dinner 7 - 9 pm (b-c)
Bed & breakfast from £22.50
Dinner B & B rates on application

Gamies mushrooms, smoked Pitfour pheasant, game pie, roast mallard duck. Clarty pudding.

STB Award Pending

Credit cards: 1, 2, 3, 5, 6

---

167   ONICH   E4
By FORT WILLIAM

Allt-nan-Ros Hotel

Onich
by Fort William
Inverness-shire
PH33 6RY
Tel: 08553 210
Fax: 08553 462

On A82, 10 miles south of Fort William.

The Macleod family welcome you to their Highland country house, set amidst landscaped gardens on the shores of Loch Linnhe. All the comfortably furnished bedrooms overlook the loch and have private facilities, telephone, colour TV, full controllable heating, hairdryers, and much more. The dining room which also overlooks the loch, has fine views from the picture windows. The cuisine is a blend of French and Highland, utilising ▶

the best of local game, salmon and seafood. There is a varied and interesting wine list, and a good range of malt whiskies. A good centre from which to explore the West Highlands and islands.

Open mid Mar to late Oct
Rooms: 21 with private facilities
Dining Room/Restaurant Lunch 12.30 - 2 pm (b)
Dinner 7 - 8.30 pm (c)
No dogs
No smoking in dining room
Bed & breakfast from £32.75
Dinner B & B from £48.75
A modern style Taste of Scotland menu with a French influence, featuring fruit, vegetables and herbs from the hotel gardens, supplemented by home-baking and best local produce.
STB 4 Crown Commended
Credit cards: 1, 2, 3, 5, 6
Proprietor: James Macleod

The Lodge On The Loch
Onich, by Fort William
Inverness-shire
PH33 6RY
Tel: 08553 237/238
Telex: 94013696
Fax: 08552 629
On A82, 1 mile north of the Ballachulish Bridge.
Rest for a while in a charmed world and discover for yourself the gentle elegance of this renowned family run hotel. Superbly set above Loch Linnhe and commanding panoramic views to the Morvern mountains, this Highland house is a remarkable discovery. Individually designed bedrooms feature fine woven fabrics from the islands and combine every modern comfort.

Open early Feb to end Oct and also for Christmas + New Year
Rooms: 20, 18 with private facilities
Bar Lunch 12 - 2.30 pm (a)
Dinner 7 - 9.30 pm (c)
Facilities for the disabled
No smoking in restaurant
Bed & breakfast £29.50 - £46.50
Dinner B & B £46 - £63
Scottish smoked salmon with gravadlax and poached Loch Lochy salmon, served with fresh dill and mustard vinaigrette. Local scampi wrapped in Glen Uig smoked salmon. Medallions of venison with game and rowanberry sauce. Sweet crepe with Drambuie ice-cream and Blairgowrie raspberry sauce.
STB 4 Crown Commended
Credit cards: 1, 3
Proprietors: Norman & Jessie Young

Creel Restaurant
Front Road
St Margaret's Hope
Orkney
KW17 2SL
Tel: 0856 83 311
13 miles south of Kirkwall.
A scenic drive which takes you over all the famous Churchill Barriers, relics of World War II, brings you to St Margaret's Hope Bay and the Creel Restaurant. The Creel is a simple homely and friendly little restaurant which won the Taste of Britain Award in 1986 and was listed in the AA Top 500 Restaurants in Britain 1989. Alan Craigie, the proprietor/chef, works wonders with fish and shellfish and this highly commended restaurant is one at which it is essential to book in advance.

Open Feb to Dec
Rooms: 3
Dinner 7 -10 pm except Mon (c)
Note: dinner not served Mon, Tue, Wed + Thu in low season
Bed & breakfast from £18
Smoked lamb, fish soups, Orkney crab, scallops, salmon. Prime Orkney beef. All Orkney products, local fresh vegetables and potatoes.
Credit cards: 1, 3
Proprietors: Alan & Joyce Craigie

Foveran Hotel
nr Kirkwall
St Ola
Orkney
KW15 1SF
Tel: 0856 2389
On A964 Orphir road, 2½ miles from Kirkwall.
This modern purpose built hotel, all on the one level, is set in 32 acres with spectacular views over Scapa Flow. It has a reputation for its friendly personal atmosphere. Open-fired sitting room for pre-dinner drinks and after-dinner coffee. The Scandinavian-style dining room is bright and attractive. The hotel has its own private beach.

Open all year
Rooms: 8 with private facilities
Dinner 7 - 9 pm (c)
Bed & breakfast from £26
Home-made soups and pâtés; prawns, scallops, lobster, sea trout, fresh Orkney lamb, beef, game, farm-cheese – all as

available. New dishes from traditional raw materials.
STB 3 Crown Commended
Credit cards: 1, 3
Proprietors: Ivy & Bobby Corsie

PRICE CATEGORIES

(a)	under £10.00
(b)	£10.00 - £15.00
(c)	£15.00 - £20.00
(d)	£20.00 - £25.00
(e)	£25.00 - £30.00
(f)	over £30.00

The Foresters
107 Main Street
Pathhead
Midlothian
EH37 5PT
Tel: 0875 320273
In the main street of the village just 12 miles south of Edinburgh on A68.
The Foresters was one of the original horse changeover points on the Edinburgh-York-London route and the character of the time has been maintained. A family run pub restaurant offering good, inexpensive food.

Open all year
Dining Room/Restaurant Lunch 12 - 3 pm: 12.30 - 3 pm Sun (a)
Dinner 5 - 11 pm: 6.30 - 11 pm Sun (a)
Specialities include pastry dishes – five different pies all cooked to order; chicken, pork and steak all wrapped in crisp puff pastry. Local fish and venison.
No credit cards
Proprietor: David Birrell

The Peat Inn
Peat Inn
Fife
KY15 5LH
Tel: 033 484 206

At junction of B940/941, 6 miles south-west of St Andrews.

An 18th century village inn, situated in the village which bears its name, just six miles from St Andrews. An outstanding restaurant now recognised as one of Britain's finest, featuring the very best Scottish produce served stylishly in the intimate, beautifully furnished dining rooms. Well worth a detour.

Open all year, except 2 wks Jan + 2 wks Nov
Rooms: 8 with private facilities
Dining Room/Restaurant Lunch from 1 pm (c)
Dinner 7 - 9.30 pm (f)
Closed Sun + Mon
No smoking in dining room
Bed & breakfast from £40
Dinner B & B rates on application

Breast of pigeon in a pastry case with wild mushrooms. Whole lobster in sauce with coriander and ginger. Caramelised apple pastry with a caramel sauce.

Credit cards: 1, 2, 3

In A Class of Its Own 1989

Proprietors: David & Patricia Wilson

Cringletie House Hotel
Peebles
EH45 8PL
Tel: 072 13 233

A703, 2½ miles north of Peebles.

Scottish baronial mansion set in 28 acres of gardens and woodland, in beautiful and peaceful surroundings. Magnificent views from every room. Scottish meat and fish always used, with fresh fruit and vegetables in season from own two acre walled kitchen garden, and from market. The kitchen garden is featured in "The Gourmet Garden" by Geraldene Holt. Imaginative home-cooking at its best.

Open mid Mar to 1 Jan

Rooms: 13 with private facilities
Light lunch except Sun (a)
Dining Room/Restaurant Lunch Sun only (b) 3 courses + coffee/petit fours
Afternoon Tea 3.30 - 4.30 pm
Dinner 7.30 - 8.30 pm (d) 4 courses + coffee/petit fours
No smoking in restaurant
Bed & breakfast £36 - £39
Dinner B & B £56 - £59

Haggis stuffed mushrooms with whisky sauce, hot cheese mousse baked with cream, roast duckling with blackberry and gin sauce, casseroled haunch of venison with red wine and prunes. Toffee cheesecake.

STB 4 Crown Commended

Credit cards: 1, 3

Proprietors: Stanley & Aileen Maguire

Drummore
Venlaw High Road
Peebles
EH45 8RL
Tel: 0721 20336

In a quiet cul-de-sac off the Edinburgh road (A703) in Peebles.

Hillside house with panoramic views over Peebles and the Tweed Valley. Set among trees on Venlaw Hill, the house is in an ideal situation for walkers, and mountain bikes are available for hire for the more adventurous guest. For the less energetic – the peaceful surroundings are ideal for a relaxing break.

Open Easter to Oct: advance bookings only Apr + May

Rooms: 2
Dinner 6.30 - 7.30 pm (a)
Unlicensed
Bed & breakfast from £10.50
Dinner B & B from £18

Fresh local poultry, lamb and beef. Trout fresh from the farm. Variety of salads. Oatcakes and a selection of Scottish cheeses.

STB 2 Crown
No credit cards
Proprietor: Jean Phillips

Kailzie Garden Restaurant
Kailzie
Peebles
EH45 9HT
Tel: 0721 22807

2½ miles from town centre. *on B7062.*

Situated in 17 acres of beautiful gardens by the River Tweed this attractive but unpretentious little restaurant is housed in the old stable square and has been carefully converted to retain as many of the original features as possible. The main dining area in the old coach room still has the original wood panelling. The old stalls and loose boxes form an extension to this area. The menu is simple and great emphasis is placed on good home-cooking and baking using local produce, fresh fruit and vegetables from the gardens during the season.

Open Mar to late Oct
Dining Room/Restaurant Lunch 12.15 - 2 pm (a)
Afternoon Tea 3 - 5 pm
Dinner from 7.30 pm Sat only (b)
Facilities for the disabled
No smoking area in restaurant

Home-made soups, pâté, lamb and fish. Selection of home-baked sweets including meringues.

No credit cards

Proprietors: Grace & Ewen Innes

Kingsmuir Hotel
Springhill Road
Peebles
EH45 9EP
Tel: 0721 20151

On quiet south side of Peebles.

Charming, century-old house standing in own leafy grounds. Family run hotel, specialising in Scottish cooking, using the best of local produce in a wide variety of dishes, served in dining room, lounge or bar, lunchtime and evenings. Smaller portions of most dishes can be served for children and those with smaller appetites. Ideal centre for touring Edinburgh and stately homes of the Borders, golfing and fishing.

Open all year

Rooms: 10 with private facilities
Bar Lunch 12 - 2 pm (a)
Dining Room/Restaurant Lunch 12 - 2 pm (a)
Bar Supper 7 - 9.30 pm (a)
Dinner 7 - 8.30 pm (b)
No smoking in dining room
Bed & breakfast from £29
Dinner B & B from £40

Home-made soups (especially Cullen skink) and pâtés. Kingsmuir steak pie. Salmon – Tweed Kettle a speciality – trout, seafish and shellfish. Roasts of beef, lamb, venison, chicken (with skirlie). Fresh selection of home-made sweets daily.

STB 3 Crown Commended

Credit cards: 1, 2, 3

Proprietors: Elizabeth, Norman & May Kerr

Peebles Hotel Hydro

Innerleithen Road
Peebles
Tweeddale, EH45 8LX
Tel: 0721 20602

A large, imposing chateau-style hotel with lofty ceilings, wide corridors and plenty of space, set in 30 acres of ground overlooking River Tweed Valley and Border hills. The hotel's bedrooms are comfortable and up-to-date – all rooms having private facilities, TV, hospitality tray, direct dial telephones and most with hairdryers and trouser presses. Leisure centre with pool, jacuzzi, saunas, solarium, steam bath, beauty salon, gymnasium, etc. Tennis, squash, riding.

Open all year
Rooms: 137 with private facilities
Bar Lunch 12.30 - 4 pm (a)
Dining Room/Restaurant Lunch 12.45 - 2 pm (a-b)
Dinner 7.30 - 9 pm (b-c)
Bed & breakfast £29.50 - £33.50
Dinner B & B £38 - £43.50

Fresh trout from local fish farm. Best of Scottish smoked salmon, Border lamb, beef and other Scottish produce.
STB 4 Crown Commended
Credit cards: 1, 2, 3, 5

PERTH

172   F6

The Bein Inn

Glenfarg
nr Perth, PH2 9PY
Tel: 057 73 216

10 minutes south of Perth. Exit M90, junction 8 northbound/9 southbound, in the Glen.

Traditional coaching inn set in the beautiful Glen of Glenfarg. Character restaurant serving à la carte and vegetarian menus. Cosy lounge bar, "hideaway" snack bar (May to Oct). Well appointed accommodation, most en suite.

Open all year
Rooms: 13, 11 with private facilities
Bar Lunch 12 - 2 pm (a)
Dinner 7 - 9.30 pm (c)
Bed & breakfast from £19
Dinner B & B from £34

Cullen skink, Scottish smoked trout and salmon. Highland game soup. Sirloin Rabbie Burns. Venison casserole, Tayside salmon, local Scottish lamb, pheasant Blairgowrie. Cloutie dumpling.
STB 3 Crown Commended
Credit cards: 1, 3, 6
Proprietors: Mike & Elsa Thompson

Huntingtower Hotel

Crieff Road
Perth
PH1 3JT
Tel: 0738 83771
Fax: 0738 83777

On A85, 3 miles west of Perth

Set in 3½ acres of beautiful landscaped gardens, the Huntingtower Hotel acts as a perfect base as a gateway to the Highlands. Facilities such as salmon fishing and game shooting are available close by. The oak-panelled restaurant with its high ceiling, quality furnishing and table appointments creates an almost grand feeling, whilst retaining the relaxed and comfortable atmosphere which pervades this country house.

Open all year
Rooms: 19 with private facilities
Bar Lunch 12 - 2.30 pm (a)
Dining Room/Restaurant Lunch 12 - 2.30 pm (b)
Dinner 7 - 9.30 pm (c)
Bed & Breakfast £39.50 - £59
Dinner B & B £56.50 - £76

Locally caught game and salmon. Fresh local produce prepared carefully and imaginatively.
STB 4 Crown Commended
Credit cards: 1, 2, 3, 6

Murrayshall Country House Hotel

Scone
Perthshire
PH2 7PH
Tel: 0738 51171
Telex: 76197
Fax: 0738 52595

4 miles out of Perth, 1 mile off A94.

Murrayshall Hotel is a sumptuously appointed and elegant country house with high standards of quiet, unobtrusive efficient service. It is set in 300 acres of parkland and with a challenging 6,420 yards golf course. Bruce Sangster, an award winning chef, uses produce from the hotel's four acre garden to produce a Taste of Scotland with a hint of French cuisine for the Old Masters Restaurant. French and Spanish spoken.

Open all year
Rooms: 19 with private facilities
Bar Lunch (Club House) 12 - 3 pm (a)
Bar Supper (Club House) 5.30 - 9 pm (b)
Dinner 7 - 9.30 pm (f)
Gourmet evenings and weekends
No dogs
Bed & breakfast £70 - £120
Dinner B & B rates on application

Breast of locally shot pigeon with red cabbage compote. Parcel of wild Tay salmon and turbot with langoustine tails. Perthshire raspberries.
STB 5 Crown Highly Commended
Credit cards: 1, 2, 3, 5, 6

Best Restaurant 1988

Number Thirty Three Seafood Restaurant

33 George Street
Perth
PH1 5LA
Tel: 0738 33771

Perth city centre.

Opened in 1987, this fashionably pink and grey art deco theme restaurant specialises in all types of fish and shellfish. Light meals are served in the Oyster Bar and main meals in the relaxing mirrored Dining Area. Everything from mussels and a cup of coffee to a three course à la carte meal is available at lunch and dinner from Tuesday to Saturday.

Open all year except 10 days over Christmas/New Year period
Bar Lunch 12.30 - 2.30 pm (a)
Dining Room/Restaurant Lunch 12.30 - 2.30 pm (a)
Bar Supper 6.30 - 9.30 pm (a)
Dinner 6.30 - 9.30 pm (c)
Closed Sun + Mon

Mary's seafood soup. Creamy crab and prawn terrine. Monkfish and spring vegetables en papillote. Seafood casserole. Sticky toffee pudding.
Credit cards: 1, 2, 3
Proprietors: Gavin & Mary Billinghurst

Parkland House Hotel

St Leonards Bank
Perth
PH2 8EB
Tel: 0738 22451
Fax: 0738 22046

Junction of St Leonards Bank and Marshall Place in centre of Perth adjoining the South Inch Park.

We are taking an exceptional course in listing Parkland House in the Guide before it opens and we do so because of the fine reputation of its proprietors Pat and Allan Deeson who also own Nivingston House Hotel at Cleish.

Parkland House, the original home of the Lord Provost of Perth, is a good ►

example of a classical Town House with fine woodwork and cornices. It is ideally situated in this historic old city, the ancient capital of Scotland, with lots of interesting places nearby. Emphasis is placed on the quality of the food in both the restaurant and the Conservatory, and the Parkland should prove a very valuable addition to the quality hotel scene in and around Perth.

Opening Spring 1991

Open all year

Rooms: 14 with private facilities
Dining Room/Restaurant Lunch 12 - 2 pm (b)
Dinner 7 - 9 pm (f)
Bed & breakfast from £60
Dinner B & B from £80
Special weekend breaks

Speciality – lunchtime seafood buffet.

STB Award Pending

Credit cards: 2, 3, 6

Proprietors: Pat & Allan Deeson

Scone Palace
Perth
PH2 6BD
Tel: 0738 52300

On A93 Braemar road, 2 miles out of Perth.

Ancient crowning place of Scotland's kings – now the historic home of the Earl and Countess of Mansfield. See the antique treasures, explore the grounds, enjoy lunch beside the range in the 'Old Kitchen' restaurant, or a snack in the coffee shop. Take home the excellent produce from the shop. To arrange special off-season visits contact the Administrator.

Open Good Friday to mid Oct

Dining Room/Restaurant Lunch 11.30 am - 2 pm except Sun (a)
Sun Lunch served Jul + Aug only, unless pre-booked
Dinner (d-e) by arrangement only

Fresh Tay salmon, home-made soup always available on the lunch menu. Home-baking, chutney and marmalade a speciality.

No credit cards

Waterside Inn
Fraserburgh Road
Peterhead
Aberdeenshire, AB4 7BN
Tel: 0779 71121
Telex: 739413
Fax: 0779 70670

30 miles north of Aberdeen on A952. 1 mile north of Peterhead.

Scotland's most north-easterly hotel and leisure club – swimming pool, spa bath, sauna, Turkish steam room, keep-fit – is the ideal haven for rest and luxury for the business executive, conference delegate or the whole family. Ogilvies Restaurant offers an exciting adventurous four course table d'hote menu which allows Tony Jackson and his team to show the high standard of dishes that has won them many awards. The Grill Room still offers an extensive menu – with meals served all day – plus a special children's menu and vegetarian corner.

Open all year

Rooms: 110 with private facilities
Meals served all day (Grill Room)
Bar Lunch 12 - 2.30 pm (a)
Dining Room/Restaurant Lunch 12 - 2.30 pm (b)
Dinner 7 - 10 pm (c)
Bed & breakfast £50 - £65
Dinner B & B rates on application

Beef and fish dishes from Europe's premier fishing port and rich Buchan hinterland.

STB 5 Crown Commended

Credit cards: 1, 2, 3, 5, 6

Pittodrie House Hotel
Pitcaple
Aberdeenshire
AB5 9HS
Tel: 04676 444
Telex: 739935
Fax: 04676 648

Off A96 near Pitcaple – 21 miles north of Aberdeen, 17 miles north of airport.

A castle style turreted mansion at the foot of Bennachie which was originally the home of the owner, Theo Smith, and which has been skilfully and sympathetically extended in the last year to give an additional 15 bedrooms and

function room. The original character of the public rooms has been maintained with antiques and family portraits. There is a beautifully kept three acre walled garden.

Open all year

Rooms: 41 with private facilities
Dining Room/Restaurant Lunch 12.30 - 2 pm: 12.30 - 1.30 pm Sun (a) prior booking essential
Dinner 7.30 - 9 pm (b)
Bed & breakfast £45 - £60
Dinner B & B rates on application

Menu changes daily featuring fresh game and salmon.

STB 4 Crown Commended

Credit cards: 1, 2, 3, 5

Proprietor: Theo Smith

Auchnahyle Farm
Tomcroy
Pitlochry
Perthshire
PH16 5JA
Tel: 0796 2318
Fax: 0796 3657

On outskirts of Pitlochry.

Auchnahyle, the delightful secluded 18th century farmhouse home of Penny and Alastair Howman, is a "Wolsey Lodge" and recommended by Karen Brown (US visitors note) and Chris Gill in his "Charming Small Hotels Guide". Elegant four course candlelit dinners are served for up to six guests who are treated as friends and offered every comfort. Dogs, and children over 12, welcome. Booking ahead advisable.

Open Easter to end Sep

Rooms: 3, 1 with private facilities
Picnic Lunches on request
Theatre Suppers 6.45 pm (c)
Dinner from 7.30 pm (c)
Unlicensed – guests welcome to take own wine
No children under 12
No smoking in dining room
Bed & breakfast from £20
Dinner B & B from £35.50

Own quail and quail eggs with exclusive sources for trout and venison. Everything fresh and vegetables usually from the garden. Own goat cheese, and honey.

Credit cards: 1, 3

Proprietors: Penny & Alastair Howman

Birchwood Hotel

East Moulin Road
Pitlochry
Perthshire, PH16 5DW
Tel: 0796 2477

200 yards off the Atholl Road on Perth side of Pitlochry.

Beautiful stone-built Victorian manor house on wooded knoll surrounded by four acres of attractive grounds. Noted for food and hospitality. Open to non-residents for all meals. Choice of à la carte and table d'hôte menus with extensive wine list. All bedrooms with private facilities, colour TV, telephone and courtesy trays. Dogs accepted by arrangement.

Open Mar to Nov
Rooms: 16 with private facilities
Dining Room/Restaurant Lunch 12 - 1.30 pm (a)
Dinner 6.30 - 8 pm (b-c)
No smoking in restaurant
Bed & breakfast rates on application
Dinner B & B £36 - £41

Smoked venison with pear, trout Faskally, Highland steak, sirloin steak with haggis stuffing, creamed smokie, pork Edradour, cranachan.

STB 3 Crown Commended
Credit cards: 1, 3
Proprietors: Brian & Ovidia Harmon

Castlebeigh House

Knockard Road
Pitlochry
Perthshire, PH16 5HJ
Tel: 0796 2925

Just off Pitlochry-Moulin road.

Castlebeigh is a good example of the large houses built in Pitlochry in the period 1870 to 1880. These were made for confident gracious living. Castlebeigh sits high on the hillside on the north side of Pitlochry and has sweeping views over the Tummel Valley. It is well situated and convenient for the many attractions and places of interest that make the town so popular.

Open Apr to Nov – also open Christmas + New Year
Rooms: 21, 19 with private facilities
Dinner 6 - 8 pm (b)
No smoking in restaurant
Bed & breakfast £25 - £35
Dinner B & B £35 - £45

Salmon mousse with cucumber sauce. Deep fried Scottish brie with cranberry sauce. Great favourites are the home-made sweets.

STB 3 Crown Commended
Credit cards: 1, 2, 3, 5, 6
Proprietors: Alistair & Diane McMenemie

Craigmhor Lodge, Hotel & Restaurant

27 West Moulin Road
Pitlochry
Perthshire
PH16 5EF
Tel: 0796 2123

Pitlochry – on A924 Braemar road.

Craigmhor, traditional in style, is set in two acres of secluded grounds overlooking the Tummel Valley, with the town of Pitlochry nestling below. The Lodge offers guests comfortable accommodation in en suite bedrooms with tea/coffee makers and colour TV. It also features a relaxing lounge with open fire, an intimate cocktail bar and restaurant, open from 6.30 pm, enabling guests to enjoy a pre-theatre meal.

Open all year
Rooms: 11 with private facilities
Bar Lunch 12 - 2 pm (a)
Dining Room/Restaurant Lunch (b) – by arrangement
Dinner 6.30 - 8 pm (c)
Dinner for non-residents 6.30 - 8.30 pm – by arrangement
Facilities for the disabled
No smoking in restaurant
Bed & breakfast £20 – £26
Dinner B & B £32 - £38

Roast haunch of wild boar, fresh Tay salmon and local venison served with only the finest of fresh seasonal produce. Home-made desserts.

Credit cards: 1, 3
Proprietors: Jean & Sandra Hutton, Ian Mackenzie

Dunfallandy House

Logierait Road
Pitlochry
Perthshire
PH16 5NA
Tel: 0796 2648

On south side of Pitlochry, signposted off road leading to Festival Theatre.

Originally built for General Archibald Fergusson in 1790, this Georgian mansion house is now a beautifully refurbished country house hotel. It is magnificently situated within the Dunfallandy Estate and has unrivalled views of the glorious Tummel Valley, with the popular highland town of Pitlochry nestling below. This characterful house retains its historical features including marble fireplaces, log fires and the 'General's Bath' – the original Georgian ceramic bath of rather alarming depth! The elegant dining room offers imaginative food expertly prepared and presented, enhanced by fresh flowers, silver cutlery, crystal glasses and candlelight. An extensive wine list features traditional and New World wines.

Open Mar to Oct
Rooms: 9, 8 with private facilities
Dinner 6.30 - 8 pm (b)
No children
No dogs
No smoking in dining room
Bed & breakfast £23 - £30
Dinner B & B £35 - £42

Wild duck breast poached with local chanterelles, fresh garden herbs and claret. Varied selection of vegetarian dishes always available.

Credit cards: 1, 2, 3
Proprietors: Jane & Michael Bardsley

East Haugh Country House Hotel & Restaurant

East Haugh
by Pitlochry
Perthshire
PH16 5JS
Tel: 0796 3121

On old A9 road, 1 mile south of Pitlochry.

East Haugh House is a beautiful 17th century turreted stone Clan house, set in two acres of lawned gardens, which has been sympathetically refurbished to offer a high standard of accommodation. The restaurant and conservatory bar are complemented by the individually designed and furnished bedrooms, one featuring an antique pine four-poster bed and an open fire. Neil McGown, the proprietor/chef, takes the greatest pride in preparing his dishes which are becoming renowned, and he may even shoot or catch the ingredients for you himself!

Open all year
Rooms: 6, 4 with private facilities
Bar Lunch 11.30 am - 2.15 pm (a)
Dining Room/Restaurant Lunch (a) – by reservation only
Bar Supper 6 - 11 pm (a)
Dinner 6.30 - 11 pm (c)
Bed & breakfast £20 - £40
Dinner B & B £37 - £56

Mix of traditional Scottish and classic French. Game in season, an abundance of fresh fish and shellfish. Original vegetarian dishes.

STB 3 Crown Commended
Credit cards: 1, 3
Proprietors: Neil & Lesley McGown

The Green Park Hotel
Clunie Bridge Road
Pitlochry
Perthshire
PH16 5JY
Tel: 0796 3248

North side of Pitlochry.

Set in its own grounds on the banks of Loch Faskally, the Green Park Hotel has 37 bedrooms all with private facilities. The spacious lounges, restaurant and cocktail bar all boast breathtaking views of the loch and the hills beyond.

Open late Mar to Oct

Rooms: 37 with private facilities
Bar Lunch 12 - 2 pm (a)
Dining Room/Restaurant Lunch (a-b) by arrangement only
Bar Supper 7 - 9 pm
Dinner 6.30 - 8.30 pm (c)
No smoking in restaurant
Bed & breakfast from £32
Dinner B & B from £43

Full Scottish dinner served every Fri. Choice of over 30 hors d'oeuvres Sat. Cold buffet table Sun dinner.

Credit cards: 1, 3, 6

Proprietors: Graham & Anne Brown

Knockendarroch House Hotel
Higher Oakfield
Pitlochry
Perthshire
PH16 5HT
Tel: 0796 3473

High on hill overlooking village – just off Atholl Road.

Splendidly confident large Victorian house standing squarely on its hill looking over the Tummel Valley and Pitlochry. Recommended by Karen Brown's Hotel Guide. Bookings advised and essential for non-residents.

Open mid Mar to Nov

Rooms: 12 with private facilities
Dinner 6.15 - 7.15 pm (c)
Bed & breakfast from £20.50
Dinner B & B from £30

Good home cooking – pan-fried chicken with pickled apple and red cabbage, butterfly of trout, cucumber cream. Home-made soups and pâtés. Crème caramel in a sugar nest.

STB 3 Crown Commended

Credit cards: 1, 2, 3, 5

Proprietors: Mary & John McMenemie

Mill Pond Coffee Shop
Burnside Apartments
19 West Moulin Road
Pitlochry
PH16 5EA
Tel: 0796 2203

Around 300 yards north of junction of A924 Pitlochry/Braemar road and Atholl Road, Pitlochry.

A delightful little coffee shop within a recently completed apartment hotel, situated in a convenient quiet location. An imaginative menu is served throughout the day, with home-made soups and hot dishes, cold buffet, tasty snacks and sandwiches, vegetarian dishes, home-baking and speciality ices. Selection of teas, coffee and health drinks.
Children welcome.

Open all year

Continuous food service from 10 am - 7 pm daily (b)
No smoking in restaurant

Open sandwiches - Tay salmon, local smoked gammon; from the buffet – smoked trout, salmon, game pâté. Ginger cream meringues, butter shortbread, gateaux with local seasonal fruits, Scottish cheeses.

Credit cards: 1, 2, 3, 5, 6

Proprietors: Bill & Jessie Falconer

Torrdarach Hotel
Golf Course Road
Pitlochry
Perthshire
PH16 5AU
Tel: 0796 2136

On road signposted to golf course at north end of town.

Torrdarach offers a high standard of personal service and traditional home cooking. The hotel is in a quiet and peaceful woodland setting overlooking Pitlochry. This is a good centre for touring, walking and fishing, and, of course, the famous Festival Theatre.

Open Easter to mid Oct

Rooms: 7, 3 with private facilities
Dinner at 6.45 pm (a)
Residents only
No dogs
No smoking in dining room
Bed & breakfast from £16.50
Dinner B & B from £23

Kipper pâté, fresh Scottish salmon, home-made soups and desserts, together with local beef and lamb provide interesting and varied menus.

No credit cards

Proprietors: Muriel & Robert How

Westlands Hotel (formerly 'Airdaniar')
160 Atholl Road
Pitlochry
Perthshire
PH16 5AR
Tel: 0796 2266

On old A9 north of town centre.

Refurbished, extended and re-named for 1991, Westlands is situated close to the centre of Pitlochry yet enjoys fine views over the surrounding mountains and Vale of Atholl. The proprietors' policy of continual improvement now provides 16 bedrooms (all en suite) with colour TV, tea/coffee tray, radio, hairdryers and direct dial telephones, and central heating throughout. The new Westlands Restaurant opens early in 1991, offering distinctive cuisine in tasteful surroundings using the best products Scotland has to offer. 'Taste of Scotland' dishes are a particular feature. Reduced rates for Spring/Autumn are available as are Winter and theatre packages.

Open mid Feb to Jan

Rooms: 16 with private facilities
Lunch 12 - 2 pm (a)
Dinner 6.30 - 9 pm (c)
Bed & breakfast from £24.50
Dinner B & B from £39.50

Atholl Skewer – pieces of tender lamb marinated with fresh ginger and spices, baked on skewers. Sauté of Scottish lambs liver with lime and sage butter.

STB 3 Crown Commended

Credit cards: 1, 3

Proprietors: Andrew & Sue Mathieson

PLOCKTON
176   D3

The Haven Hotel
Innes Street
Plockton
Ross-shire, IV52 8TW
Tel: 059 984 223

In the village of Plockton.

In the lochside village of Plockton, originally a 19th century merchant's house, the Haven has been carefully converted into a charming small hotel set in the centre of one of Scotland's most ▶

beautiful villages. The hotel features three lounges – one with open fire, two 'no smoking'. Bedrooms are furnished to the highest standard.

Open Feb to 20 Dec

Rooms: 13 with private facilities
Bar Lunch 12.30 - 2 pm (a)
Dining Room/Restaurant Lunch 12.30 - 2 pm (a) – last order 1.45 pm
Dinner 7 - 8.30 pm (c)
No smoking in restaurant
Bed & breakfast from £25
Dinner B & B from £31

Plockton prawns, pheasant, local salmon, venison, haggis, kippers, local black pudding, wild duck, Scottish lamb, beef and pork. Home-made sweets.

STB 4 Crown Highly Commended

Credit cards: 1, 3

Proprietors: Marjorie Nichols & John Graham

PORT OF MENTEITH
177 F5

Lake Hotel
Port of Menteith
Perthshire, FK8 3RA
Tel: 08775 258
Fax: 08775 671

On A81 – at Port of Menteith – 200 yards on road to Arnprior.
The Lake Hotel stands right on the shore of Scotland's only lake (the others are all lochs). It has been converted from a 19th century manse and has delightful views over the lake to the hills of the Trossachs. Completely refurbished it has been fitted out to a high standard of comfort. There is a new large conservatory and an elegant lounge. Altogether this is a most attractive establishment in lovely surroundings serving quality fresh food.

Open 1 Feb to 25 Dec

Rooms: 14 with private facilities
Bar Lunch 12 - 2 pm (a)
Dining Room/Restaurant Lunch 12.30 - 2 pm (c)
Bar Supper 7 - 10 pm (a)
Dinner 7 - 9 pm (c)
No smoking area in restaurant
Bed & breakfast rates on application
Dinner B & B rates £36

West coast smoked fish and shellfish. Isle of Mull loin of lamb. Shortbread with local berries. Orkney goats cheese.

STB 4 Crown Commended

Credit cards: 1, 3

Proprietor: J L Leroy

PORTPATRICK
178 I4

The Fernhill Golf Hotel
Heugh Road
Portpatrick
nr Stranraer, DG9 8TD
Tel: 077 681 220
Fax: 077 681 596

Portpatrick's leading hotel is spectacularly situated with views over the town and the Irish Sea. Continually developing, this popular three star hotel added six executive bedrooms and a new reception area in 1990. The conservatory is especially attractive and is a fashionable eating area for à la carte and bar meals. The restaurant offers a fine selection of food and wine, and the patronage of local people is a pointer to the high quality of the cuisine. Smoking is discouraged in the restaurant and conservatory but permitted in the bar extension. Ample overnight parking is available within the walled grounds.

Open all year except Christmas Day + Boxing Day

Rooms: 21 with private facilities
Bar Lunch 12 - 2 pm (a)
Dining Room/Restaurant Lunch – by special arrangement
Bar restaurant meals 6 - 10 pm
Dinner 7 - 9 pm (c)
No dogs in public rooms
No smoking in restaurant + conservatory
Bed & breakfast from £30
Dinner B & B from £44.50

Only finest meat, fish and local produce used in season and when available. All meals are cooked to order.

STB 4 Crown Commended

Credit cards: 1, 2, 3, 5

Proprietors: Anne & Hugh Harvie

RAASAY
ISLE OF
179 D3

Isle of Raasay Hotel
Raasay Island
by Kyle of Lochalsh
IV40 8PB
Tel: 047 862 222/226

Between Skye and mainland. Easy access by car ferry from Sconser (Skye).
Small, comfortable hotel situated in woodlands on the totally unspoiled beautiful Isle of Raasay, overlooking the Sound of Raasay to the mountains of Skye. The hotel itself is a remarkable blend of old and new in a renovated old stone mansion. Ideal for naturalists, geologists, hill-walkers and all those who wish to "get away from it all". The food is good and wholesome. Spectacular views of the Cuillins.

Open Apr to Sep

Rooms: 12 with private facilities
Bar Lunch 12.30 - 2 pm (a)
Dinner from 7 pm (d)
No smoking in restaurant
Bed & breakfast from £27
Dinner B & B from £42

Home-made soups and sweets a speciality. Fresh Raasay salmon in season, best Scottish beef, local fish, cranachan, Strathbogie mist, Raasay wild brambles and peach brulee with cream.

STB 3 Crown Commended

No credit cards

Proprietor: Isobel Nicholson

ROTHES
180 D7

Rothes Glen Hotel
Rothes
Morayshire
IV33 7AF
Tel: 034 03 254

On north side of Rothes, on road to Elgin.
A delightful turreted and compact Victorian mansion, standing in 40 acres of grounds maintaining a herd of long-haired Highland cattle. The public rooms are imposing, with marble fire places and 18th century furniture.

Open Feb to Dec

Rooms: 16, 13 with private facilities
Bar Lunch 12.30 - 2 pm (a)
Dining Room/Restaurant Lunch 12.30 - 2 pm (a-b)
Dinner 7.30 - 9 pm (c)
Bed & breakfast from £50.25
Dinner B & B from £69.50

Fresh fish and shellfish from the Moray Firth and salmon from the River Spey.

Credit cards: 1, 2, 3, 5, 6

Proprietors: Donald & Elaine Carmichael

The Grange Inn
Grange Road
St Andrews
Fife
KY16 8LJ
Tel: 0334 72670

Grange Road is off A917 to Crail on exit from St Andrews.

Charming old world inn beautifully situated on a hillside overlooking the town, St Andrews Bay and the Tay estuary. The restaurant features the best of local produce in season, such as East Neuk haddock, Tay salmon, Perthshire venison, local beef and lamb. There is also a daily selection of home-cooked meals served in the bar.

Open all year
Rooms: 2 with private facilities
Bar Lunch 12.30 - 2 pm (a)
Dining Room/Restaurant Lunch 12.30 - 2 pm except Mon (b)
Bar Supper 7 - 10 pm (b)
Dinner 7.30 - 9.30 pm except Mon (c)
Note: Restaurant closed Mon - only Bar Meals available.
Dinner menu changes weekly.
No smoking in restaurant
Bed & breakfast rates on application
Dinner B & B rates on application

Mixed salad leaves with fine strips of smoked quail and chicken breast in red wine vinegar dressing. Baked fresh sea trout in filo pastry with a garden sorrel sauce. Hot cherry pancake laced with Kirsch.

Credit cards: 1, 2, 3, 5
Proprietors: Ann Russell & Peter Aretz

Parkland Hotel & Restaurant
Kinburn Castle
Double Dykes Road
St Andrews
Fife, KY16 9DS
Tel: 0334 73620

Near centre of St Andrews.

Parkland Hotel occupies part of a fine castle-style mansion, set in its own grounds. Close to all amenities of the town. Golf course, beach and shopping are all within a few minutes walk. The restaurant is renowned for its five course gourmet dinners. The finest fresh fish and meat are used as well as exotic fruit and vegetables. The chef/proprietor makes good use of locally caught fish and shellfish.

Open all year
Rooms: 15, 9 with private facilities
Dining Room/Restaurant Lunch 12.30 - 2 pm (b) except Sun
Dinner 6.30 pm daily, table d'hôte for residents
Dinner 7.30 - 8.30 pm except Sun + Mon (c)
Residents only Sun
Reservations essential
Bed & breakfast £22.50 - £31
Dinner B & B from £34.50 - £43.50

STB 3 Crown Commended

Credit cards: 1, 3

Proprietors: Brian & Rosemary MacLennan

Rufflets Country House Hotel
Strathkinness Low Road
St Andrews
Fife
KY16 9TX
Tel: 0334 72594

On B939, 1½ miles west of St Andrews.

Rufflets is set in ten acres of award winning gardens, 1½ miles from the town centre and famous golf courses. This Heritage hotel's bedrooms all have private bathrooms/showers, radio, colour TV, tea/coffee-making facilities and hairdryers. The kitchen team has won a gold medal at a St Andrews salon culinaire cookery competition and was awarded the Blue "R" restaurant award by the RAC in 1990. The Garden Restaurant is well known for the use of fresh Scottish produce and innovative combinations of ingredients.

Open all year except 6 Jan to 18 Feb (incl)
Rooms: 21 with private facilities
Bar Lunch 12.30 - 2 pm (a)
Dining Room/Restaurant Lunch 12.30 - 2 pm (b)
Dinner 7 - 9 pm (c)
Menu changes daily
Bed & breakfast from £34
Dinner B & B from £48

Fresh salmon and horseradish mousse with avocado pear and Highland oatcakes; a brace of boned quail baked with chestnut and orange stuffing, served in a port wine sauce. Rufflets raspberries in an almond cup with Drambuie cream on a coulis of summer fruits.

STB 4 Crown Commended

Credit cards: 1, 2, 3, 5

Proprietor: Ann Russell.

St Andrews Golf Hotel
40 The Scores
St Andrews
Fife, KY16 9AS
Tel: 0334 72611
Telex: 94013267
Fax: 0334 72188

Forth Bridge/M90, take A91 for St Andrews. Turn left for golf course.

Situated on the cliffs with magnificent views over the Links and St Andrews Bay, 200 yards from the world famous "Old Course". The building is Victorian, tastefully modernised with most comfortable bedrooms and elegant public rooms. Quality prints of the best of Scottish artists line the walls. The oak-panelled restaurant offers a fine selection of dishes prepared from the best of local produce and complemented by an extensive and carefully selected wine list. Golf arranging is a speciality, either using one of the hotel's packages or having a holiday tailored to your requirements. The hotel is family owned and run. Children welcome. Dogs accepted – small charge. Italian and some French spoken.

Open all year
Rooms: 23 with private facilities
Bar Lunch 12 - 2.30 pm (a)
Dining Room/Restaurant Lunch 12.30 - 2.30 pm Sun only (b)
Dinner 7 - 9.30 pm (c)
No smoking in restaurant
Bed & breakfast from £45
Dinner B & B from £56

Petite eclairs filled with a delicate trout mousse, served with a natural yoghurt and horseradish dressing; fresh Tay salmon poached in white wine, finished with orange and vermouth sauce; strips of Perthshire venison sauted with a julienne of fresh vegetables, served with smoked oysters.

STB 4 Crown Commended

Credit cards: 1, 2, 3, 5, 6

Proprietors: Maureen & Brian Hughes

Eastertown Farm
Sandilands
Lanark, ML11 9TX
Tel: 055588/286

2½ miles east from M74 taking A70 Edinburgh/Ayr exit.

Tastefully modernised traditional stone built farmhouse on working sheep farm, set in commanding situation in

▶

beautiful countryside. TV, tea/coffee-making facilities in all rooms. Seven miles from Lanark, convenient to M74 road link. Scottish Farmhouse of the Year Winner 1987.

~~Open all year~~

~~Rooms: 5, 2 with private facilities~~
~~Dinner at 6.30 pm (a)~~
~~Bed & breakfast rates on application~~
~~Dinner B & B from £18~~

~~Home-made Scottish dishes using home-produced lamb, pork and vegetables.~~

~~STB 2 Crown Highly Commended~~

~~No credit cards~~

~~Proprietor: Janet Tennant~~

[WITHDRAWN]

---

183 — SELKIRK — H7

Philipburn House Hotel
Selkirk
TD7 5LS
Tel: 0750 20747
Fax: 0750 21690

A707 Moffat-Peebles. 1 mile from A7.

Award winning country house hotel and restaurant, set in the heart of the romantic Scottish Borders. Imaginative bar meals, home-baked afternoon teas. 1751 Georgian house with swimming pool and five acres of beautiful grounds – garden gained "Grounds for Delight" Award 1989. Special breakaway packages available.

Open all year

Rooms: 16 with private facilities
Bar Lunch 12 - 2 pm (a)
Dining Room/Restaurant Lunch 12.30 - 2 pm (a)
Children's High Tea 5.30 - 6 pm
Dinner 7.30 - 9.30 pm (b)
No smoking area in restaurant
Bed & breakfast from £37
Dinner B & B from £44

Medallions of roe deer Monanie – with a blueberry sauce and poached pear. Fillet of Border lamb Philipburn – cooked rosy pink on a crisp potato galette with gooseberry and mint sauce.

STB 4 Crown Commended

Credit cards: 1, 2, 3, 5

Proprietors: Jim & Anne Hill

---

184 — SHETLAND ISLES OF — B9

Busta House Hotel
Busta
Brae
Shetland
ZE2 9QN
Tel: 080622 506
Fax: 080622 588

On the Muckle Roe road – 1 mile off the A970 Hillswick road.

The impressive but slightly severe external appearance of Busta House gives no hint of the charm and elegance of the interior. This is reputedly the oldest continuously inhabited building in Shetland and it enjoys a commanding site overlooking Busta Voe. The public rooms are impressive and have been furnished with good taste while the bedrooms have every thoughtful facility that one would except for caring hosts. The food lives up to the standard of the rest of the hotel concentrating on the plentiful harvest of good local produce from both land and sea, and there is a well chosen wine list and a stock of over 100 malt whiskies. Peter and Judith Jones can arrange holiday packages including flights or ferry from the UK mainland, and organise car hire, with a car to meet you at the airport or ferry terminal.

Open all year except 23 Dec to 3 Jan

Rooms: 21 with private facilities
Bar Lunch 12 - 2 pm (a)
Bar Supper 7 - 9.30 pm (a)
Dinner 7 - 9 pm (d)
No smoking in dining room
Bed & breakfast from £32.50
Dinner B & B from £45 (min. 3 nights stay)

Roast leg of Shetland lamb with blackcurrant and ginger wine sauce. Shetland salmon baked with oranges and fresh thyme. Supreme of chicken stuffed with prawns in puff pastry, served with a puree of red pepper.

STB 4 Crown Commended

Credit cards: 1, 2, 3, 5, 6

Proprietors: Peter & Judith Jones

Da Peerie Fisk
Busta, Brae
Shetland
ZE2 9QN
Tel: 080622 679

On west side of Busta Voe. Turn left off A970 onto Muckle Roe road and then after 600 yards first left again.

Da Peerie Fisk ("The Little Fish") is as its name suggests a restaurant devoted to local seafoods. It stands right on the shoreline and though the buildings have been recently converted, the site itself, as a trading post, goes back to Hanseatic times. It has been well fitted out and tastefully furnished and the owners are very much in evidence and pride themselves on the quality of their food. Probably the most northerly restaurant of its type in Britain, it is a welcome addition to quality catering in the Shetland Isles.

Open all year

Dinner 6.30 - 10 pm (c)
Facilities for the disabled
No smoking in restaurant

Lobster flamed with Drambuie. Shetland oysters and mussels. Monkfish tails in Dijon sauce. Halibut steaks and turbot with selected sauces.

Credit cards: 1, 2, 3, 5

Proprietors: Major & Mrs E G Wise

St Magnus Bay Hotel
Hillswick
Shetland
ZE2 9RW
Tel: 080623 372

36 miles north of Lerwick.

A timber clad Norwegian built hotel erected at the turn of the century with a more recently added extension. It occupies a splendidly dominating position in the village and must rank as one of the most northerly hotels in the British Isles. There is an impressive stairway and a comfortable pine-lined dining room with a separate coffee or supper room and a public bar. The chef relies heavily – and rightly – on a copious supply of fresh fish and local shellfish. Children are welcome.

Open all year

Rooms: 26 with private facilities
Bar Lunch 12.30 - 1.45 pm (a)
Dining Room/Restaurant Lunch 12.30 - 2 pm (b)
Dinner 7.30 - 8.45 pm (c)
Bed & breakfast £27 - £30
Dinner B & B £41.50 - £44.50

Fresh seafood – lobster, scallops, etc. Smoked salmon roulade with a creamy walnut sauce. Shetland lamb pan-fried with juniper berries. Sherry ginger log.

STB 3 Crown Approved

Credit cards: 1, 3, 6

Proprietors: Peter & Adrienne Titcomb

SKELMORLIE
185   **G4**

Manor Park Hotel
Skelmorlie
Ayrshire, PA17 5HE
Tel: 0475 520832

Off A78 halfway between Largs and Wemyss Bay piers.

Gracious Victorian manor situated in hillside overlooking Firth of Clyde. Panoramic views from all public rooms. Luxuriously furnished throughout. Hairdryer and tea-making facilities in bedrooms. First class cuisine. Unique cocktail bar with renowned malt whisky collection.

Open Mar to early Jan
Rooms: 23, 22 with private facilities
Bar Lunch 12.45 - 2.30 pm (a)
Dining Room/Restaurant Lunch 12.45 - 2.30 pm (b)
Dinner 7 - 9.30 pm (c)
Bed & breakfast from £44
Dinner B & B from £61
The best of local meat and fish predominate. Scampi Laphroaig, venison Macallan.
STB Award Pending
No credit cards
Proprietors: Alan Williams

SKYE
186   **ISLE OF**   **D3**

Ardvasar Hotel
Ardvasar, Sleat
Isle of Skye, IV45 8AS
Tel: 04714 223

Opposite Mallaig – ½ mile from Armadale ferry.

Small white, traditional, whitewashed stone building overlooking mountains and Sound of Sleat water to Mallaig. Cosy small rooms, sitting room with log fire. Traditionally furnished to give warm homely atmosphere.

Open Mar to Dec
Rooms: 10 with private facilities
Bar Lunch 12 - 2 pm (a)
Bar Supper 5 - 7 pm
Dinner 7.30 - 8.30 pm (c)
Bed & breakfast from £25
Dinner B & B from £36
Fresh lobster, scallops, prawns. Princess scallops. All locally caught – on availability. Daily changing menus.
Credit cards: 3
Proprietors: Bill & Gretta Fowler

Atholl House Hotel
Dunvegan
Isle of Skye
IV55 8WA
Tel: 047 022 219

A863 Dunvegan Village.

Family run hotel in the village of Dunvegan with magnificent views of mountains and loch. The tastefully decorated bedrooms, all have colour TV, direct dial telephones, tea/coffee-making facilities and duvets. Ideal centre for touring the Isle of Skye.

Open all year except Nov
Rooms: 9, 7 with private facilities
Morning Coffee 10 - 11.30 am:
Dining Room/Restaurant Lunch 12 - 2 pm (a)
Afternoon Tea 3 - 5 pm
Dinner 7 - 9.30 pm (c)
Restricted licence
No smoking in restaurant
Bed & breakfast £23.50 - £28
Dinner B & B £38.50 - £43
Scottish beef steaks, local seafoods. Skye lamb, trout and venison. Home-made soups and sweets. Highland wines, jellies and cheeses.
STB 3 Crown Commended
Credit cards: 1, 3
Proprietors: Cliff & Barbara Ashton

Glenview Inn
Culnacnoc
by Portree
Isle of Skye
IV51 9JH
Tel: 047 062 248

13 miles north of Portree on A855.

Fine example of a traditional Skye house, pleasantly converted to a small and friendly family run inn, north of Portree in one of the loveliest areas of Skye. The proprietors take great enjoyment in their cooking and helping guests' waistlines expand in comfort. Calorie counters beware!

Open Easter to end Oct
Rooms: 6, 4 with private facilities
Bar Lunch 12.30 - 2.30 pm (a)
Dinner from 8 pm (c)
Bed & breakfast from £22
Dinner B & B from £38
Fresh bread with unusual soups; rich pâtés; skewered scallops, roast lobsters and Skye oysters; whiskied steaks; crab stuffed chicken; calorie-laden puddings.
STB 4 Crown Commended
Credit cards: 1, 3
Proprietors: Harper Family

Harlosh Hotel
by Dunvegan
Isle of Skye
IV55 8ZG
Tel: 047 022 367

4 miles south of Dunvegan off A863.

Perfectly positioned on the shores of Loch Caroy the Harlosh commands one of the finest views of the Cuillins, MacLeods Tables and the Islands of Loch Bracadale. This small cosy hotel offers an elegant but homely atmosphere with an emphasis on peace and tranquillity.

Open Easter to Oct
Rooms: 8, 2 with private facilities
Dinner 6.30 - 9 pm (a-b)
No dogs
No smoking area in restaurant
Bed & breakfast from £21
Dinner B & B from £32
Local fish and shellfish – fresh whenever possible on a constantly changing menu dependent on what is available. Cooked sympathetically to any requirement.
STB 2 Crown Commended
Credit cards: 1, 3
Proprietor: Peter Elford

Kinloch Lodge
Sleat
Isle of Skye
IV43 8QY
Tel: 047 13 214

6 miles south of Broadford on A851 and 8 miles north of Armadale on A851.

Kinloch Lodge is an isolated converted shooting lodge at the south end of the island. It is set a mile from the main road at the foot of a mountain at the head of a sea loch. Spectacular panoramic views of the mainland at one side and the Cuillin range at the other. Personally run by Lord and Lady Macdonald.

Open Mar to mid Jan except 11 to 27 Dec
Rooms: 10 with private facilities
Dinner from 8 pm (c)
Residents only
Bed & breakfast £35 - £48
Dinner B & B £56 - £70
Lady Macdonald pays particular attention to the food served both at breakfast and on the small dinner menus, using the very best of the wide range of ingredients available locally.
Credit cards: 1, 3
Proprietors: Lord & Lady Macdonald

Portree House

Home Farm Road
Portree
Isle of Skye, IV51 9LX
Tel: 0478 2796

5 minutes walk from the centre of Portree village.

Bar/Restaurant within Georgian mansion house with views over Portree Loch to the Cuillins – open all year round to residents and non-residents, serving lunches and evening meals seven days a week. Families welcome – large garden area including children's playground. Five self-catering cottages available.

Open all year

Bar Lunch 12 - 4.30 pm: 12 - 2.30 pm Winter (a)
Dinner 5.30 - 10 pm (a)

Home-made soups, pâté and delicious real ice-cream. Local fish, Highland venison, Aberdeen Angus steaks, Ross-shire lamb – all beautifully served with freshly baked potatoes.

No credit cards

Proprietors: N & M Wilson &
                P & F Gooch

Skeabost House Hotel

Skeabost Bridge
Isle of Skye, IV51 9NP
Tel: 047 032 202

4 miles north of Portree on Dunvegan road.

Turning into the drive to Skeabost House is like entering a new world. In direct contrast to the stark countryside around it, Skeabost is an oasis of cultivated serenity. A former hunting lodge, this delightful country house hotel stands in 12 acres of secluded woodlands and garden, wonderfully positioned on the shore of Loch Snizort. This is a comfortable and relaxing family run hotel with good lounges, a billiard room, cocktail bar and an attractive restaurant. The staff go all out to make guests welcome and to attend to their every need and the chefs make good use of an abundance of fresh produce from sea and farm.

Open Apr to mid Oct

Rooms: 26 with private facilities
Bar Lunch 12 - 1.30 pm (a)
Buffet Lunch 12 - 1.30 pm (a)
Dinner 7 - 8 pm (a)
Bed & breakfast £31 - £40
Dinner B & B £45 - £54
Fresh salmon, venison, Skye lamb.
STB 4 Crown Commended
No credit cards
Proprietors: Stuart/McNab/Stuart

Three Chimneys Restaurant

Colbost
nr Dunvegan
Isle of Skye
IV51 9SY
Tel: 047 081 258 (Glendale)

4 miles west of Dunvegan on B884 road to Glendale. Look out for Glendale Visitor Route signs.

Very old crofter's cottage with cosy, candlelit, stone-walled interior, beamed ceilings and open fires. Widely acclaimed restaurant, close by the sea on the shores of Loch Dunvegan. Remote and beautiful spot on scenic road to Glendale and most westerly point of Skye. Spectacular views and glorious sunsets over the Outer Isles. Excellent accommodation within walking distance, as well as in and around Dunvegan village. Macallan/Decanter Restaurant of the Year 1990.

Open Easter to mid Oct

Dining Room/Restaurant Lunch 12.30 - 2 pm (a)
Dinner from 7 pm (b)
Closed Sun
No smoking in restaurant

Local shellfish – fresh Skye oysters, langoustine and lobster; fresh fish and wild Skye salmon; fresh Scottish beef, lamb and venison dishes, including steaks; vegetarian selection.

Credit cards: 1, 3

Proprietors: Eddie & Shirley Spear

Ullinish Lodge Hotel

Struan
Isle of Skye
IV56 8FD
Tel: 047 072 214

Off A863 between Sligachan and Dunvegan.

18th century country house beautifully set overlooking the Cuillins and the shores of Loch Bracadale. Ideally situated for walking and climbing. Brown trout fishing in the three lochs, salmon fishing in two rivers. Rough shooting over 27,500 acres. John and Claudia Mulford are welcoming hosts. There is a pleasant restaurant with a no smoking area and a large lounge with open fire for the cooler evenings. The bedrooms are tastefully decorated and traditionally furnished. The menu is changed every day and usually features a mixed bag throughout the week, with at least four main dishes each evening from which to choose. John is also willing, given a little notice, to cook any specially requested dish in the range on any other day. The hotel has a fine range of malt

whiskies and a good selection of wine including a range of Scottish wines and liqueurs. German spoken.

Open Easter to mid Oct

Rooms: 8, 6 with private facilities
Dining Room/Restaurant Lunch 12 - 2 pm (a)
Bar Supper 6 - 9 pm (a)
Dinner 7 - 9 pm (c-e) or by arrangement
No smoking area in restaurant
Bed & breakfast from £25.50
Dinner B & B £40 - £45

Venison in red wine; pheasant with redcurrants and walnuts; Bracadale scallops in Talisker sauce and dressed crab. House speciality – seafood dish for two, featuring lobster, local prawns and a range of local shellfish.

STB 3 Crown ~~Approved~~   Commended
No credit cards

Proprietors: John & Claudia Mulford

Chapeltoun House Hotel

Stewarton
Ayrshire
KA3 3ED
Tel: 0560 82696

On B769 Stewarton-Irvine road (access via A77 Glasgow-Kilmarnock road).

Chapeltoun – a gracious country house hotel set in beautiful Ayrshire countryside. The hotel has an inviting restaurant renowned for its excellent cuisine and service complemented by an extensive cellar of fine wines. The chef selects only the finest fresh produce to create interesting and appetising menus.

Open all year except first 2 wks Jan

Rooms: 8 with private facilities
Bar Lunch 12 - 2 pm (a)
Dining Room/Restaurant Lunch 12.30 - 2 pm (c)
Dinner 7 - 9.15 pm (e)
Bed & breakfast £42.50 - £65
Dinner B & B £62.50 - £85

Best of local meat, fish, game and vegetables.

STB 4 Crown Highly Commended

Credit cards: 1, 2, 3

Proprietors: Colin & Graeme McKenzie

The Topps Farm
Fintry Road
Denny
Stirlingshire
FK6 5JF
Tel: 0324 822471

On B818 Denny-Fintry road, off M80.

New farmhouse in superb scenic position. Working sheep and cashmere goat farm in easy reach of Glasgow, Edinburgh, Perth, Trossachs and Loch Lomond. Fishing, walking. Nine and 18 hole golf courses nearby. Also horse riding by arrangement. Non-smokers only.

Open all year
Rooms: 8 with private facilities
Dinner from 7 pm (b)
Residents only
No smoking throughout
Bed & breakfast from £15
Dinner B & B from £25

Breakfast trout, porridge, local haggis, black pudding, etc. Glenmorangie gateau, rosewater meringues. Grumphies and neeps. Roast garlic lamb.

STB 3 Crown Commended

No credit cards

Proprietors: Jennifer & Alistair Steel

Tolbooth Restaurant
Old Pier
Stonehaven Harbour
Stonehaven
Tel: 0569 62287

Off A92, 10 miles south of Aberdeen.

Situated in 16th century old building, the Tolbooth is the oldest building in Stonehaven, with picturesque views of Stonehaven harbour. This restaurant specialises in seafood. There is a permanent exhibition of Royal Scottish Academy artists on the whitewashed stone walls. Afghan rugs enhance the beautifully polished wooden floors.

Open Apr to Dec

Closed Christmas to Easter

Dining Room/Restaurant Lunch 12 - 2.30 pm except Mon (b)
Dinner 7 - 9.30 pm except Mon (d)
Apr to Oct open Tue to Sun
Weekday lunches from Jun
Nov + Dec open weekends only

North sea bouillabaisse – local fish, mussels and prawns simmered in a saffron broth, Orkney scallops, langoustines, oysters, lobster, turbot, halibut. Vegetarian and meat dishes also available. Organic herbs and vegetables used.

Credit cards: 1, 3

Proprietor: Moya Bothwell

The Creggans Inn
Strachur
Argyll, PA27 8BX
Tel: 0369 86 279
Fax: 0369 86 637

1½ hours from Glasgow on A83 then A815.

This is an inn with a difference! The food is superb and the atmosphere in the friendly comfortable luncheon bars delightful. At night in the pretty dining room looking down the loch, dinner is more formal, with a large selection of original Scottish country house dishes from Lady MacLean's cookbooks.

Open all year
Rooms: 21, 17 with private facilities
Bar Lunch 12.30 - 2.15 pm (a)
Dinner 7.30 - 9.30 pm (d)
Bed & breakfast from £40
Dinner B & B from £54

Loch Fyne oysters, smoked salmon, local lobster, mussels, prawns and kippers.

STB 3 Crown Commended

Credit cards: 1, 2, 3, 5, 6
Proprietors: Sir Fitzroy MacLean,
The Hon Lady MacLean &
Charles E MacLean

The Bay House Restaurant & Bar
Cairnryan Road
Stranraer
Wigtownshire, DG9 8AT
Tel: 0776 3786

Overlooking Loch Ryan on A77 – ½ mile from Sealink Ferry terminal, Stranraer.

Bay House Restaurant – originally the golf clubhouse – is situated on the shores of Loch Ryan. This family owned and run establishment welcomes children and aims to cater for individual tastes and appetites.

Open all year
Bar Lunch 12 - 2.15 pm (a)
Bar Supper 6 - 9.15 pm (a)
Dinner 6 - 9.15 pm (b)
No meals served on New Year's Day
Facilities for the disabled
Credit cards: 1, 2, 3, 6
Proprietor: T Pearson

North West Castle Hotel
Portrodie
Stranraer
DG9 8EH
Tel: 0776 4413
Telex: 777088
Fax: 0776 2646

Seafront – opposite harbour.

Anyone who has ever travelled on the Stranraer-Larne ferry – and thousands who have not – will know and love the North West Castle Hotel. A superbly managed resort hotel which seems to incorporate everything that anyone could possibly want. In its own grounds overlooking the harbour it has an indoor swimming pool, jacuzzi, multi-gym, saunas, sunbeds, bowls, a curling rink, table tennis, darts, pool, snooker. It naturally follows that the bedrooms have colour TVs, radio, trouser press, hairdryer and coffee-making facilities. For those on inclusive rates there is even free golf at two local courses. A pianist plays during dinner.

Open all year
Rooms: 78 with private facilities
Bar Lunch 12 - 2 pm (a)
Dining Room/Restaurant Lunch 12 - 2.30 pm (b)
Dinner 7 - 9.30 pm (c)
Bed & breakfast from £33
Dinner B & B from £45

Smoked salmon cornet filled with prawns. Fillet of beef Wellington. Poached escalope of Cree salmon Hollandaise. Vegetarian dishes available.

STB 5 Crown Commended

No credit cards

Best Town Hotel 1989

Proprietor: H C McMillan

STRATHLACHLAN
192   G4

Inver Cottage Restaurant
Strathlachlan
by Cairndow
Argyll
PA27 8BU
Tel: 036 986 396/275

B8000, 6 miles past Strachur.

Rosemary MacInnes has established an excellent little restaurant in delightful surroundings on the shores of Loch Fyne overlooking the ruins of old Castle Lachlan. A charming hostess, she makes everyone warmly welcome and the staff take their cue from her. There is a nice relaxed atmosphere about this place with its open log and peat fires, and it is very much a pleasant place to tarry.

Open Mar to Oct
Bar Lunch 11.30 am - 2.30 pm (a)
Dining Room/Restaurant Lunch 11.30 am - 2.30 pm (a)
Dinner 6 - 10 pm (b)
Wide variety of home-made bar meals. In the evenings also an à la carte menu specialising in local seafood. Only fresh produce used. Renowned for its pudding trolley, home-made tablet and truffles.
Credit card: 3
Proprietor: Rosemary MacInnes

STRATHYRE
193   F5

Creagan House
Strathyre
Perthshire
FK18 8ND
Tel: 087 74 638

On A84, ¼ mile north of Strathyre.

In a lovely country setting, Creagan is a family owned 17th century farmhouse with five charming bedrooms. The baronial dining hall with its grand open fire provides a unique setting in which to enjoy good food and fine wines. A mixture of experience, caring and friendliness contribute to your enjoyment.

Open Mar to Jan
Rooms: 5, 3 with private facilities
Dining Room/Restaurant Lunch from 1 pm Sun only (b)
Lunch parties on other days by arrangement
Dinner 7.30 - 8.30 pm (b-c)
Booking essential for all meals
No smoking in dining hall or bedrooms
Bed & breakfast £17.50 - £21.50
Dinner B & B £28 - £32
Mushrooms Dunsyre, ragout of seafood, venison Beananach, wee collops. Flora McDonald steamed pudding, strawberry and chestnut roulade.
Credit cards: 1, 3
Proprietors: Gordon & Cherry Gunn

STRONTIAN
194   E3

Kilcamb Lodge Hotel
Strontian
North Argyll
PH36 4HY
Tel: 0967 2257

Strontian, south-west of Fort William.

A family run country house hotel, owned and managed by John and Suzanne Bradbury, situated in 30 acres of secluded grounds on the shores of Loch Sunart facing south. The house is a former 18th century hunting lodge and former home of Fraser Darling, the naturalist and author. Natural lawns slope gently down to the waters edge with the Morvern Hills rising steeply in the background. Most of the bedrooms have a loch view and all have their own facilities. Ideally situated for hill-walking, fishing, bird-watching and most other outdoor pursuits.

Open Easter to Oct
Rooms: 9 with private facilities
Bar Lunch 12.30 - 1.45 pm (a)
Dinner from 7.30 pm (d)
No smoking in restaurant
Bed & breakfast from £35
Dinner B & B from £45
Traditional cuisine prepared from locally caught seafood and game, with fresh fruit and vegetables.
STB 3 Crown Commended
No credit cards
Proprietors: John & Suzanne Bradbury

Loch Sunart Hotel
Strontian
Argyll
PH36 4HZ
Tel: 0967 2471

A82 to Corran Ferry. A861 to Strontian.

Delightful, family run 18th century country house, overlooking loch in a magnificent area. An ideal base for touring, walking, bird-watching or just "getting away from it all". Take advantage of the 4/7 day breaks. Reduced rates for children.

Open Easter to Oct
Rooms: 11, 10 with private facilities
Bar Lunch 12 - 2 pm (a)
Bar Supper 7.30 - 8.45 pm
Dinner 7 - 7.30 pm (c)
Facilities for the disabled
No smoking in restaurant
Bed & breakfast from £22
Dinner B & B from £38
Renowned for home-cooking to a high standard of both traditional and unusual dishes. Specialities include soups and ice-cream.
STB 3 Crown Commended
No credit cards
Proprietors: Peter & Mildred Renton

TAIN
195   D6

Morangie House Hotel
Morangie Road
Tain
Ross-shire, IV19 1PY
Tel: 0862 2281

Just off A9 Inverness-Wick road.

A fine old Victorian mansion set on the northern outskirts of the Highland town of Tain, Scotland's oldest Royal Burgh. The hotel has been extensively modernised but still maintains the character of the building with its superb collection of Victorian stained glass windows. Award winning chefs prepare meals unsurpassed in the area and served by the friendly but efficient staff.

Open all year
Rooms: 11 with private facilities
Bar Lunch 12 - 2.30 pm (a)
Dining Room/Restaurant Lunch 12 - 2.30 pm (b)
Bar Supper 5 - 10 pm (a)
Dinner 7 - 10 pm (d)
No dogs
Bed & breakfast £22 - £35
Dinner B & B £36 - £49

►

Extensive à la carte menu specialising in local beef and seafood dishes. Mussel and onion stew. Beef Wellington. Game soup. Lobster thermidor. Moules mariniere.

STB 4 Crown Commended

Credit cards: 1, 2, 3, 5

Proprietor: John Wynne

TARBERT
196   G3

The Anchorage Restaurant
Quayside, Harbour Street
Tarbert
Argyll
PA29 6UD
Tel: 0880 820881

On A83 – situated on Tarbert quayside.

Unique restaurant on the quayside at Tarbert not far from Tarbert Castle. Seafood is the order of the day offering a good selection from Arran, Islay, Gigha, Jura and numerous other places along the west coast. The owner personally selects fish from the evening sale on the quayside. The restaurant also has a direct line to a fishing boat for a resumé of the day's catch.

Open Mar to Dec

Dining Room/Restaurant Lunch 11.30 am - 2.30 pm (a)
Dinner 6.45 - 10.30 pm (b-c)
Closed Sun + Mon
Facilities for the disabled

Seafood is the speciality of this restaurant, all personally selected, direct from boat and the quayside. Brought in from Kintyre and the islands. Aberdeen Angus beef. Vegetarian dishes available.

Credit cards: 1, 3

Proprietors: David & Fiona Evamy

The Columba Hotel
East Pier Road
Tarbert
Argyll
PA29 6UF
Tel: 0880 820808

On East Pier Road, ½ mile to the left around harbour.

Superbly positioned at entrance to Tarbert Harbour. Warm, comfortable lounge bar with log fire, providing good wholesome bar meals daily. Restaurant with beautiful views over Loch Fyne. Menus with emphasis on local produce – shellfish, venison, locally supplied fish and fresh vegetables. Twelve bedrooms centrally heated, sauna, mini-gym, solarium.

Open all year

Rooms: 12, 9 with private facilities
Bar Lunch 12 - 2 pm (a)
Bar Supper 6 - 7.30 pm (a)
Dinner 7 - 9 pm (c)
Dinner not available Mon to Thu, 1 Nov to Easter
Bed & breakfast from £17.50
Dinner B & B from £32.50

Lobster and king prawns – when available. Jura venison, local fish, only fresh vegetables.

STB 3 Crown Approved

Credit cards: 1, 2, 3, 5

Proprietor: E Davison

THORNHILL
197   H6

Trigony House Hotel
Closeburn
Thornhill
Dumfriesshire
DG3 5EZ
Tel: 0848 31211

A76 – 13 miles north of Dumfries.

Trigony makes an excellent base for exploring this magnificent untouched part of Scotland. An attractive secluded country house hotel situated just off A76 in over four acres of secluded gardens and woodlands. The hotel has a friendly and welcoming atmosphere together with high standards of comfort and hospitality. Children over 10 welcome.

Open all year

Rooms: 9 with private facilities
Bar Lunch 12 - 2 pm (a)
Bar Supper 6.30 - 9 pm
Dinner 7 - 8.30 pm (b)
No children under 10
Bed & breakfast £25 - £29.50

Roast Galloway beef, local pheasant and venison, Nith salmon.

STB 4 Crown Commended

Credit cards: 1, 3

Proprietors: Frank & Mary Kerr

TIREE
198   ISLE OF   F2

The Glassary
Sandaig
Isle of Tiree
Argyll
PA77 6XQ
Tel: 08792 684

West coast of island.

Restaurant situated on the picturesque west coast of the island close to white, sandy beaches. Adjacent is the guest house which is all on one level and has a residents' lounge with TV, and tea/coffee-making facilities. The restaurant is a pine-lined converted byre with panoramic views of shore and Atlantic Ocean.

Restaurant open Easter to Oct
Guest house open all year

Rooms: 3
Dining Room/Restaurant Lunch 12 - 2 pm (a-b)
Dinner 7 - 9 pm (b-d)
Bed & breakfast from £13
Dinner B & B from £20

Extensive and imaginative à la carte menu, using Isle of Tiree reared beef and lamb, wild salmon from Mull and Atlantic seafood. Interesting sweet menu, features Carrageen pudding – a traditional island recipe, made from local seaweed.

STB Listed Approved

No credit cards

Proprietors: Mabel & Donny Macarthur

TORRANYARD
199   NEAR IRVINE   G4

Montgreenan Mansion House Hotel
Montgreenan Estate
Torranyard, Kilwinning
Ayrshire
KA13 7QZ
Tel: 0294 57733
Telex: 778525.

Off A736 Glasgow-Irvine road near Torranyard.

The character of this former country seat has remained gracious with the history of the estate dating back to 1310. All the late 18th century features, including attractive marble and brass fireplaces, decorative ceilings and plaster work, have been retained. Montgreenan has a heliport facility and a snooker room, tennis court, lawn croquet and golf course.

Open all year   ▶

Rooms: 16 with private facilities
Bar Lunch 12 - 2.30 pm (a)
Dining Room/Restaurant Lunch 12 -
2.30 pm (a)
Dinner 7 - 10 pm (c)
Bed & breakfast £44 - £100
Dinner B & B £50 - £69

*Scottish lobster Montgreenan,
Montgreenan game and whisky pie.
Locally caught salmon, trout and shellfish.*

STB 4 Crown Commended

Credit cards: 1, 2, 3, 5, 6

Proprietors: The Dobson Family

TROON
200   **G4**

Marine Highland Hotel
Troon
Ayrshire
KA10 6HE
Tel: 0292 314444
Telex: 777595
Fax: 0292 316922

*South end of Troon overlooking golf
course and sea.*

This magnificent four star hotel overlooks
the 18th fairway of Royal Troon
Championship Golf Course with
breathtaking views across the Firth of
Clyde to the Isle of Arran. An atmosphere
of quiet elegance exists throughout the
hotel combined with a standard of service
and hospitality second to none. The
Marine Leisure & Sports Club is a first
class addition to the present facilities. A
very special hotel which has admirably
blended style and tradition with
outstanding facilities.

Open all year

Rooms: 72 with private facilities
Crosbie's Brasserie open all day for meals
and snacks
Bar Lunch 12 - 3 pm (a)
Dining Room/Restaurant Lunch 12 -
3 pm (a)
Dinner 6 - 11 pm (c)
Bed & breakfast from £70
Dinner B & B from £65 (min. 2 nights stay)

*Wild boar, local wild salmon, fresh
scallops, Scotch lamb, fresh vegetables.*

STB 5 Crown Commended

Credit cards: 1, 2, 3, 5

Piersland House Hotel
Craig End Road
Troon
Ayrshire
KA10 6HD
Tel: 0292 314747

South corner of Troon.

Piersland House, built c.1899, for Sir
Alexander Walker of Johnnie Walker
whisky fame. Set in four acres of grounds
– the gardens and interior wood panelling
are special features. During 1990 a new
country house style Dining Room was
opened, in keeping with the period nature
of the Listed building. The hotel has
always had a good reputation for its food
and the new menu introduced to
complement the Dining Room conversion
should enhance this even further.

Open all year.

Rooms: 19 with private facilities
Bar Lunch 12 - 2 pm (a)
Dining Room/Restaurant Lunch 12 -
2 pm (a-b)
Afternoon Tea 3 - 5 pm
Bar Suppers 5 - 10 pm
Dinner 7 - 9.30 pm (c-d)
Bed & breakfast from £41
Dinner B & B rates on application

*A la carte includes fish and shellfish,
chicken supreme, collops in the pan. Bar
meals include local Ayrshire ham,
gammon, salmon, lamb and beef.*

STB 4 Crown Commended

Credit cards: 1, 2, 3, 5, 6

Proprietor: J A Brown

TURNBERRY
201   **H4**

Malin Court Hotel
Turnberry
Girvan
Ayrshire
KA26 9PB
Tel: 0655 31457/8

On A719 south of Maidens.

Situated between Ayr and Girvan, on the
west coast of Scotland and ideal for
touring the 'Burns Trail'. Central to a lot of
major golf courses, including the famous
Turnberry. All bedrooms have full
amenities, including colour television and
full central heating. Table d'hôte or full à la
carte menus are available in the splendid
restaurant with an excellent view of Arran
and the hills beyond. Fully refurbished.

Open all year

Rooms: 8 with private facilities
Bar Lunch 12.30 - 2.30 pm (a)
Dining Room/Restaurant Lunch 12.30 -
2.30 pm (a)
Afternoon Tea 2 - 5 pm
Dinner 7.30 - 9.30 pm (b)
Bed & breakfast £27.95 - £31.95
Dinner B & B £40 -£47

*Hotel enjoys more or less all year round
availability of fresh local beef, lamb and
pork, salmon and fresh sea produce.*

STB 4 Crown Commended

Credit cards: 1, 2, 3, 5, 6

The Turnberry Hotel &
Golf Courses
Turnberry
Ayrshire
KA26 9LT
Tel: 0655 31000
Telex: 777779
Fax: 0655 31706

A77-17 miles south of Ayr.

Turnberry Hotel is situated overlooking
Scotland's south-west Ayrshire coast.
Within its 360 acres are a luxury 115
bedroom hotel, two championship golf
courses, all weather tennis courts,
swimming pool and a billiards room
amongst other amenities. The excellent
restaurant combines elegance and
gracious service with most magical views
of Ailsa Craig and Arran.

Open all year

Rooms: 115 with private facilities
Bar meals served in Clubhouse all day
Dining Room/Restaurant Lunch 1 -
2.30 pm (b-c)
High Tea served in the Clubhouse
Dinner 7.30 - 9.30 pm (d-f)
Bed & breakfast rates on application
Dinner B & B rates on application

*Collops of venison with a farce of
hazelnuts and two sauces.*

Credit cards: 1, 2, 3, 5, 6

Best Hotel 1990

Clifton Coffee House & Craft Centre
Tyndrum
Perthshire FK20 8RY
Tel: 08384 271
Fax: 08384 330

On A85 just east of junction with A82.

A popular staging post at the eastern end of Glen Coe. A family run roadside restaurant and shopping complex surrounded by scenic splendour. The busy self-service restaurant has special facilities for the disabled and there are adjacent shops in which to browse.

Open mid Mar to late Dec

Meals and snacks served all day from end Mar to end Dec (a)
No smoking area in restaurant
No dogs except guide dogs

Fresh local produce, vegetables, salmon, brought together to give good food at budget prices.

Credit cards: 1, 2, 3, 5

Proprietors: L P Gosden,
          D D, L V & I L Wilkie

Udny Green Hotel
Udny Green
nr Ellon
Aberdeenshire
AB41 0RS
Tel: 06513 2337

Off B999 north of Aberdeen.

An 18th century family run hotel in the conservation village of Udny Green, priding itself in superb freshly prepared food from local sources and a very personal and friendly service. Udny Green is a good touring base for nearby fishing, National Trust properties, golf, whisky and castle trails, and also the beach.

Open all year except Christmas Day + New Year's Day

Rooms: 2, 1 with private facilities
Bar Lunch 12 - 2 pm (a)
Dining Room/Restaurant Lunch 12 - 2 pm (a)
Bar Supper 6 - 9.30 pm (a)
Dinner 7 - 9.30 pm: 7 - 10 pm Sat (b)
No dogs
Bed & breakfast from £20
Dinner B & B from £30

Chicken in white wine and cream. Fresh salmon in lime butter. Strips of rump steak in red wine sauce.

STB 2 Crown Commended
Credit cards: 1, 3
Proprietors: David & Maureen Mitchell

Houstoun House Hotel
Uphall
West Lothian
EH52 6JS
Tel: 0506 853831

Just off A89 (Edinburgh-Bathgate) at Uphall.

This 16th century Tower House stands in its own 26 acres of grounds, with the dining room in the old part of the building. The best of Scottish produce is used to create daily changing menus, with herbs and vegetables from the garden. An extensive wine list is offered to complement your meal, whilst there is also an excellent range of malt whiskies in the vaulted bar.

Open all year except 1 + 2 Jan (incl)

Rooms: 30 with private facilities
Dining Room/Restaurant Lunch 12.30 - 2pm (c)
Dinner 7.30 - 9.30 pm (e)
No smoking dining room available
Bed & breakfast £80 - £120
Dinner B & B from £50 (weekend break)

Crayfish and scallops with a leek tartlet on a basil flavoured sauce. Creative desserts.

STB 4 Crown Commended
Credit cards: 1, 2, 3, 5, 6

Tweed Valley Hotel & Restaurant
Walkerburn
nr Peebles
EH43 6AA
Tel: 089 687 636
Fax: 089 687 639

A72 at Walkerburn – 7 miles east of Peebles and 7 miles west of Galashiels. 32 miles south of Edinburgh.

A complete Taste of Scotland awaits you with scenic views overlooking the River Tweed and hills. After sightseeing or country pursuits, including fishing, golf and bird-watching, log fires in the lounge add that extra glow while you quietly relax with a drink before enjoying à la carte dishes including local trout, salmon and game.

Open all year

Rooms: 15 with private facilities
Bar Lunch 12 - 2 pm (a-b)
Dining Room/Restaurant Lunch 12 - 2 pm (a-c)
Dinner 7 - 9.30 pm (b-c)
No smoking in restaurant
Bed & breakfast from £33
Dinner B & B from £39.50

Trout, salmon, venison and game dishes including grouse, pheasant, duck in season and as available.

STB 4 Crown Commended
Credit cards: 1, 3
Proprietor: Charles Miller

The Leadburn Inn
Leadburn
West Linton
Peeblesshire
EH46 7BE
Tel: 0968 72952

On junction of A701, A702 and A720.

Small family run hotel, set in beautiful countryside between Edinburgh and the Borders. One of the oldest inns in Scotland – records date back to August 1777. A menu which is as extensive as any in the Borders is served all day in the lounge, the conservatory or the bar. In the evening, dinner is served in the attractive Carriage Restaurant – a luxuriously converted railway carriage. Carefully planned table d'hôte menu includes a selection of traditional Scottish dishes.

Open all year except 25 to 27 Dec + 1 to 3 Jan

Rooms: 6, 2 with private facilities
Bar meals 12 - 6 pm (a)
Dining Room/Restaurant Lunch 12 - 6 pm (a)
High Tea/Supper 6 - 10 pm (a-b)
Dinner 6 - 10 pm (a)
Bed & breakfast £15 - £20
Dinner B & B rates on application

Local game and fish a speciality.

STB Listed Commended
Credit cards: 1, 2, 3, 5, 6
Proprietors: Linda & Alan Thomson

WHITEBRIDGE
207   **E5**

Knockie Lodge
Whitebridge
Inverness-shire
IV1 2UP
Tel: 045 63 276

*On B862 – 8 miles north of Fort Augustus.
26 miles south of Inverness.*

This is one of those delightful away-from-it-all places that make one reluctant to return to the bustle of ordinary life. Formerly a shooting lodge it is now a comfortable country house hotel, and Ian and Brenda Milward go to so much trouble to make their guests feel comfortable and at home. A splendidly relaxing place with excellent public rooms including a reading/writing room and billiard room. It is set high above Loch Ness and the surrounding scenery is superb. A stay here really is an exceptional experience.

Open Apr to Oct

Rooms: 10 with private facilities
Dinner from 8 pm (e)
Booking essential for non-residents
Restricted licence
No smoking in dining room
Dinner B & B £60 - £85

STB 3 Crown Highly Commended

Credit cards: 1, 2, 3

Best Country House Hotel 1990

Proprietors: Ian & Brenda Milward

WORMIT
208   **F7**

Sandford Hill Hotel
nr Wormit
Newport-on-Tay
Fife
DD6 8RG
Tel: 0382 541802

Junction of A914 and B946.

Conveniently situated between St Andrews and Dundee, close to road which links the Tay and Forth Bridges, this picturesque country house hotel was designed by London architect Baillie Scott in a style unique to the area. Quaint narrow corridors lead to bright modernised bedrooms, most with views over the six acres of gardens. The open air courtyard restaurant with old fashioned wishing well is popular in summer.

Open all year except 1 + 2 Jan

Rooms: 15, 13 with private facilities
Bar Lunch 12 - 2 pm (a)
Dining Room/Restaurant Lunch 12 - 2 pm (b)
Bar Supper 5 - 6.45 pm except Sun + Sat, and 9 - 10 pm except Sat (a)
Dinner 7 - 9 pm (c)
Bed & breakfast £30 - £42
Dinner B & B £35 - £50

Soups – mussel and onion – cock-a-leekie; Fife coast fish, sole, local lamb, game – pheasant, duck, pigeon, venison, grouse – all in season. Hot chocolate cheese cake and nutty fudge pie.

STB 3 Crown Commended

Credit cards: 1, 2, 3, 5

Proprietor: A B Robertson

Carradale Hotel

CARRADALE, ARGYLL, SCOTLAND PA28 6RY
Telephone: Carradale (05833) 223

Our brochure is only a phone call away!

Standing in its own gardens high above the quaint fishing harbour our family-owned hotel offers you a unique combination of personal friendly service, great dining experiences and a host of modern hotel amenities. Visit us in 1991 and be enchanted by Carradale's beautiful hills, glens and beaches!

If sport is your forte, indoors and outdoors there's always lots to do at Carradale – the hotel even boasts its own indoor leisure centre, featuring two international standard glass-backed squash courts, sauna, solarium and table tennis. Outdoors, the scenic and challenging 9-hole golf course has its first tee right alongside the hotel and we can arrange river and sea fishing, pony trekking and dinghy sailing at a moment's notice to name but a few!

Children are especially welcome here at Carradale Hotel, and of course there is no accommodation charge for them when sharing a family room or suite with their parents.

Finally watch out for some great value packages in 1991 – details available in our brochure!

See entry page . . . 54

Clonyard House Hotel

Colvend, Dalbeattie, Dumfries & Galloway
Tel: Rockcliffe (055 663) 372
Proprietors: Mr and Mrs J. Thompson

A Victorian Country House, set in seven acres of wooded grounds in the centre of John Paul Jones country and 14 miles from Dumfries with its many associations with the poet Robert Burns.
We offer modern and traditional bedrooms, all with bath or shower en suite, direct dial telephones, TV and tea-making facilities. Six bedrooms are on the ground floor with private patios overlooking the garden.
Our excellent licensed restaurant specialises in home cooked Scottish produce, and we also serve bar meals in our pleasant lounge bar which is a meeting place for locals and visitors. We also cater for children with safe grounds and an "Enchanted Play Tree".

Please write or telephone for further information and brochure.

AA** STB 4 Crown Commended RAC**

See entry page . . . 56

Fine Food

in the unique Pagoda Room,
a supreme dining experience.

Luncheons, by reservation only.
Dinners, group reservations only.

Glenturret Distillery Limited
The Hosh, Crieff, Perthshire
Scotland, PH7 4HA.
Telephone: 0764 2424   Fax: 0764 4366

See entry page . . . 58

SCOTLAND'S OLDEST DISTILLERY
and AWARD-WINNING VISITOR CENTRE

The GLENTURRET

* Scotland's Oldest Highland Malt Distillery.
* Award-Winning Visitors Heritage Centre.
* Audio Visual Presentation.   * Guided Tours.
* 3-D Exhibition Museum.   * Free Taste.
* Smugglers Restaurant – Highly Recommended.
* Tasting Bar – Taste Old Glenturret, 10, 12, 15, 21 Years Old, and Glenturret Malt Liqueur.
* Large Whisky and Souvenir Shop.
* One of Scotland's Top Attractions.

VISITORS WELCOME
OPEN:
March to December
Monday to Saturday
9.30 am - 5.30 pm
Last full tour: 4.30 pm

January & February
Shop only: 2.00 pm - 4.00 pm
¾ mile north-west of Crieff, off A85

GLENTURRET DISTILLERY LTD., CRIEFF, PERTHSHIRE, SCOTLAND PH7 4HA.
Tel: 0764 2424   Fax: 0764 4366

See entry page . . . 58

The Golf View Hotel
NAIRN

In a delightful setting on the shores of the
Moray Firth and only 300 yards from
Nairn Championship Golf Course. 4 star Egon Ronay
recommended. Extensive table d' hote and
a la carte menu. Excellent wine cellar.
Chef's Bar Buffet lunch every day. Weekly features
include Decorated Buffet, Gourmet Dinners,
Cabaret Dinner Dance with Chef's specialities.
Local seafood and venison specialities.

Reservations

AA★★★★   Tel (0667) 52301   RAC ★★★
Telex 75134 Fax (0667) 55267

Norscot Hotels
Beautiful Places

See entry page . . . 94

Praban na Linne (Ltd)

Whisky Proprietors
Eilean Iarmain, An t-Eilean Sgiatheanach IV43 8QR, Scotland.
Fon Isleornsay (04713) 266. Fax (04713) 260

As a fine present for gourmet friends, who recognise a good dram when it crosses their lips, or for that special occasion, try our high quality blend "Te Bheag" which is matured in sherry casks and "married" for several months before being bottled in the traditional manner to give it its smooth and refined character. We also market a fine twelve year old vatted malt whisky, "Poit Dhubh", supplied in a handsome bilingual presentation carton.

For further information contact us at:

**Praban na Linne, An Oifig TS, Eilean Iarmain, Isle of Skye IV43 8QR.
Telephone – 047 13 266   Fax – 047 13 260**

ARRAN AROMATICS LTD

*NATURAL TOILETRY PRODUCTS
MANUFACTURED ON THE ISLE OF ARRAN
A FAMILY COMPANY, WE CARE ABOUT
OUR PRODUCTS AND THE CUSTOMERS
WHO USE THEM.*

*CHOOSE FROM OUR RANGE OF HAIR,
FACE AND BODY CARE PRODUCTS,
PLUS A VARIETY OF GIFT BOXES,
BASKETS AND NOVELTY SOAPS*

**ON SALE IN SHOPS
THROUGHOUT SCOTLAND
ALSO A PERFECT HOTEL AMENITY ITEM**
OUR PRODUCTS ARE NOT TESTED ON ANIMALS

THE WITCHERY
BY THE CASTLE

OPEN 7 DAYS
LUNCH AND DINNER
12 NOON – 11PM
352 CASTLEHILL ROYAL MILE EDINBURGH
RESERVATIONS 031 225 5613

See entry page . . . 68

THE
TRIANGLE
Brasserie & Restaurant

The Triangle offers you the choice of a
bar/bistro , a brasserie , and a formal
dining room

Fine international cuisine is served , using
predominately Scottish Produce in a modern
interpretation

Within The Triangle the walls are lined
with art , mainly by commissioned
Glasgow artists
The Triangle also incorporates many styles
of interior design , which in turn
complements the style , quality and ambience of
the place

*37
Queen Street
Glasgow G1 3EF
Tel. 041-221-8758*

See entry page . . . 74

△ *Loch Oich*

△ *Loch Lomond at Rowardennan*

Plockton, Wester Ross ▽

Glencoe

Loch Tulla, Rannoch Moor

△ Glenfinnan Monument

△ Mull from Staffa

Falls of Dockart, Killin ▽

Sanna Bay, Ardnamurchan

△ *Loch Carron*

Rannoch Moor ▽

Aberdeen

Featured on the cover . . .

△ Rufflets Country House Hotel, St Andrews
▽ Murrayshall Country House Hotel, Scone

Cromlix House, Kinbuck, by Dunblane

▽ Shieldhill Country House Hotel, Biggar

Kyles of Bute

Loch Clair in Glen Torridon

Tom Ewing, from the Anchorage Restaurant in Tarbert, celebrates with BBC Food Expert Chris Kelly after winning the Scottish Salmon Smokers' Association Culinary Competition at the Edinburgh Cookery School on 21 July 1990. Tom won £500 for his Roulade of Colonsay Whiting with Smoked Scottish Salmon flavoured with highland herbs in a Chablis sauce.

Roulade of Colonsay Whiting with Smoked Salmon Flavoured with Wild Highland Herbs in a Chablis Sauce

(From Tom Ewing, Chef, The Anchorage)

Ingredients

4 peeled and finely chopped shallots
2 oz julienne of fresh basil
2 oz picked fresh tarragon
6 sprigs of dill
6 oz fish stock
2 oz butter
2 oz fresh Scottish dairy double cream

1 oz lemon juice
Seasoning to taste
8 x 3 - 4 oz fillets of fresh whiting
4 oz sliced smoked Scottish salmon
8 fl oz Chablis or dry white wine

Serves 2

Method

1. Take fillets of fresh fish and wash/clean.
2. Peel and finely chop shallots.
3. Lay out fillets of fish onto clean surface top.
4. Trim the smoked salmon to equal sizes of white fish fillets (keep smoked salmon trimmings).
5. Place one piece of smoked salmon on each fillet of whiting (on darker side).
6. Roll whiting and smoked salmon and secure with cocktail stick giving 4 parcels of whiting and smoked salmon.
7. Butter and season cooking tray and place in chopped shallots.
8. On top of this place 4 parcels of fish.
9. Cover with fish stock, white wine and lemon juice. Bring to a slight tremble and poach for 3 to 4 minutes.
10. Remove cooked parcels and place on large plate – cover with foil and place in warm oven.
11. Reduce cooking liquor, blend in the cream and butter and reduce to correct consistency (this can be tested by pouring over back of serving spoon – if it clings to spoon a good consistency prevails).
12. Add the prepared herbs (**not** the dill)
13. Removed cooked fish parcels from the oven and place on warm presentation plates.
14. Two fish parcels per person.
15. Coat the fish with prepared sauce.
16. To finish garnish with sprigs of fresh dill and fine strips of smoked salmon (cut from trimmings).

The Anchorage Restaurant
Quayside, Harbour Street,
Tarbert, Argyll PA29 6UD

Tel: (0880) 820881
Proprietors: David & Fiona Evamy

Smoked Salmon Parcels

(From Ann Nicoll, Dunain Park Hotel)

Ingredients

6-8 oz sliced smoked salmon
4 tablespoons cream cheese
1 tablespoon mayonnaise
cream to bind
Juice of ½ lemon
1 teaspoon dill

Serves 4

Sauce

½ cup cream
1 tablespoon mayonnaise
Juice of ½ lemon
Tomato juice to colour

Method

1. Line and overlap 4 ramekins with smoked salmon slices.
2. Cream together cream cheese, mayonnaise, cream and lemon juice.
3. Fill ramekins and fold over the overlapping salmon.
4. Place in refrigerator to set.
5. Place salmon parcels onto a plate and pour round sauce.
6. Garnish with dill.

Dunain Park Hotel
Dunain Park
Inverness IV3 6JN

Tel: (0463) 230512
Proprietors: Edward & Ann Nicoll

Crowdie Cheese and Herb Pate

(served with avocado fan and a strawberry vinaigrette)

(From Sandra Pollock, Head Chef, Newton House Hotel)

Ingredients

8 ozs Crowdie cheese
1 or 2 cloves of garlic
2 oz melted butter
3 oz chopped herbs (parsley, chives and chervil)

Salt and pepper to taste
1-2 avocado pears

Strawberry Vinaigrette

½ lb of strawberries
Juice of 1 lemon
1 teaspoonful of sugar

Serves 4

Method

1. Finely chop the herbs and garlic.
2. Place this in a food processor with the cheese and mix thoroughly – add the melted butter.
3. Add seasoning to taste.
4. Place in a refrigerator to chill.

Strawberry Vinaigrette

5. Puree the strawberries with lemon juice in a food processor.
6. Add sugar – taste for sharpness and adjust with sugar or juice.

Presentation

7. Place a dessertspoonful of the vinaigrette on a plate and arrange 5 thin slices of avocado pear around as a fan.
8. Arrange 2 scoops of pate in the centre and garnish with a sprig of parsley.

Newton House Hotel
Glencarse, by Perth
PH2 7LX

Tel: (073 886) 250
Proprietors: Geoffrey & Carol Tallis

Tomato, Basil and Sesame Flan

(From Barry Cottam, Ard-Na-Coille Hotel)

Ingredients

Tomato Base

1 lb ripe flavoursome tomatoes, skinned and
    seeded (otherwise substitute tinned
    tomatoes, drained)
3 oz shallots or onion, finely chopped
½ oz root ginger, very finely chopped
1 tablespoon wine vinegar
1 teaspoon muscovado sugar
1 teaspoon Worcestershire sauce
Good pinch of salt
Olive oil

Pastry

3 oz butter, softened
4 oz wholemeal flour
1 oz medium oatmeal
1 tablespoon cold water

Topping

2 large eggs
5 fl oz fromage frais
3 fl oz double cream
(or 3 fl oz cream cheese and
    5 fl oz double cream)
1 tablespoon chopped fresh basil leaves
Salt and pepper
2 tablespoons sesame seeds

Serves 6-8 as a starter; 4 as a luncheon dish

Method

1. Saute onion and ginger in olive oil till soft.
2. Add tomatoes, salt and reduce any liquid.
3. Add wine vinegar, reduce, then sugar and Worcestershire sauce.
4. Allow to cool.
5. Cream butter in mixer.
6. Add half flour and oatmeal mix to butter with mixer running, add water.
7. Gradually add remaining flour and oatmeal till it forms a ball.
8. Roll pastry and line 9 inch flan dish. (**Note:** this pastry can be quite difficult to handle, in which case simply press into flan dish).
9. Bake blind at GM 7/425°F/220°C for 10 minutes till firm to touch, then cool.
10. Mix all ingredients for topping, except sesame seeds, in blender.
11. Put tomato base into cooled pastry case and carefully pour on the topping.
12. Bake at Gas 6/400°F/200°C for approx. 10 minutes until topping is just set.
13. Remove from oven and sprinkle top with sesame seeds.
14. Replace in oven and continue to bake for a further 10-15 minutes until firm to touch.
15. Serve with a tomato and basil side salad.

Ard-Na-Coille Hotel
Kingussie Road, Newtonmore
Inverness-shire PH20 1AY

Tel: (054 03) 214
Proprietors: Nancy Ferrier & Barry Cottam

Finnan Haddock Pate with a Watercress Sauce Served with Crispy Ayrshire Bacon

(From Jeffrey Purves, Green Inn)

Ingredients

Pate

1 lb Finnan haddock
½ pint milk
1 oz butter
1 oz flour
Pinch saffron
¼ pint double cream
2 sheets gelatine
Milled pepper to taste

Serves 4

Sauce

2 oz watercress leaves
3 fl oz double cream
2 fl oz chicken stock
Pinch salt
Milled pepper to taste
2 oz Ayrshire bacon

Method

1. Poach haddock in milk.
2. Make white sauce with butter, flour and the milk in which haddock was cooked.
3. Soak gelatine for 10 minutes, and add to white sauce, then season sauce with saffron and milled pepper.
4. Remove bones and skin of haddock, add to sauce and place in a food processor for two minutes then cool.
5. Lightly whip cream and fold into haddock mixture. Place into mould and set in refrigerator.

Sauce

6. Wash watercress and liquidise with chicken stock.
7. Lightly whip cream, fold in watercress and season sauce. Chill.
8. Cut 2oz of Ayrshire bacon into strips and fry in very hot oil, drain well.

Presentation

9. Turn out pate and cut into slices.
10. Arrange two slices of pate and two pools of sauce on each plate.
11. Place bacon on top of sauce.
12. Garnish dish with chives and small bunches of watercress and serve with hot buttered brown bread.

The Green Inn
9 Victoria Road
Ballater AB35 5QQ

Tel: (033 97) 55701
Proprietors: Jeffrey & Carol Purves

Terrine of Smoked Wood Pigeon

(Lightly smoked pigeon, layered with tender leeks, set in a game consomme and served on a mixed lentil sauce.)

(From Kevin MacGillivray, Chef, Chapeltoun House Hotel)

Ingredients

1 pint game consomme
7 leaves gelatine
3 smoked pigeons
8 young leeks
Seasoning

Sauce

1 oz brown lentils
1 oz green lentils
1 oz red lentils
¼ pint consomme
1 leaf gelatine

Serves 4

Method

1. Warm consomme; soak gelatine then add to consomme. Mix until totally dissolved. Allow to cool.
2. Remove pigeon breast from bone and then thinly slice.
3. Clean and blanch young leeks, then cut into strips.
4. Now line 1 pint terrine. Begin with a layer of consomme, set, next pigeon, allow to set, then finally a layer of leek. Repeat until complete. Place in refrigerator to set.
5. For the sauce, dissolve gelatine in consomme. (This will allow the sauce to hold on the plate.)
6. Cook each type of lentil separately, as each has a different cooking time. Once cooked, refresh.

To Serve

7. Turn out terrine and slice. Use a selection of salad leaves to accompany the terrine. Finish with the sauce and lentils.

Chapeltoun House
Stewarton
Ayrshire KA3 3ED

Tel: (0560) 82696
Proprietors: Colin & Graeme McKenzie

Pickled Wild Spey Salmon

(Two salmon recipes from Stewart Anderson, Head Chef, Muckrach Lodge Hotel.)

Ingredients

2 lb fresh salmon fillet cut into ½ inch cubes
1 tablespoon fresh dill

Marinade

6 fl oz water
6 fl oz white wine vinegar
3 tablespoons granulated sugar

½ teaspoon salt
1 onion – finely sliced
1 lemon – finely sliced
1 tablespoon mustard seeds
1 tablespoon black peppercorns
2 bay leaves

Serves 8-10 as a starter

Method

1. Combine all marinade ingredients in saucepan and bring through the boil.
2. Pour (still hot) over the salmon and dill in an earthenware dish.
3. Stir, cool and refrigerate for 4 days – stirring at least once a day.
4. Best served with Scottish oatcakes or bannocks and crisp salad.

Lime Cured Wild Spey Salmon

Ingredients

1 lb fresh salmon
5 oz chopped red onion
½ teaspoon granulated sugar
2 teaspoons salt

1 teaspoon tabasco
Juice of 10 limes
10 oz tomato concasse
1 tablespoon fresh chopped coriander

Serves 6-8 as a starter

Method

1. Fillet salmon and half freeze for 2 hours (this facilitates next step of cutting into ¼ inch dice.)
2. Place diced salmon in base of plastic tray, combine all other ingredients except tomato concasse. Pour over salmon – ensure that all fish is covered. Cover with cling film and refrigerate for 5-7 hours.
3. Before serving combine with tomato concasse
4. Serve with salad and Scottish oatcakes or hot crusty bread.

Both these recipes may be used with halibut, scallops or fresh prawns if desired.

Muckrach Lodge Hotel
Dulnain Bridge
Grantown-on-Spey PH26 3LY

Tel: (047 985) 257
Proprietors: Roy & Pat Watson

Terrine of Seafood with a Vermouth Flavoured Aspic

(From Clive Lamb, Head Chef, Invery House)

Ingredients

6 crepes (5 inch diameter)
8 large spinach leaves
8 oz salmon
8 oz turbot
8 oz lemon sole
8 prawn tails
1 x 6 oz monkfish tail
8 asparagus spears (medium)
3-4 bay leaves
½ pint fish stock
½ pint dry vermouth
1 oz aspic granules

Serves 8-10

Method

1. Line a terrine mould with tinfoil and line the inside with the crepes, allowing them to overlap slightly.
2. Blanch the spinach leaves in boiling salted water for a few seconds, refresh in cold water, drain well and pat dry with a cloth.
3. Repeat process with asparagus, allowing slightly longer in the boiling water to cook.
4. Brush the crepes with a little egg white and cover with the spinach leaves.
5. Cut the fish into strips and shell the prawn tails.
6. Place in the terrine alternate layers of fish and asparagus, lightly seasoning each layer with salt and black pepper.
7. Bring to the boil the vermouth and fish stock, add the aspic and stir until dissolved. Pour over the fish until completely covered.
8. Fold over the crepes, place the bay leaves on top, cover with a lid and stand in a bain marie (if one of these is not available use a baking tin with water to halfway up dish), place in oven for 40 minutes at GM 4/350°F/180°C.
9. Remove from oven and cool.
10. Refrigerate for 8 hours before removing from terrine mould
11. Serve with a dill mayonnaise or tomato coulis.

Invery House
Bridge of Feugh
Banchory, Kincardineshire AB3 3NJ

Tel: (03302) 4782
Proprietors: The Spence Family

Trout with a Horseradish and Walnut Stuffing

(From Frances Evans, Bayview Hotel)

Ingredients

4 whole trout or trout steaks depending on the size of the fish
2 oz walnuts – roughly chopped
2 tablespoons creamed horseradish
1 tablespoon fine oatmeal
¼ pint cream
1 teaspoon lemon juice
Salt and freshly ground black pepper
walnut oil for grilling

Serves 4

Method

1. Mix together walnuts, horseradish, cream, oatmeal, lemon juice and seasoning.
2. Stuff the gutted trout, brush with a little oil and grill each side for about 5 minutes.
3. Spread remaining mixture on top, grill until brown.
4. Sprinkle with chopped parsley and garnish with lemon.

Bayview Hotel & Restaurant
Cullen
Banffshire AB5 2SU

Tel: (0542) 41031
Proprietors: David & Frances Evans

Supreme of Halibut with Grated Potatoes and Woodland Mushrooms

(From Alan Hill, Executive Chef, Gleneagles Hotel)

Ingredients

4 x 4 oz halibut fillets
Salt and freshly ground pepper
2 tablespoons olive oil
1 oz butter
4 oz potato strips
½ oz mixed herbs
Nutmeg
2 egg whites
1 oz butter
1 oz shallots

¼ pint madeira wine
½ pint fish stock
¼ pint lobster stock
½ oz oregano
2 oz butter to finish
1 oz bacon
4 oz woodland mushrooms
½ oz pine kernels
½ oz chopped marjoram
12 button onions
4 pluches of oregano to garnish

Serves 4

Method

1. Season the halibut fillets with a little salt and freshly ground pepper.
2. Seal the fillets in a little hot oil and butter then allow to cool.
3. Drain the washed potato strips and blanch in a little boiling salted water, remove, refresh and dry.
4. Place the potato into a stainless steel bowl and season with salt and freshly ground pepper and a touch of nutmeg.
5. Whisk the egg whites until stiff and add to the mixed herbs.
6. Fold this mixture into the potatoes and place upon the top of the halibut and roast the fish through a hot oven until the potato is golden brown and the fish cooked.
7. Remove, dry and keep warm.
8. Place some butter into saucepan and cook the shallots with no colour.
9. Add the madeira wine and reduce by one half.
10. Pour in the fish stock and continue the process gradually adding the lobster stock.
11. Infuse the oregano and once the correct consistency is reached allow to cool for a few seconds and then finish with the butter.
12. Saute the bacon and mushrooms together with the glazed onions and chopped marjoram.
13. Add the pine kernels and remove, dry and keep warm.
14. Pass the sauce through a fine strainer and check the seasoning and consistency then pour upon the serving plate.
15. Sprinkle the garnish upon the top, keeping the button onions together.
16. Place the fish into the centre and garnish with the oregano flowers.
17. Serve immediately.

The Gleneagles Hotel
Auchterarder
Perthshire PH3 1NF

Tel: (0764) 62231
Proprietors: Gleneagles Hotel PLC

Filo Purses of Queen Scallops with Leek and White Wine Sauce

(From George Kelso, Head Chef,
Ardsheal House Hotel)

Ingredients

24 queen scallops
2 medium leeks, blanched and cut into julienne strips
2 sheets filo pastry
¾ pint double cream
¾ pint fish stock
melted butter
2 oz chopped butter
Seasoning
1 cup white wine
2 fl oz whipped cream

Serves 4

Method

1. Saute scallops very lightly, drain and keep warm. Reserve a few scallops for garnish.
2. Mix scallops and julienne of leeks with a little whipped cream and season to taste.
3. Brush melted butter on two sheets of filo pastry and place one sheet on top of the other. Cut into four circles.
4. Spoon on scallop and leek mixture, gather into a purse or parcel, and tie with a strip of leek.
5. Reduce wine, stock and cream to a sauce consistency, add seasoning and finish with butter.
6. Bake scallop purses on a buttered tray at GM 7/425°F/220°C for 8 -10 minutes or until golden brown.
7. Place on plates and pour sauce around. Arrange reserved scallops on plates and garnish with a herb.

Ardsheal House
Kentallen of Appin
Argyll PA38 4BX

Tel: (063 174) 227
Proprietors: Bob & Jane Taylor

Poached Spey Salmon in Pink Champagne with Raspberries and Mint Sauce

(From Brian Mutch, Head Chef, Craigellachie Hotel)

Ingredients

4 x 5 oz pieces of salmon (bone, skin and fat removed)
½ bottle good quality rose champagne
¼ pint of fish stock
¼ pint double cream
1 bunch of mint
1 small punnet of raspberries
Seasoning to taste
Wine vinegar
Chopped basil

Serves 4

Method

1. Poach fish for 5-7 minutes in champagne.
2. Remove fish and keep warm.
3. Boil fish stock and reduce by half with champagne, add cream and cook for further 10 minutes.
4. Season to taste.
5. Chop mint finely and add it with the raspberries at the last minute.
6. Serve immediately.

Craigellachie Hotel
Craigellachie, Speyside
Banffshire AB3 9SS

Tel: (0304) 881204
Proprietors: Tomas Gronager & Stephen Goodchild

Arran Chicken

(Supreme of chicken stuffed with smoked salmon and goats milk cheese and lightly panfried in butter)

*(From Robin McIlwraith, Head Chef,
The Pickwick Hotel)*

Ingredients

4 fresh chicken breasts
8 oz smoked salmon
½ lb butter
4 oz goats milk cheese
½ pint milk
2 eggs   } whisked together to make egg wash
1 lb plain flour
1 lb white breadcrumbs

Serves 4

Method

1. Slice each breast of chicken, stuff with 1 oz goats milk cheese and 2 oz smoked salmon.
2. Slowly melt butter.
3. Pass prepared chicken through flour, egg wash and breadcrumbs.
4. Place in melted butter and cook slowly for approximately 20 minutes turning frequently.
5. Serve with tossed salad or a selection of fresh vegetables and Ayrshire potatoes.

**The Pickwick Hotel
19 Racecourse Road
Ayr KA7 2TD**

**Tel: (0292) 260111
Proprietor: Robert S. Gilmour**

Oban Bay Scallops in Cream Cheese Sauce with Strips of Vegetables

(From Brian Graham, Executive Chef, Shieldhill Country House Hotel)

Ingredients

16 pieces of fresh cleaned scallops cut in half
4 sprigs of dill
½ pint double cream
1 measure of white wine
½ finely chopped onion
2 oz cream cheese
1 small piece of carrot, leek, courgette and turnip
    cut into matchstick shapes
Salt and pepper
1oz unsalted butter
1 teaspoon whipped double cream
2 egg yolks
8 leaves cut cleaned spinach

Serves 4

Method

1. Melt half the butter in a thick bottomed pan, add scallops and strips of vegetables.
2. Cook lightly without colouring the scallops.
3. Add white wine to pan and bring to boil.
4. Remove scallops and vegetables and put to one side.
5. Reduce cooking wine by two-thirds. Add pouring cream and season.
6. When sauce has reached consistency to coat the back of a wooden spoon, remove from heat and add the scallops and vegetables to the sauce.
7. Cook off spinach and onions in a little butter and place pile of spinach on each plate.
8. Put sauce back on heat and add cream cheese then add more seasoning if needed.
9. Remove sauce from heat, add whipped cream and egg yolks slowly stirring.
10. Place scallops and sauce onto spinach. Place each plate under grill and glaze.
11. Garnish plates with a sprig of fresh dill, then serve.

Shieldhill Country House Hotel
Quothquan, Biggar
Lanarkshire ML12 6NA

Tel: (0899) 20035
Proprietors: C. Dunstan & J. Greenwald

Stuffed Orange Peppers

(From Isobel Steven, Ardchoille Farm Guest House)

Ingredients

4 orange peppers
1 cup of brown and wild rice
2 cups of water
6 small mushrooms
½ oz butter
6 dried apricots, cooked in a little water till soft
1 oz sultanas
1 oz chopped walnuts
Juice of 1 fresh orange
Pinch of mixed herbs
Salt and freshly ground black pepper

Serves 4

A vegetarian main course or as an accompaniment to pork or ham.

Method

1. Cut peppers in half and remove seeds. Place in buttered dish.
2. Cook rice in slightly salted water until tender and drain.
3. Toss chopped mushrooms in butter in a pan until tender and golden brown.
4. Chop apricots into small pieces and retain syrup.
5. Combine all ingredients, season lightly. Put the mixture into peppers and cover with foil.
6. Cook in a moderate oven for 15 minutes until peppers are tender.
7. Garnish with fresh parsley.

Ardchoille Farm Guest House
Dunshalt
Auchtermuchty KY14 7EY

Tel: (0337) 28414
Proprietor: Isobel J. Steven

Gateau of Venison with a Compote of Cabbage and Apple

(From Stewart Cameron, Executive Chef, Turnberry Hotel)

Ingredients

12 thin mignons of venison fillets
x 1½ ozs each
2 oz finely shredded cabbage
1½ oz finely grated apple
Turned apples (20 pieces-small)

Venison Sauce

4 oz venison trimmings
1 pint venison stock and glace
¼ pint venison marinade

Serves 4

Honey Cream

1 shallot
2 oz honey
4 fl oz cream

Mignonette

1 oz redcurrant jelly
½ onion
12 peppercorns   } Reduce together
1 bay leaf
¼ pint red wine

Method

1. Take shredded cabbage and grated apple and braise in a little white wine vinegar until cooked.

Venison Sauce

2. Taking the trimmings, seal off in hot fat, add the stock and reduce by half. Add sufficient amount of glace, add mignonette and reduce to the correct consistency. Pass through muslin and finish with butter in last minute.

Honey Cream

3. Sweat off a small amount of shallots. Add the honey, reduce slightly, add the cream and reduce to consistency required. Pass through a sieve.

4. Seal off the mignons of venison in a hot pan, cook as required. Heat up the cabbage in a little butter. Place one of the mignons as the base, a layer of cabbage, venison, cabbage and finally venison, so that you have a gateau effect about 2½ inches high.

5. To serve, place this 'gateau' in the centre of the plate, coat with the rich venison sauce.

6. Place a teaspoonful of honey cream on top of the gateau. Garnish with the turned apples, sauteed in butter.

Note: Venison mignons should be batted out thin, then cut out with a round cutter (2½ inch diameter), to give a neat gateau presentation.

The Turnberry Hotel
Turnberry
Ayrshire KA26 9LT

Tel: (0655) 31000

Casserole of Scotch Beef with Highland Whisky and Fresh Herbs

(From Chris Bentley, Head Chef, Coul House Hotel)

Ingredients

3 lbs shoulder steak sliced into 2 oz pieces
1 oz whisky
2 large onions sliced
1 teaspoon tomato puree
1 pint beef stock or 1 pint of water and 1 stock cube
Large handful of fresh herbs as available, parsley, thyme, marjoram, sage, rosemary, chives
Salt and pepper
1 oz flour
1 oz suet or lard

Serves 4

Method

1. Melt suet in pan.
2. Roll the slices of steak in flour then fry in the hot fat.
3. Add the onion slices and cook until transparent.
4. Stir in the tomato puree, then half of the whisky, slowly add the stock.
5. Layer the bottom of a casserole dish with the coarsely chopped herb selection.
6. Pour the meat mixture over the herbs, season with salt and pepper to taste.
7. Cover and cook in the oven slowly for 1½ hours, pour the rest of the whisky over the top before serving.

Coul House Hotel
Contin, by Strathpeffer
Ross-shire IV14 9EY

Tel: (0997) 21487
Proprietor: Martyn Hill

Breasts of Perthshire Wood Pigeon with a Raspberry Vinegar and Port Wine Sauce

(From Bill Kerr, Chef/Proprietor, Croftbank House Hotel)

Ingredients

4 wild pigeons – plucked
1 fl oz raspberry vinegar
1 oz butter
4 fl oz port wine
½ pint brown pigeon stock
12 fresh raspberries with stock
4 baby leeks
8 fresh asparagus heads
1 carrot
1 onion
1 bay leaf

Serves 4

Method

1. Bone breast from pigeon carcass and leave to side.
2. To make stock – roast pigeon carcass till brown with carrot, onion and bay leaf.
3. Add butter to a saute pan, add pigeon breasts to brown butter, season, cook till pink. Remove from pan, keep warm. Let them rest in warm oven.
4. Pour off residue, add raspberry vinegar, reduce, then add port wine deglace. Finally add the reduced pigeon stock, whisk in knob of butter, taste.
5. Sauce plates, slice pigeon breast and place on top. Finally arrange raspberries, baby leeks, fresh asparagus heads around plate. Serve.

Croftbank House Hotel
30 Station Road
Kinross, Fife KY13 7TG

Tel: (0577) 63819
Proprietors: Bill & Diane Kerr

Ballantine of Young Grouse

*(From Martin J. Hoefkens, Head Chef,
Cairndale Hotel)*

Ingredients

4 young grouse (boned as for ballantine)
4 oz butter
4 finely chopped shallots
Livers and hearts of grouse finely chopped
2 level tablespoons oatmeal
2 level tablespoons breadcrumbs
2 dessertspoons heather honey
4 measures malt whisky
¾ pint demi-glace
3 oz grouse pate
4 shortcrust pastry barquettes (approx. 4 inches long)
4 sprigs heather
Salt and pepper to taste

Serves 4

Method
Stuffing

1. Sweat off shallots, liver and hearts in butter. Add oatmeal, breadcrumbs, half the honey, seasoning and some of the demi-glace to make a soft paste.
2. Stuff the birds and tie up so as to make a sealed oval parcel. Roast at GM 7/425°F/220°C for approx. 20 minutes.
3. Line the barquettes with grouse pate, place a grouse on each one, de-glaze roasting tin with whisky and remainder of honey, add rest of demi-glace, check for seasoning, strain sauce over each bird and garnish with sprigs of heather.

   Sauce should be thick enough to coat birds — if not reduce and whisk in some butter.

Cairndale Hotel
English Street
Dumfries DG1 2DF

Tel: (0387) 54111
Proprietors: The Wallace Family

Medallions of Maize-fed Guinea Fowl with a Pistachio Nut and Chive Filling

(From Bruce Sangster, Executive Chef, Murrayshall Country House Hotel)

Ingredients

4 Guinea fowl supremes
(chicken supremes may be
substituted)
2 oz chicken breast
1 carrot
1 oz pistachio nuts blanched
 and skinned
Fresh chives
½ pint double cream

Serves 4

Sauce

1 pint stock made from the carcass of
 Guinea fowl or chicken
¼ pint red wine
¼ pint ruby port
1 onion
cold butter to finish sauce

Method

1. Remove the fillets from the supremes and place with the chicken meat in a liquidiser. Process them, remove and rub through a sieve. Place in a bowl and set over ice with a little salt and gradually work in the double cream. Allow to rest.
2. Prepare a fine dice of carrot and blanch in boiling salted water.
3. Finely chop the pistachio nuts.
4. Mix the carrot, nuts and chives into the mousse, adjust the seasoning.
5. Bat out the supremes with a meat hammer between plastic sheets.
6. Butter 4 sheets of tin foil and place one supreme on each sheet, season with salt and pepper.
7. Add some of the mousse down the centre of the supremes then carefully roll up and secure in the foil, allow to rest.
8. Meanwhile prepare the light sauce by browning the onion which should be finely sliced then add the stock and reduce quickly by half.
9. Add both port and red wine and again reduce by half.
10. Strain and pass through a fine muslin, keep warm.
11. In a thick bottomed pan with a little oil seal the tin foil parcels and place in the oven GM 6/7 approx. 400°F/200°C for 8-10 minutes. Remove and allow to rest.
12. Finish the sauce by bringing to the boil and adding cold butter. Do not reboil as sauce will separate.
13. Remove the foil from the supremes and carve into 8-9 thin slices, arrange on hot plates and nap with the sauce.
14. Serve with vegetables of your choice.

Murrayshall Country House Hotel
Scone
Perthshire PH2 7PH

Tel: (0738) 51171
Proprietors: MacOlsen Ltd

Noisettes of Lamb with a Bramble Sauce

(From Elma Barrie, Hawkcraig House)

Ingredients

8 noisettes of lamb
4 oz mushrooms – finely sliced
2 oz onions – finely chopped
4 tablespoons port
3 tablespoons brandy
¼ pint lamb stock
6 oz brambles
Oil, butter and seasoning to taste

Serves 4

Method

1. Saute lamb in a little sunflower oil to seal, transfer to warm oven and cook till tender.
2. Add stock to deglaze pan, simmer and reduce.
3. Add butter, mushrooms, onions and cook till tender.
4. Add port and brandy – flambe and reduce.
5. Add brambles and cook gently for 2 minutes.
6. Pour sauce over or beside noisettes, and garnish with fresh mint.
7. Serve with new potatoes and fresh vegetables in season.

Hawkcraig House
Aberdour
Fife KY3 0TZ

Tel: (0383) 860335
Proprietor: Elma Barrie

Marrannoch

(From Anita Steffen, Cuilmore Cottage)

Ingredients

1 tin unsweetened chestnut puree
3 oz butter
4 oz ground almonds
4 oz dark rum
1 tablespoon brown sugar
4 oz chopped nuts

Serves 4

Method

1. Process all ingredients except chopped nuts until smooth.
2. Stir in 4 oz chopped nuts.
3. Spoon into 1 pint pudding basin lined with cling film and refrigerate overnight.
4. Remove from bowl, peel off film.
5. Cut into wedges. Decorate by trickling 1 teaspoon raspberry puree over the ridge edge of each wedge. Surround with cream.
6. Garnish with a strawberry leaf and a sliced fanned strawberry.

Cuilmore Cottage
Kinloch Rannoch
Perthshire PH16 5QB

Tel: (08822) 218
Proprietor: Anita Steffen

Mansfield White Stag

(From Sheila MacKinnon, Mansfield House Hotel)

Ingredients

Mousse
4 egg yolks
½ pint cream
½ lb white chocolate
Stags Breath Liqueur

To Complete

Some sponge cake
4 egg whites
Caster sugar
Stags Breath Liqueur

Serves 8

Method

1. Beat egg yolks with sugar until thick and creamy, then add liqueur.
2. Whip cream until almost thick.
3. Melt chocolate in bowl over water.
2. Combine mixtures together, then fill half ramekins and freeze.
5. Cut sponge cake with a plain medium scone cutter – one for each mousse. Brush with liqueur and place one on each plate.
6. Unmould chocolate mousse and place on top of sponge. Make a meringue with egg white and sugar and pipe all over each dessert then flash under a hot grill to light brown. Decorate as desired with cherries and angelica.

Mansfield House Hotel
Weensland Road
Hawick TD9 9EL

Tel: (0450) 73988
Proprietors: Ian & Sheila MacKinnon

Passion Fruit Nougat

*(From Alfie Murray, Head Chef,
Ardoe House Hotel)*

Ingredients

2 egg whites
3¼ cups cream
2 tablespoons Drambuie
3 passion fruits
Toasted almonds
Angelica
Glace cherries
2½ oz loaf sugar
2½ oz caster sugar

Serves 4

Method

1. Dissolve 2 oz of loaf sugar in water and bring to the boil at a temperature of 250°F.
2. Whisk egg white and 2½ oz caster sugar until stiff and add the boiling syrup. Whisk until cool and whip cream until stiff.
3. Chop the cherries and angelica, fold the fruit cream, egg white, passion fruit and Drambuie together.
4. Pour into terrine and set in freezer until required.

Presentation

Place some passion fruit coulis on the plate with 2 slices of nougat and a fan of strawberries and fresh blackcurrants.

Ardoe House Hotel
South Deeside Road
Blairs, Aberdeen AB1 5YP

Tel: (0224) 867355
Proprietors: Waterside Inns Ltd

A Tayberry and Redcurrant Souffle Glacé with a Tart Blackcurrant Coulis

Ingredients

6 egg yolks
4 oz caster sugar
¾ pint double cream
4 egg whites
1 lb fresh tayberrries or raspberries
8 oz fresh redcurrants
½ tablespoon redcurrant jelly
Juice ¼ lemon

Serves 8-10

Garnish

4 oz white chocolate
8 oz fresh tayberries or raspberries
8 oz fresh blackcurrants
2 fl oz stock syrup
Juice ½ lime or lemon
4 tablespoons Framboise (raspberry liqueur)
    or strawberry liqueur – per portion

Method

1. Line a deep rectangular pate/terrine mould with cling wrap.
2. Melt the white chocolate and line or brush the inside of small individual cup shape moulds (1 per portion) and refrigerate.
3. Prepare souffle mix by whisking the egg yolks, lemon juice and half the raspberry liqueur with the fresh redcurrants and tayberries (which have previously been hulled liquidised and strained) with the other half of the raspberry liqueur.
4. When the mix is thick and shows marks of the whisk, beat further until cold.
5. Beat the cream lightly until slightly thick and fold through carefully into the cold sabayon mix.
6. Beat egg whites until it shows peaks (not too stiff) and fold this also into the souffle mix.
7. Pipe or spoon mixture into the lined terrine mould. Cover with more cling wrap and deep freeze for at least 12 hours.
8. Liquidise the fresh blackcurrants (which have been washed and hulled) with the stock syrup and lime or lemon juice and strain through a fine strainer.
9. Assemble the dessert by removing the chocolate cups from the moulds, place a few fresh tayberries in each one and a teaspoon of raspberry or strawberry liqueur and garnish with lemon balm or mint.
10. Serve a thin slice of souffle glace cut with a warm knife, garnish with chocolate cup and coulis of blackcurrant with a few whole blackcurrants sprinkled over the coulis.
N.B. This type of dessert should only be prepared with fresh berries. Raspberries can be substituted for tayberries.

Bouquet Garni
51 High Street
Elie, Fife KY9 1BZ

Tel: (0333) 330374
Proprietors: Andrew & Norah Kerracher

The 1992 TASTE OF SCOTLAND GUIDE
is scheduled to be published in
November 1991.

To reserve a copy at the 1991 price of £2.80 (including post & packaging), complete the coupon below and send it with your cheque or postal order, made payable to TASTE OF SCOTLAND, to

Taste of Scotland (Guide Sales)
33 Melville Street
Edinburgh EH3 7JF

You will be placed on the priority list to receive the Guide as soon as it is published.

- - - - ✂ - ✂

To: TASTE OF SCOTLAND (GUIDE SALES)
    33 MELVILLE STREET
    EDINBURGH EH3 7JF

Please send_____copy/copies of
the 1992 Guide.
Cheque / Postal Order enclosed for_____

NAME:_____

ADDRESS:_____

_____

_____Post Code_____

BLOCK CAPITALS, PLEASE!

SAMPLE POST INCLUSIVE PRICES FOR OVERSEAS ON NEXT PAGE.

GUIDE
1991

Overseas prices including post & packaging:

£5 (Europe) : US$15 (air mail – North America)

Eurocheques in £ sterling preferred, but
personal cheques/checks in local currency acceptable.

---

*On your travels have you visited
a restaurant or hotel which you
feel merits inclusion in the
Taste of Scotland Guide?*

We welcome your recommendations.

COMMENTS on meals in places listed in
The Taste of Scotland Guide are welcomed.
Send to: Taste of Scotland, 33 Melville Street, Edinburgh EH3 7JF

91
O
E

Establishment visited

Date   Meal

Comments

Name

Address

COMMENTS on meals in places listed in
The Taste of Scotland Guide are welcomed.
Send to: Taste of Scotland, 33 Melville Street, Edinburgh EH3 7JF

91
O
E

Establishment visited

Date   Meal

Comments

Name

Address

Send to: Taste of Scotland, 33 Melville Street, Edinburgh EH3 7JF

Caithness Glass *Prestige Award 1991*

I nominate_____[ESTABLISHMENT]
for a Caithness Glass Prestige Award for the following category:

(Categories)   (Please tick <u>one</u> category only)

☐ Best Hotel   ☐ Best Country House Hotel

☐ Best Restaurant   ☐ Best Newcomer

☐ Best Hospitality & Welcome

Name_____

Address_____

_____

Date of visit_____

Meal (if appropriate)_____

Closing date for entries: 15 September 1991.

------------------------✂---

Send to: Taste of Scotland, 33 Melville Street, Edinburgh EH3 7JF

Caithness Glass *Prestige Award 1991*

I nominate_____[ESTABLISHMENT]
for a Caithness Glass Prestige Award for the following category:

(Categories)   (Please tick <u>one</u> category only)

☐ Best Hotel   ☐ Best Country House Hotel

☐ Best Restaurant   ☐ Best Newcomer

☐ Best Hospitality & Welcome

Name_____

Address_____

_____

Date of visit_____

Meal (if appropriate)_____

Closing date for entries: 15 September 1991.

160

COMMENTS on meals in places listed in
The Taste of Scotland Guide are welcomed.
Send to: Taste of Scotland, 33 Melville Street, Edinburgh EH3 7JF

91
O
E

Establishment visited

Date   Meal

Comments

_____

_____

_____

_____

Name

Address

_____

COMMENTS on meals in places listed in
The Taste of Scotland Guide are welcomed.
Send to: Taste of Scotland, 33 Melville Street, Edinburgh EH3 7JF

91
O
E

Establishment visited

Date   Meal

Comments

_____

_____

_____

_____

Name

Address

_____

Send to: Taste of Scotland, 33 Melville Street, Edinburgh EH3 7JF

Caithness Glass *Prestige Award 1991*

I nominate_____[ESTABLISHMENT]
for a Caithness Glass Prestige Award for the following category:

(Categories)   (Please tick <u>one</u> category only)

☐ Best Hotel   ☐ Best Country House Hotel

☐ Best Restaurant   ☐ Best Newcomer

☐ Best Hospitality & Welcome

Name_____
Address_____
_____
Date of visit_____
Meal (if appropriate)_____
Closing date for entries: 15 September 1991.

✂- -

Send to: Taste of Scotland, 33 Melville Street, Edinburgh EH3 7JF

Caithness Glass *Prestige Award 1991*

I nominate_____[ESTABLISHMENT]
for a Caithness Glass Prestige Award for the following category:

(Categories)   (Please tick <u>one</u> category only)

☐ Best Hotel   ☐ Best Country House Hotel

☐ Best Restaurant   ☐ Best Newcomer

☐ Best Hospitality & Welcome

Name_____
Address_____
_____
Date of visit_____
Meal (if appropriate)_____
Closing date for entries: 15 September 1991.

CAITHNESS GLASS/TASTE OF SCOTLAND PRESTIGE AWARDS 1990
WINNERS WITH MAGNUS MAGNUSSON AT CALEDONIAN HOTEL, EDINBURGH
MONDAY 15 OCTOBER 1990

Picture shows: (L to R)

Standing: Keith Allison, Turnberry Hotel
Alistair Mair, MD Caithness Glass
John Minaur, Chairman Taste of Scotland Board
Magnus Magnusson (with award)
Jack MacMillan, Chief Executive, Taste of Scotland
David Cowan, The Triangle, Glasgow
Jonathan Brown, Ardanaiseig Hotel, Kilchrenan

Seated: Christine Dunstan, Shieldhill Hotel, nr Biggar
Brenda Milward, Knockie Lodge, Whitebridge
Anita Steffen, Cuilmore Cottage, Kinloch Rannoch
Vivien Sirotkin, The Gleneagles Hotel

INDEX

Editor	:	**Nancy K Campbell BA**
Published by	:	**Taste of Scotland Scheme Ltd,** a non-profit making company limited by guarantee trading as Taste of Scotland Registered in Scotland No. 90836
Typeset and printed in Scotland by	:	**Inglis Allen Kirkcaldy**
Inside colour photography	:	Courtesy of **George Young Photographers, Gourock Scottish Tourist Board (Aberdeen, Loch Laggan, Montrose, Sweetheart Abbey) William McDonald Dunn (View from the shore at Ullapool)**

□□□□□□□□□□□□

The details quoted in this guidebook are as supplied to Taste of Scotland Scheme Limited and to the best of the Company's knowledge are correct. They may have been amended subsequently and all users are advised in their own interests to check when making a reservation.

TASTE OF SCOTLAND SCHEME LIMITED accepts no responsibility for any errors or inaccuracies.

□□□□□□□□□□□□

TASTE OF SCOTLAND SCHEME LTD
33 Melville Street
Edinburgh
EH3 7JF
Telephone: 031 220 1900
Fax: 031 220 6102

ISBN 1 871445 01 9

Notes